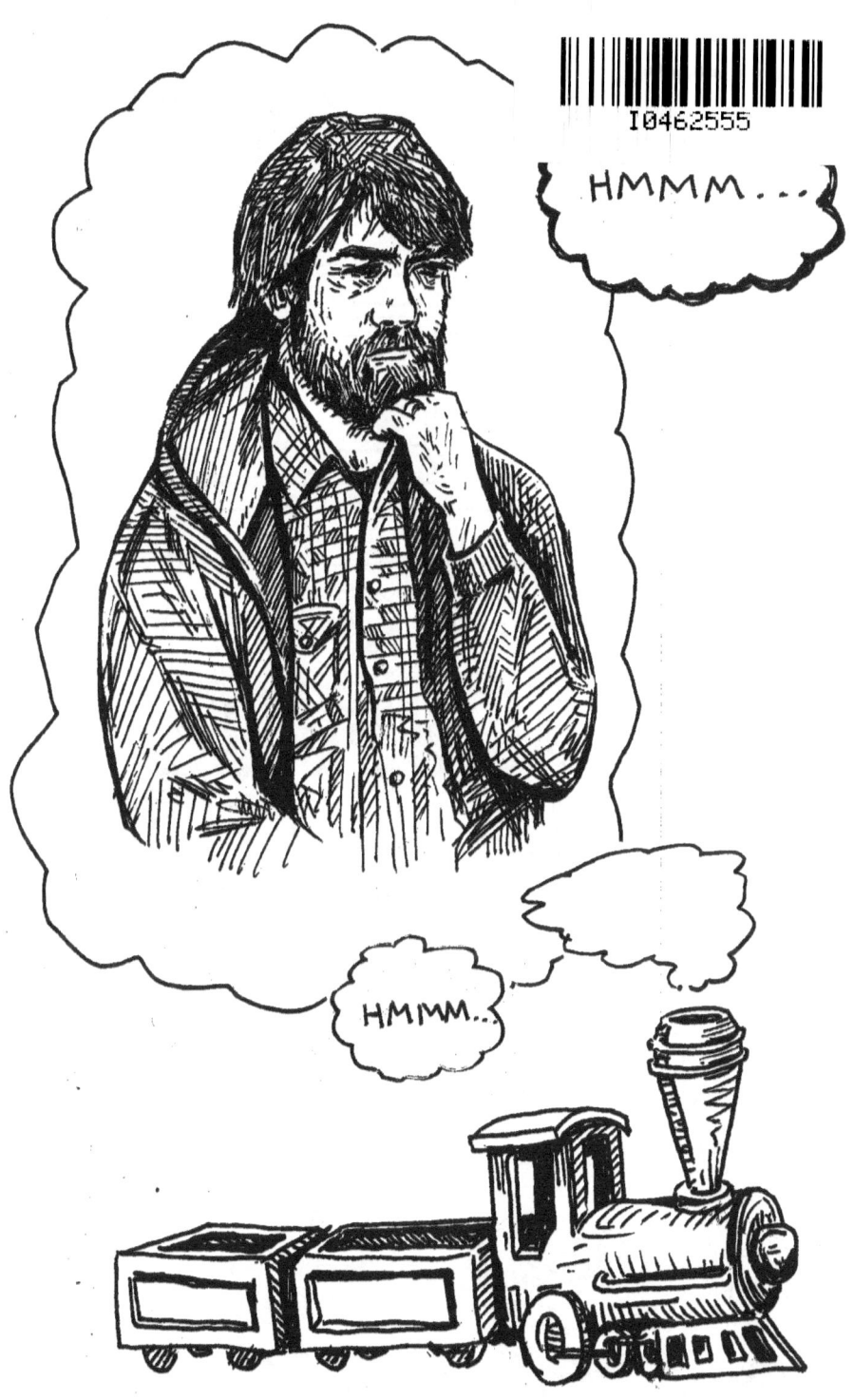

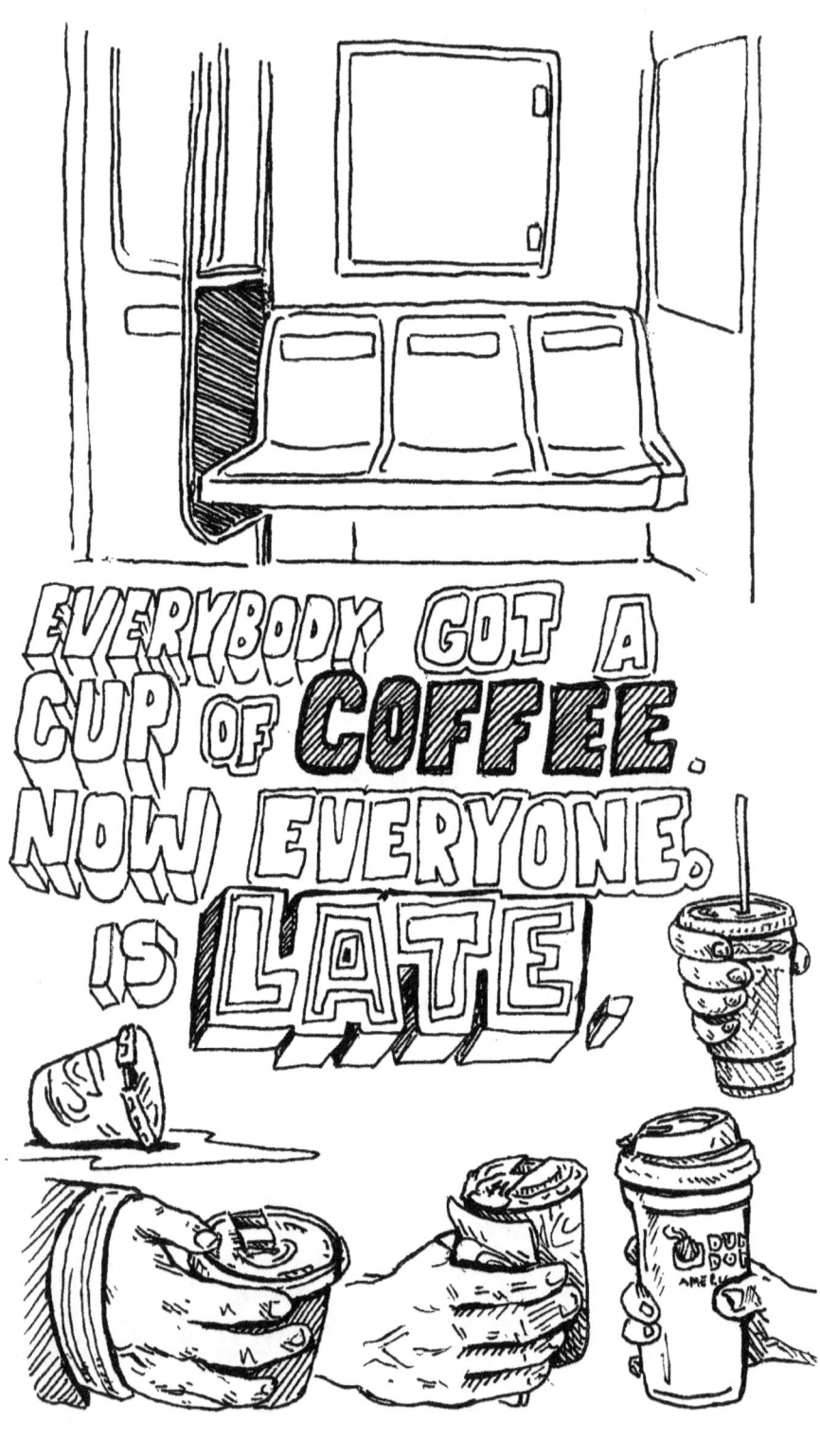

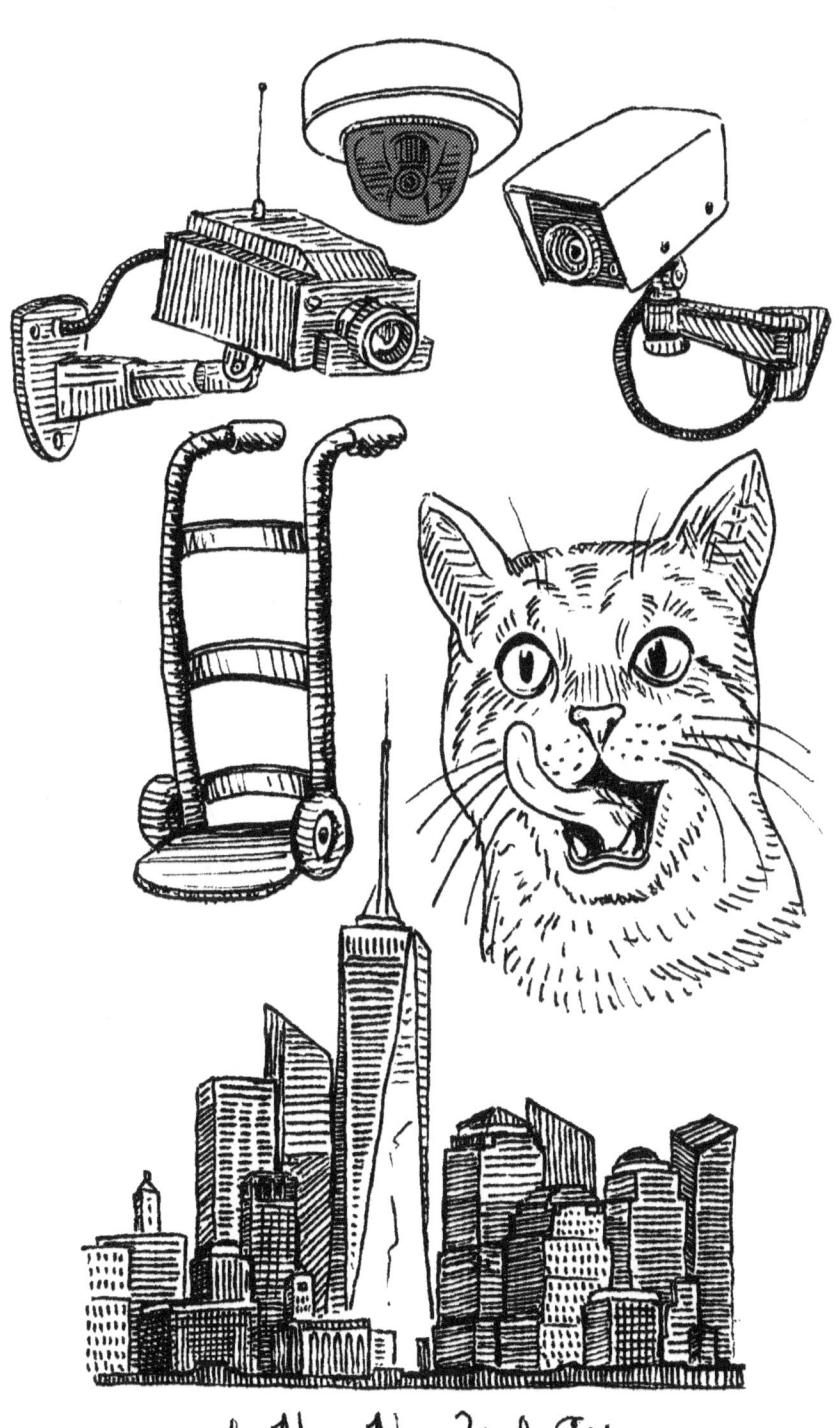

the New New York City

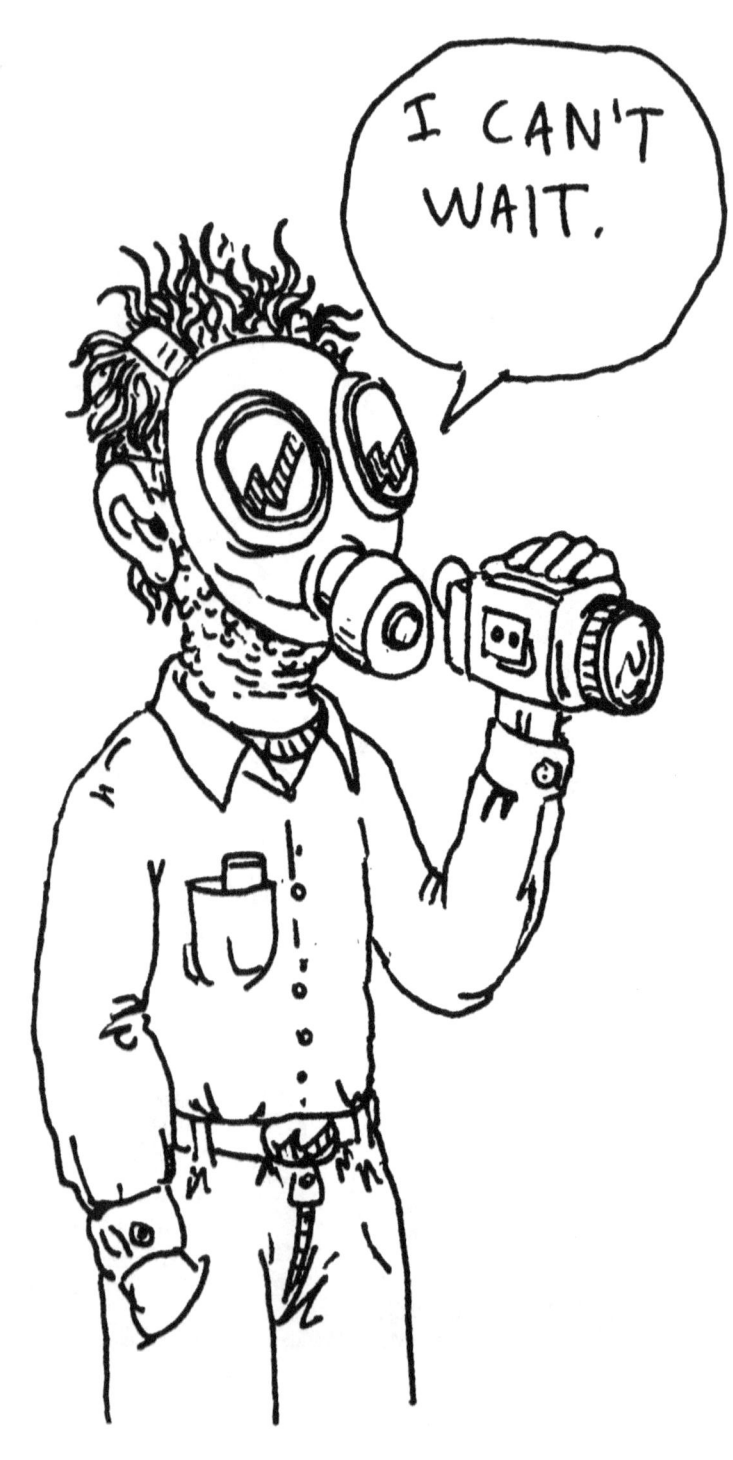

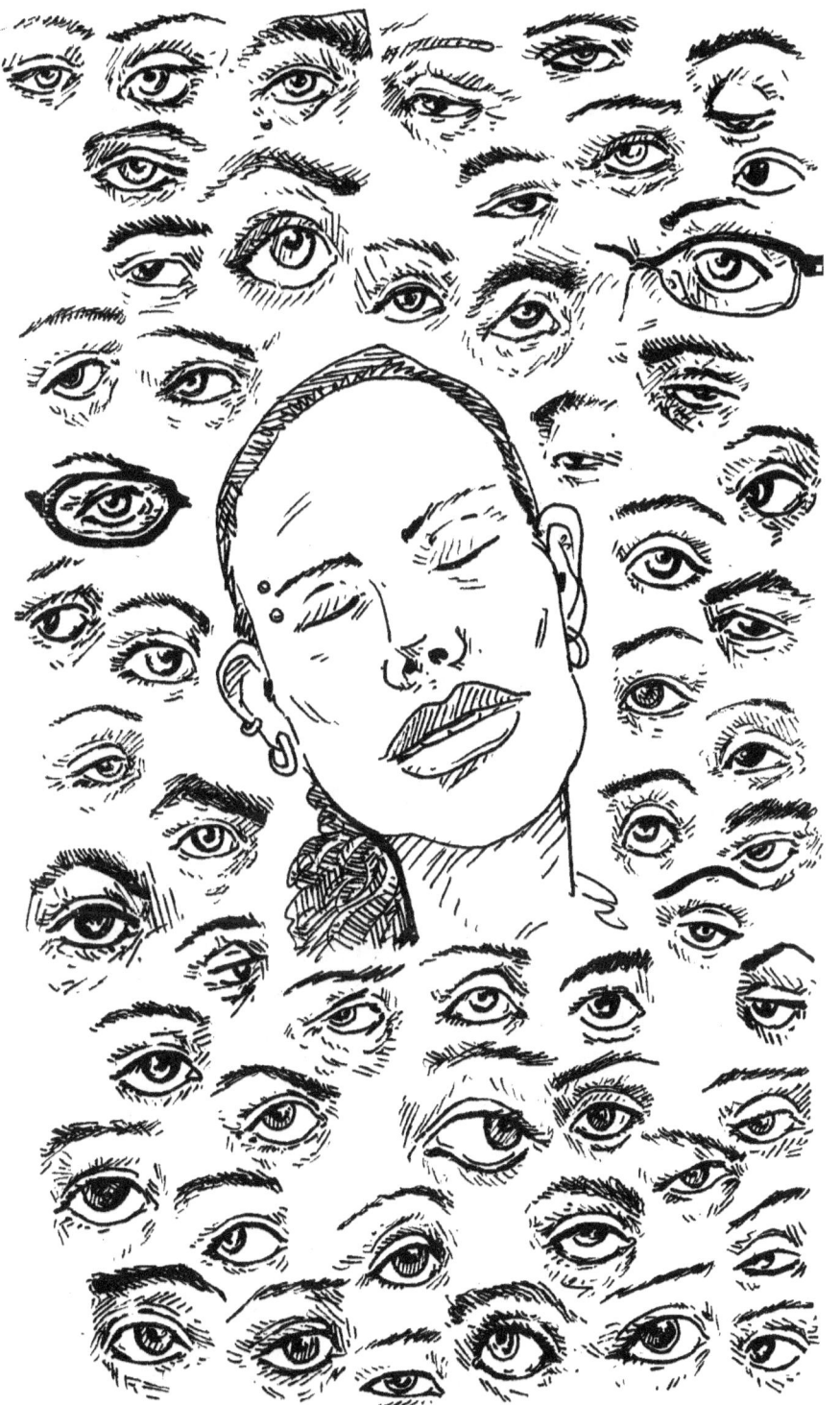

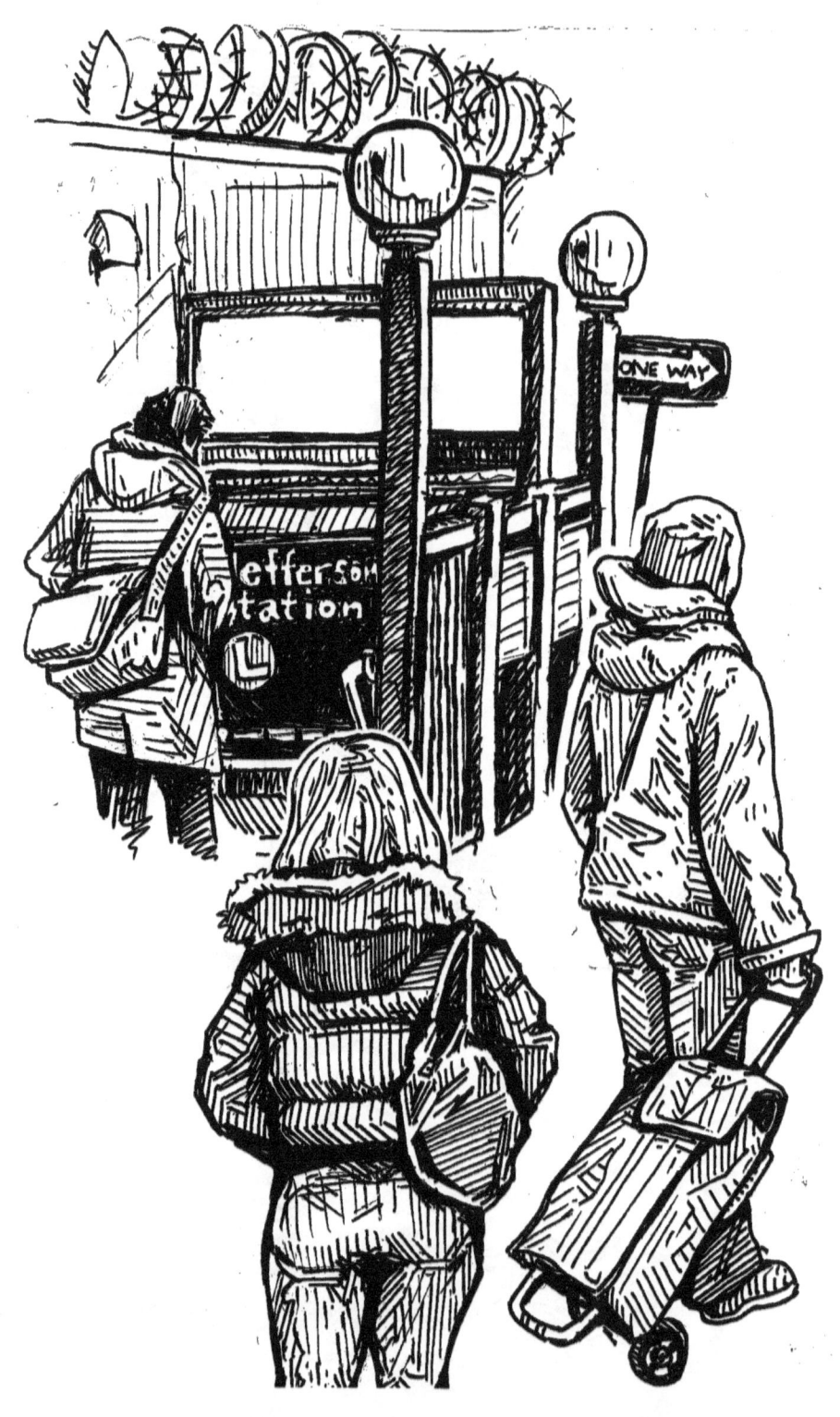

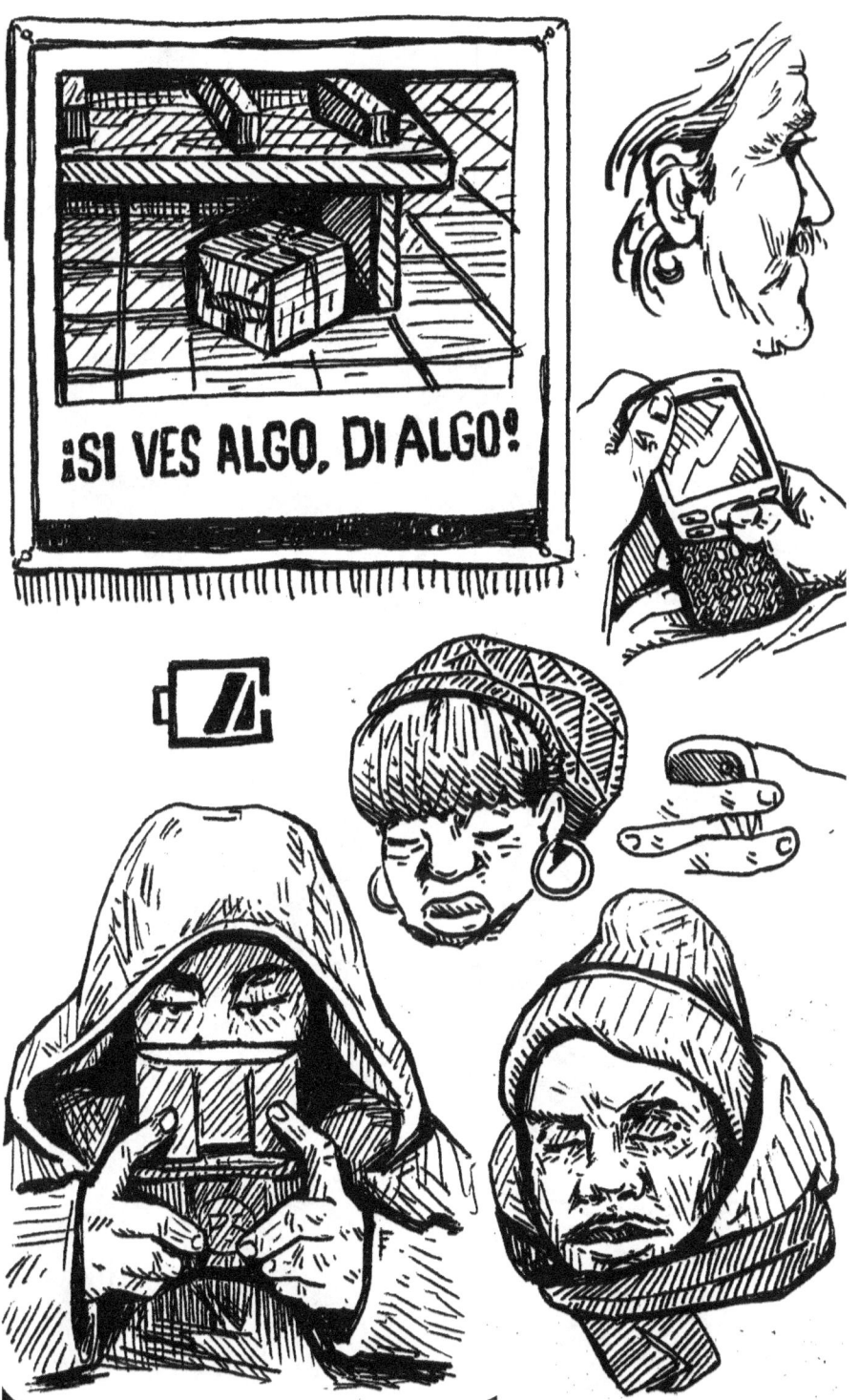

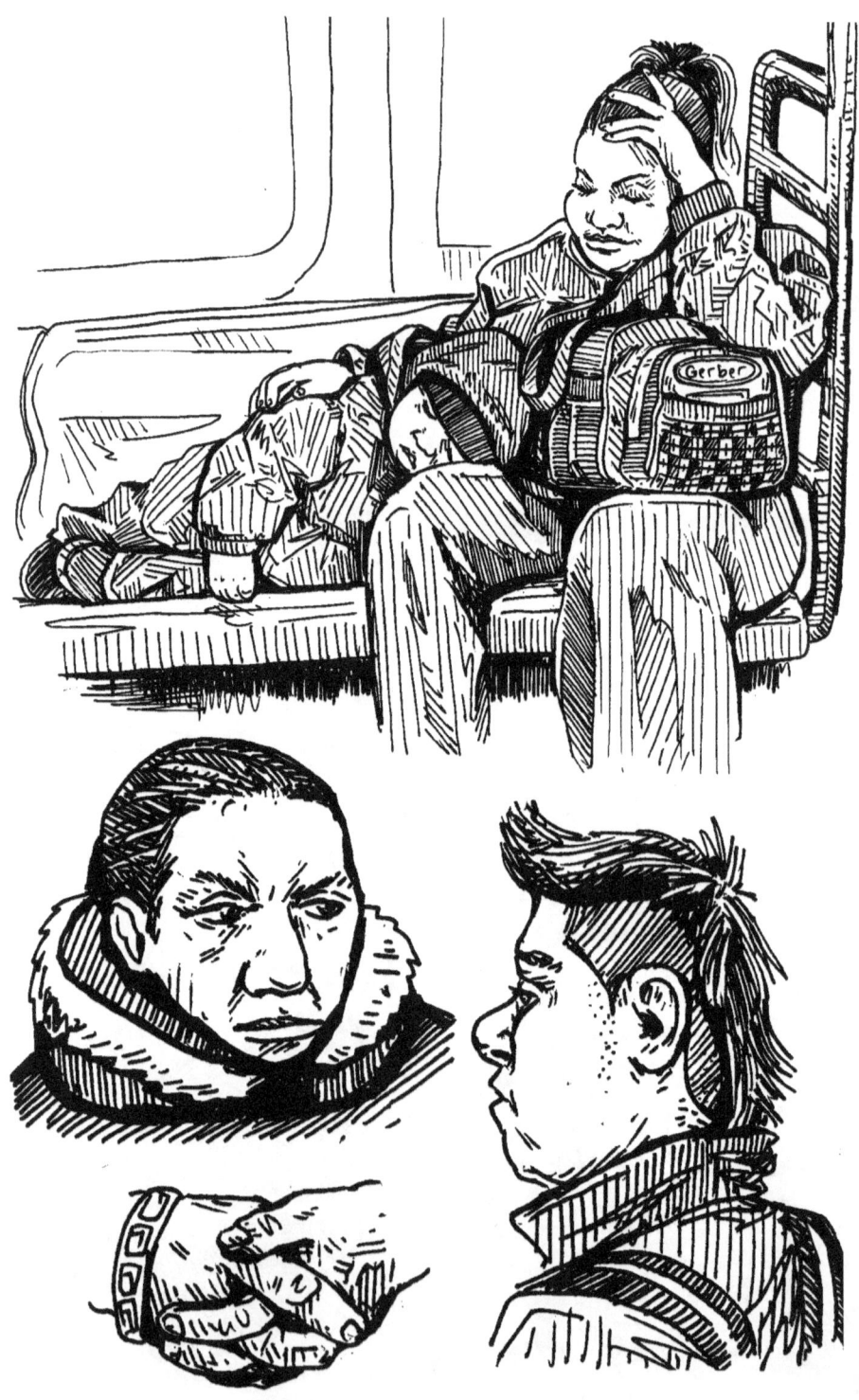

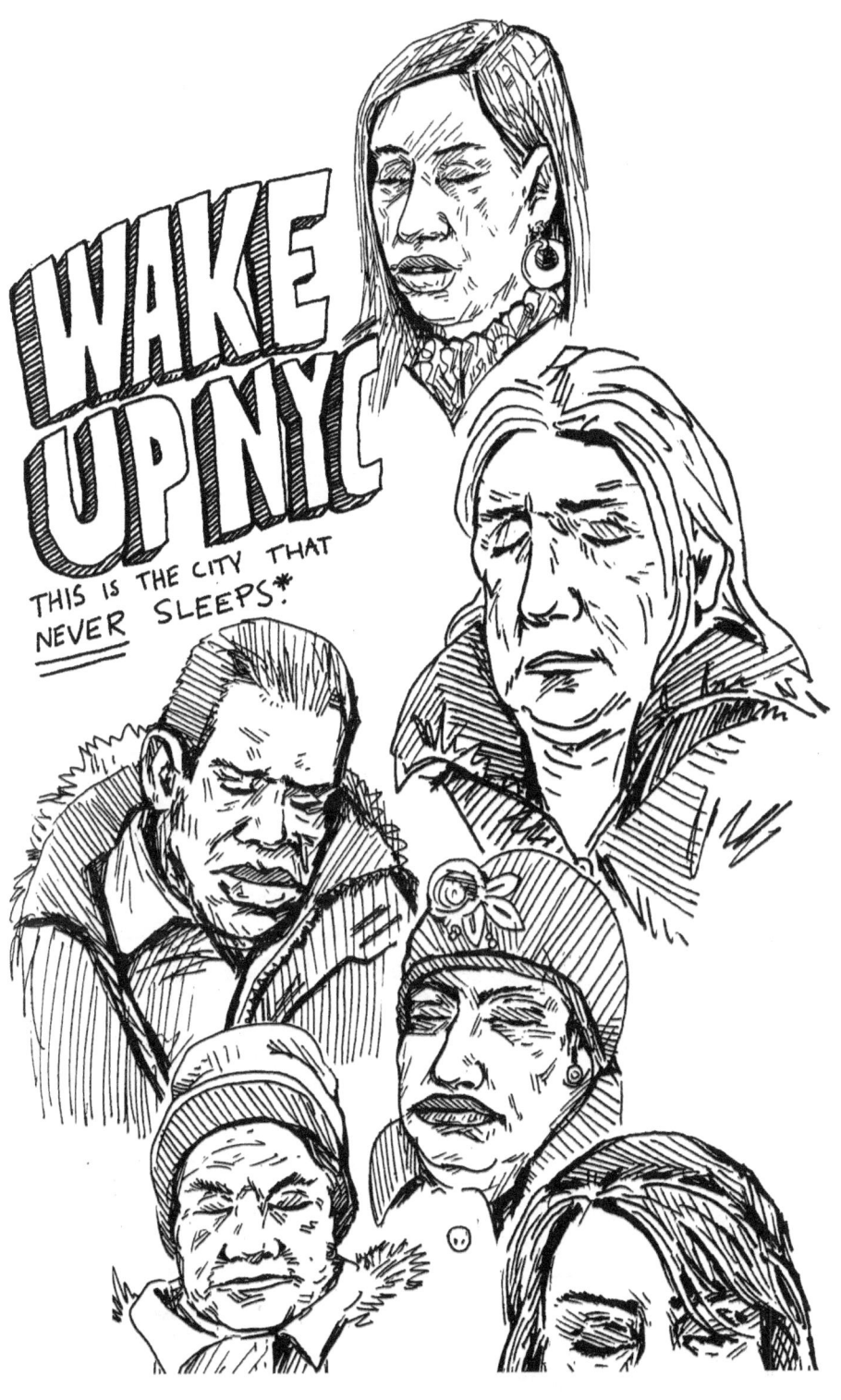

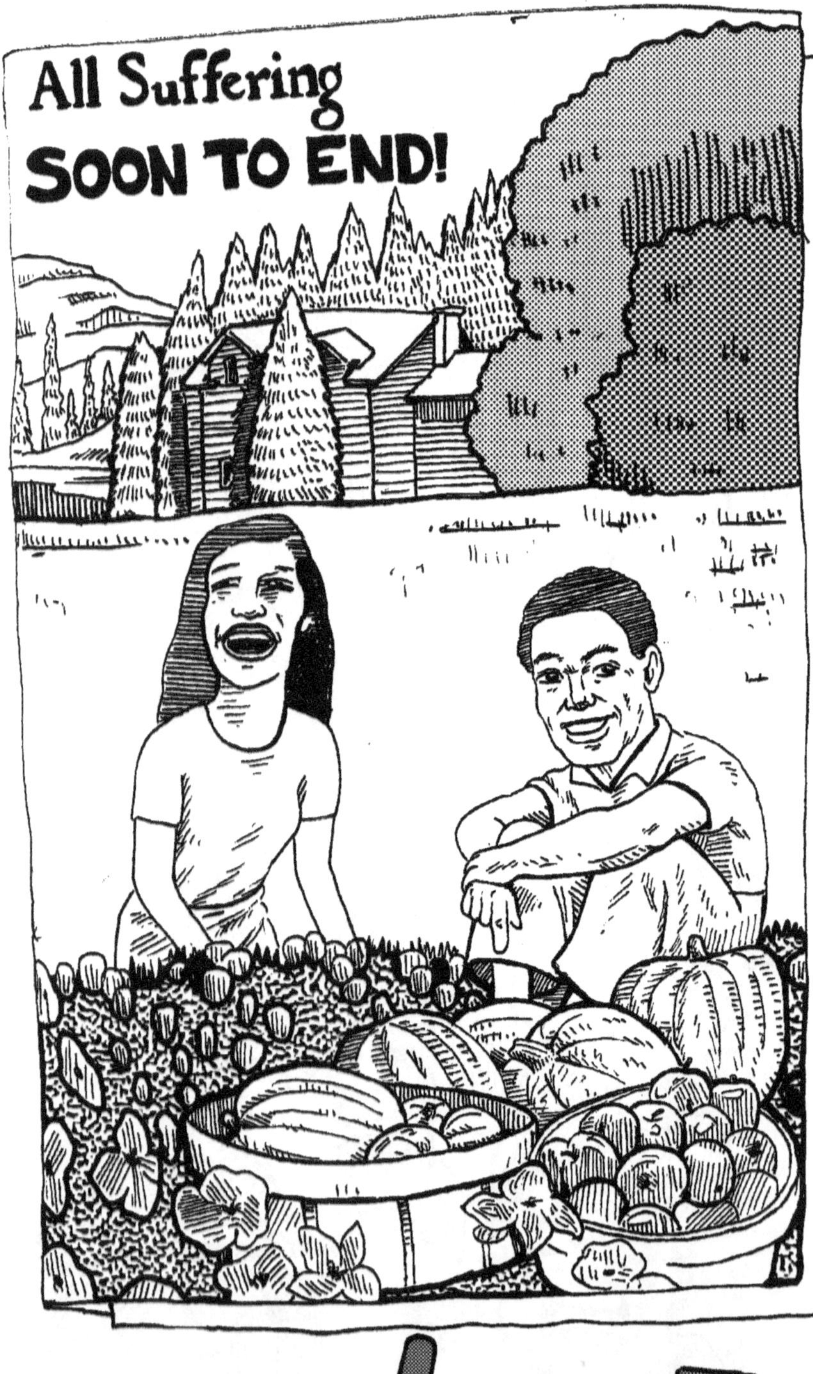

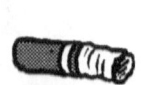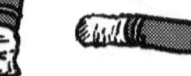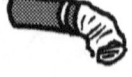

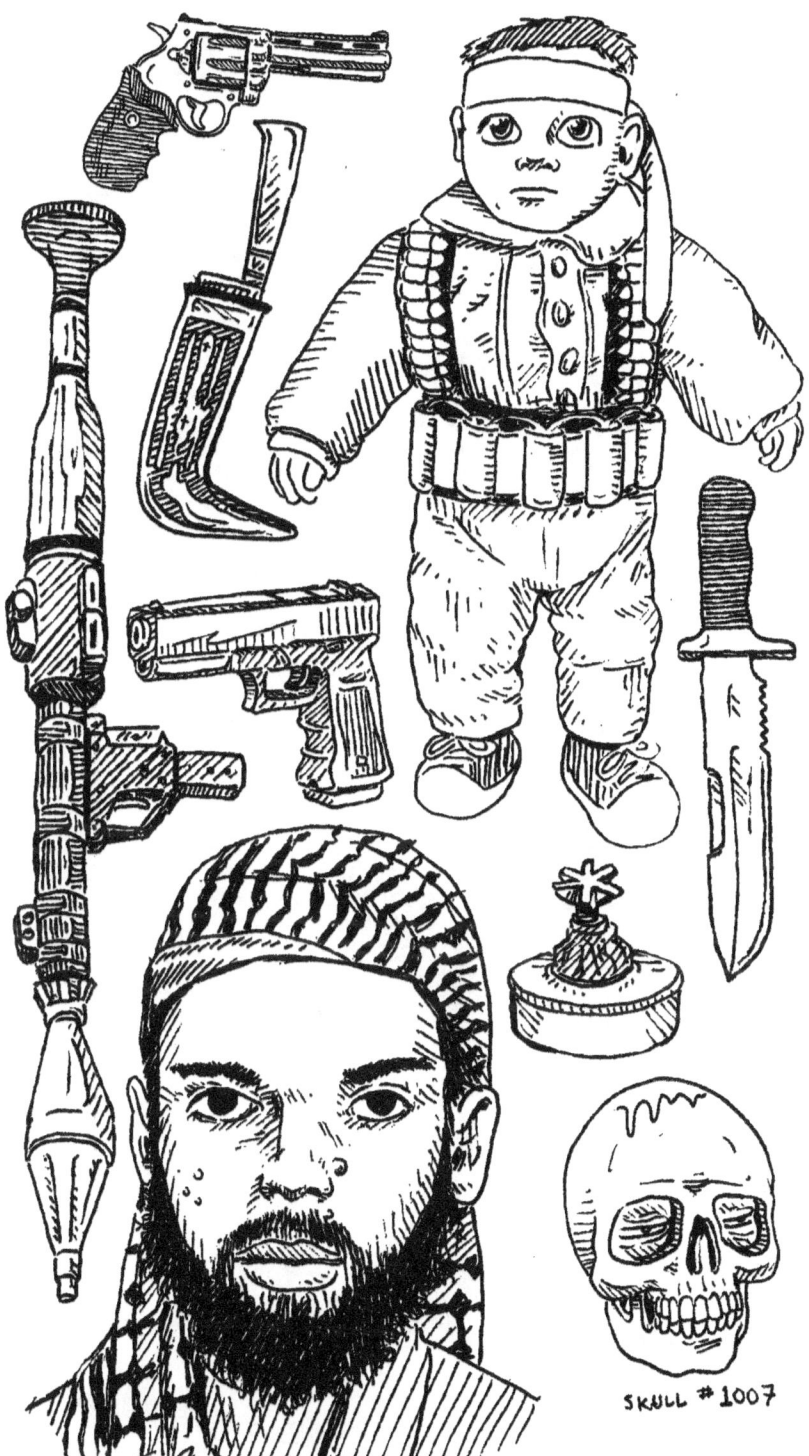

SKULL # 1007

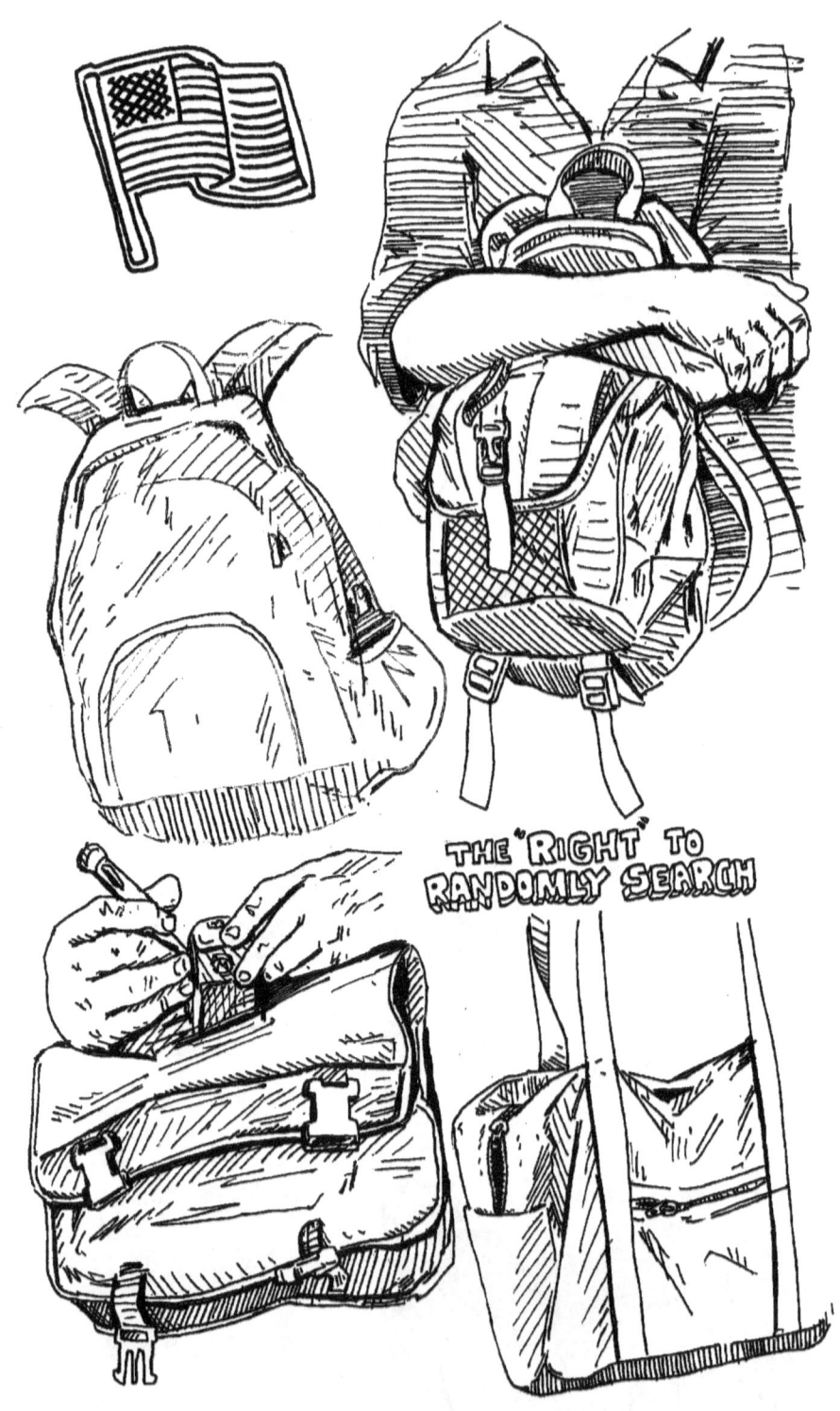

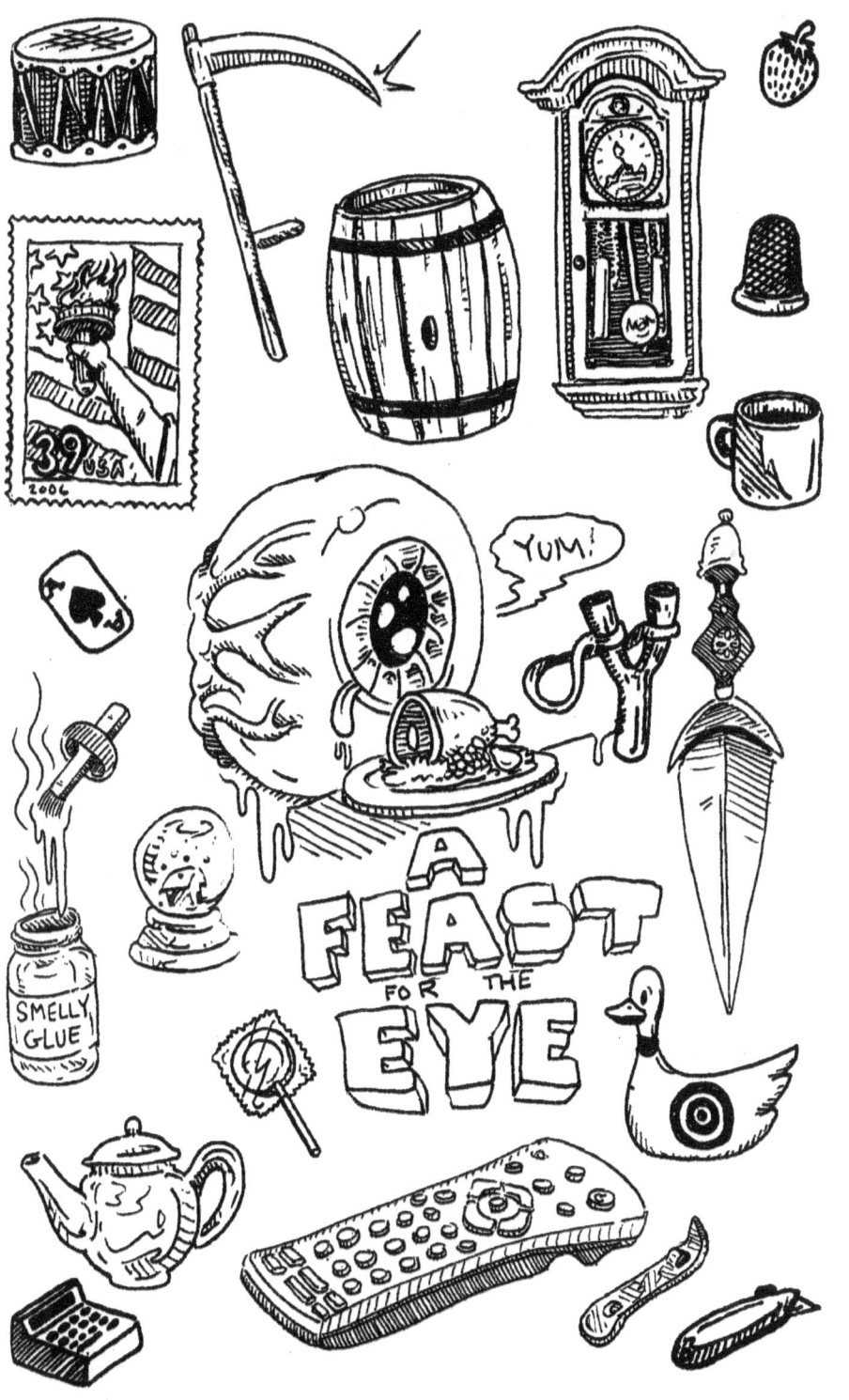

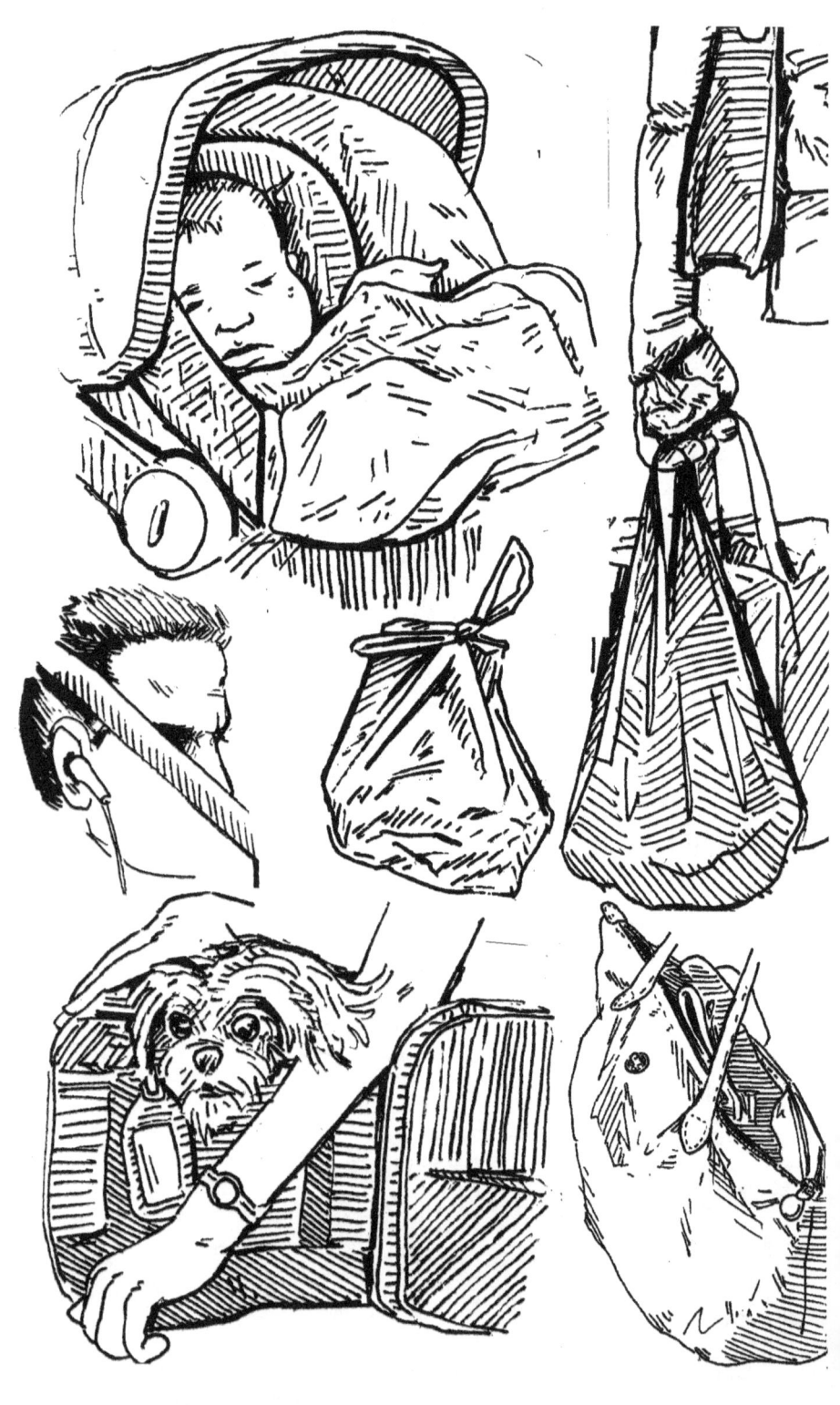

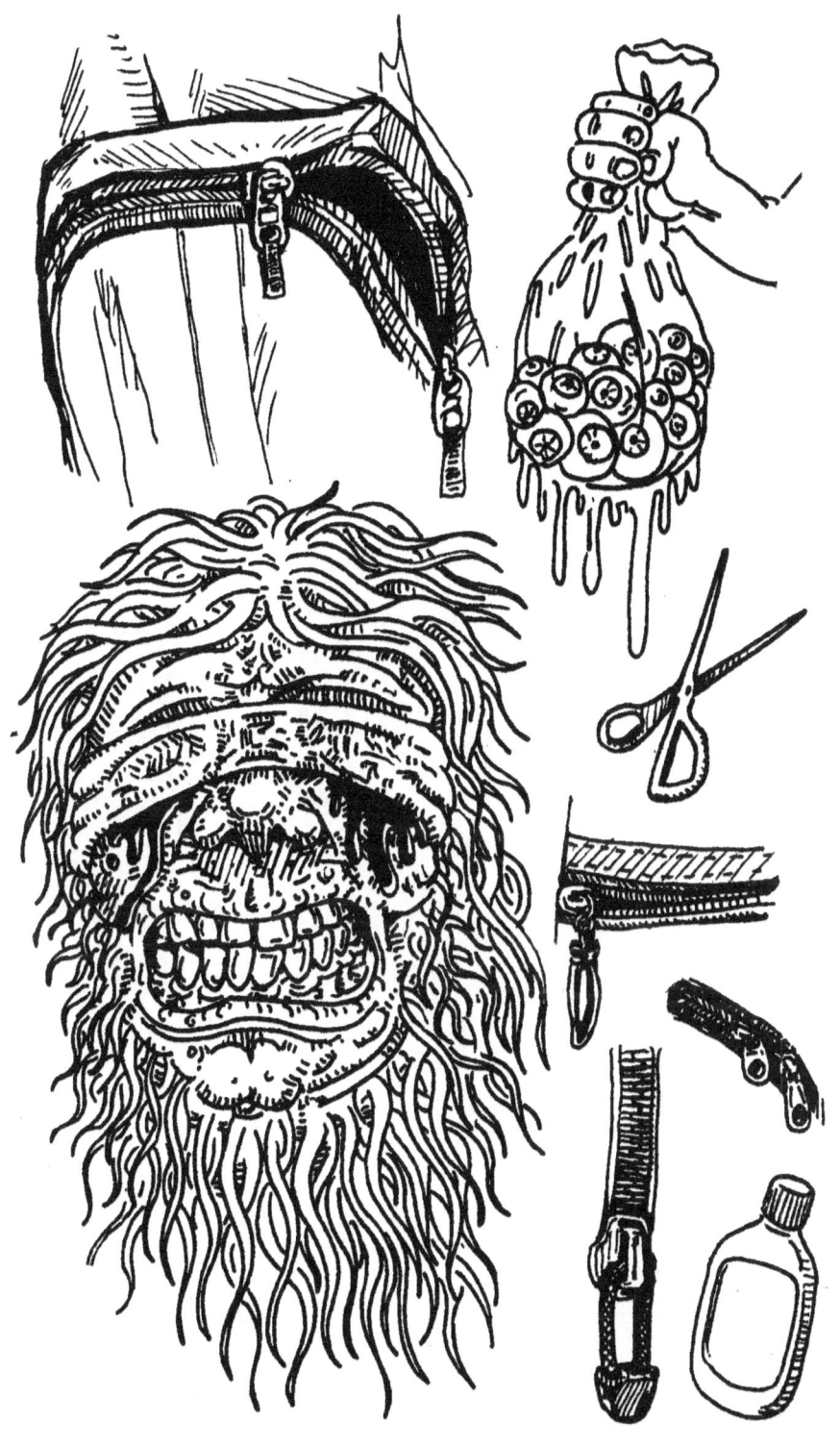

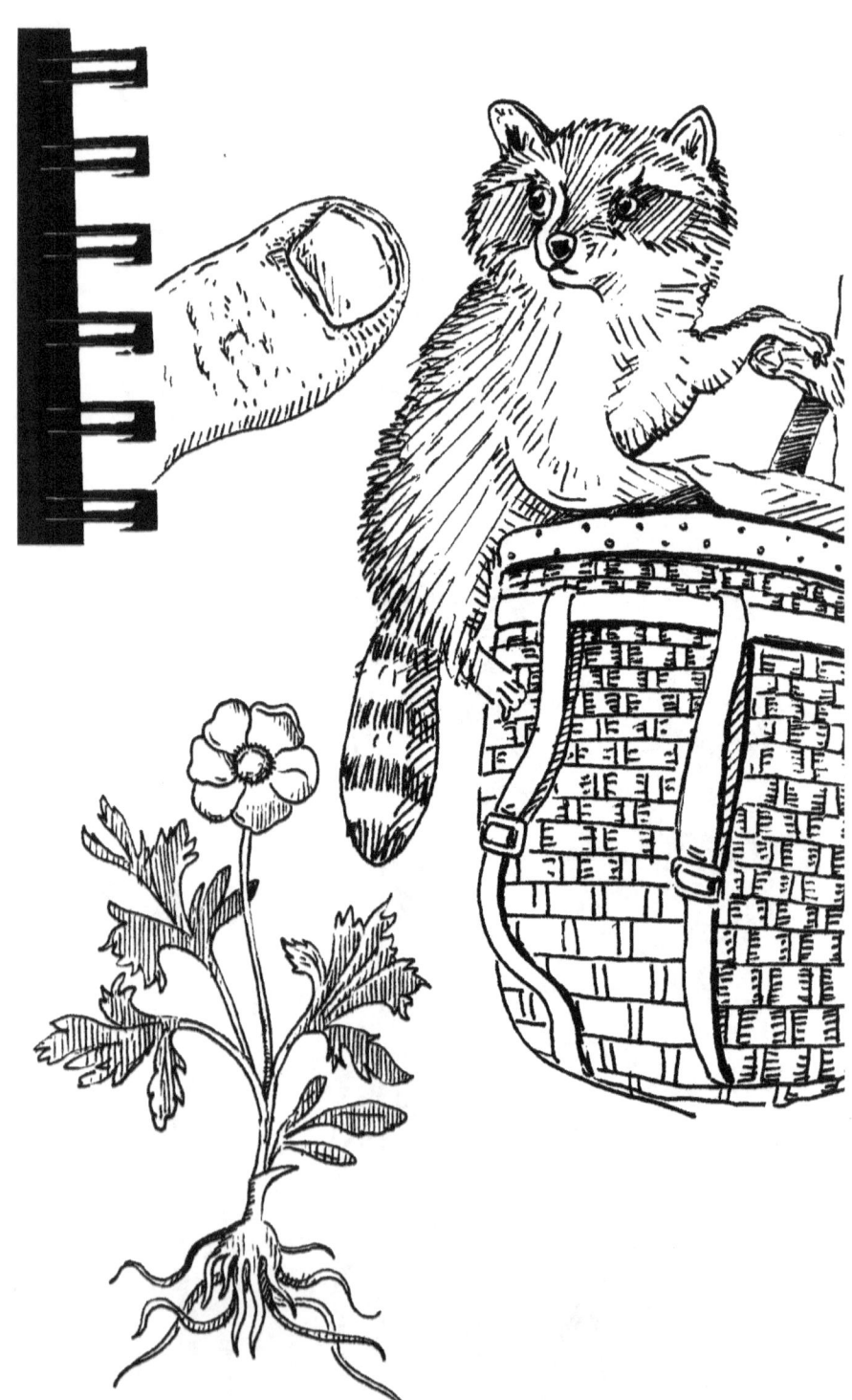

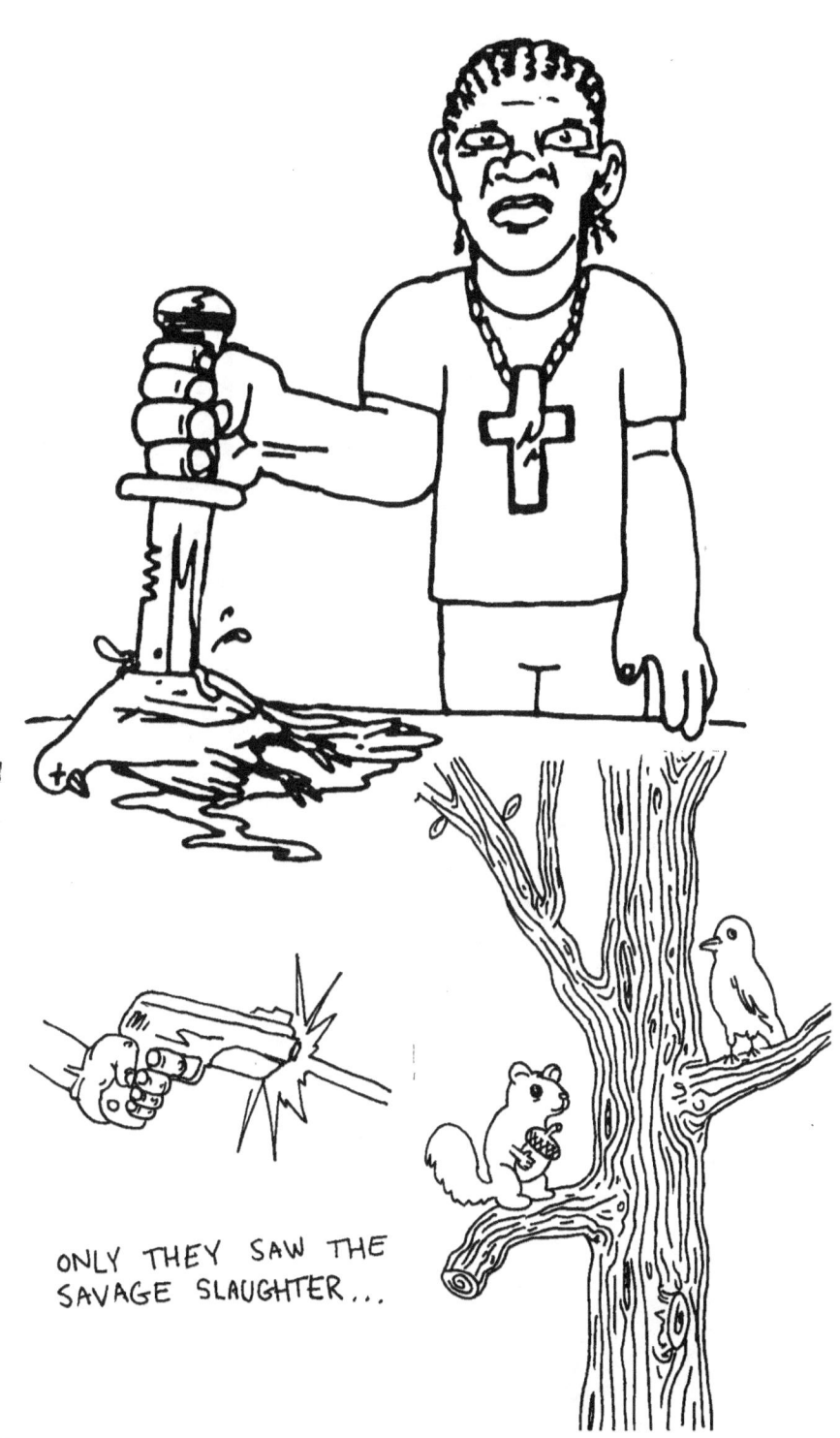

ONLY THEY SAW THE
SAVAGE SLAUGHTER...

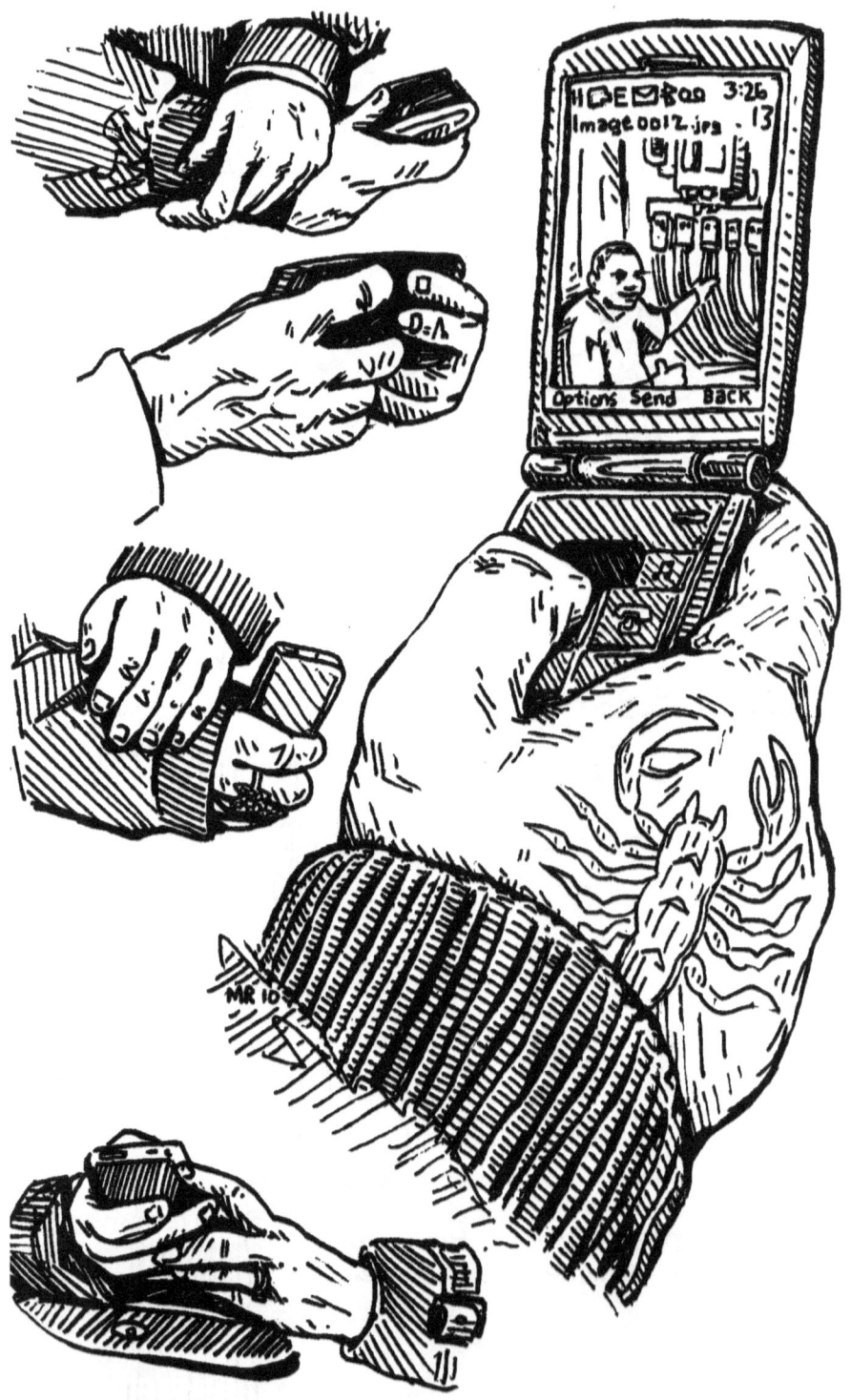

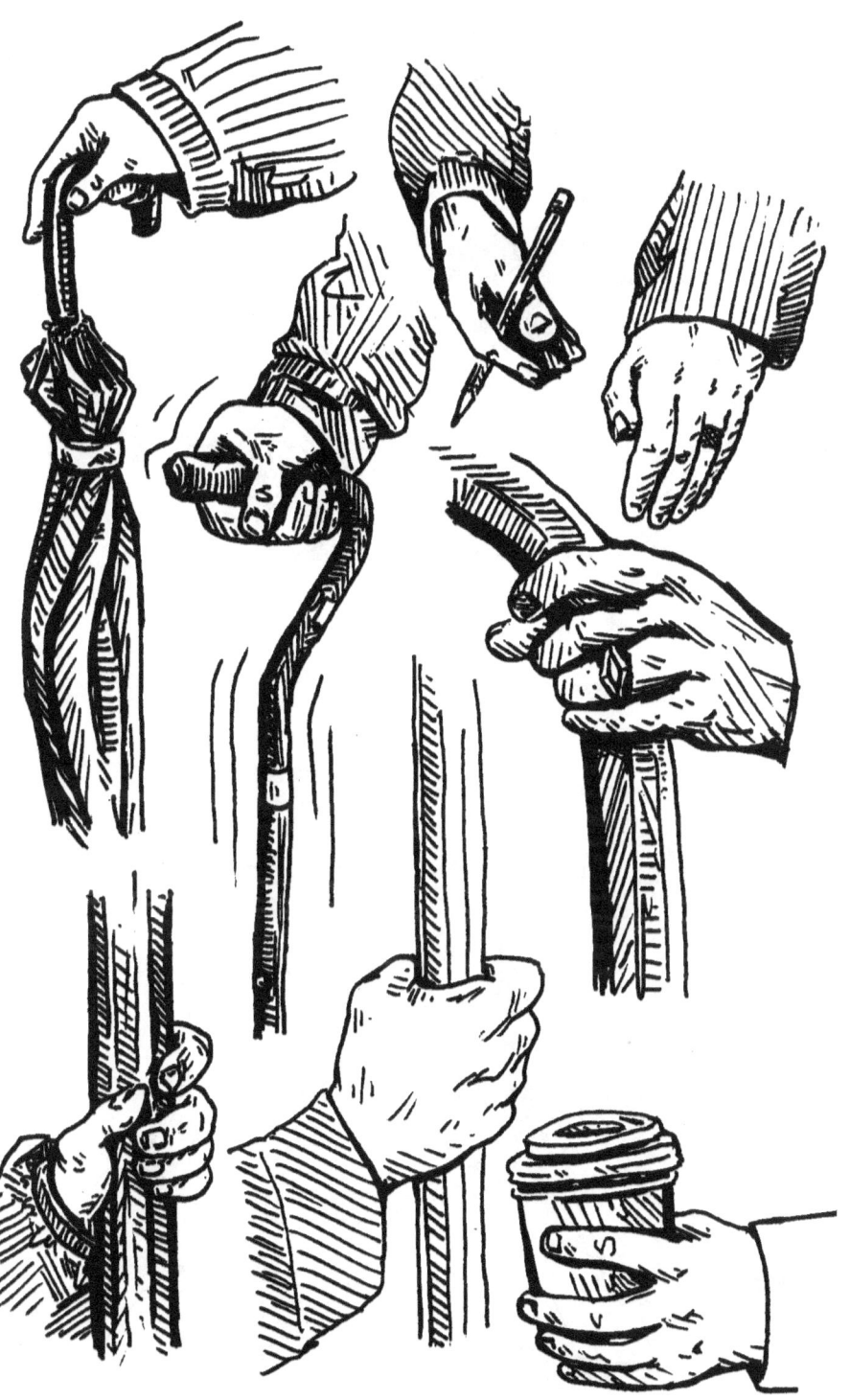

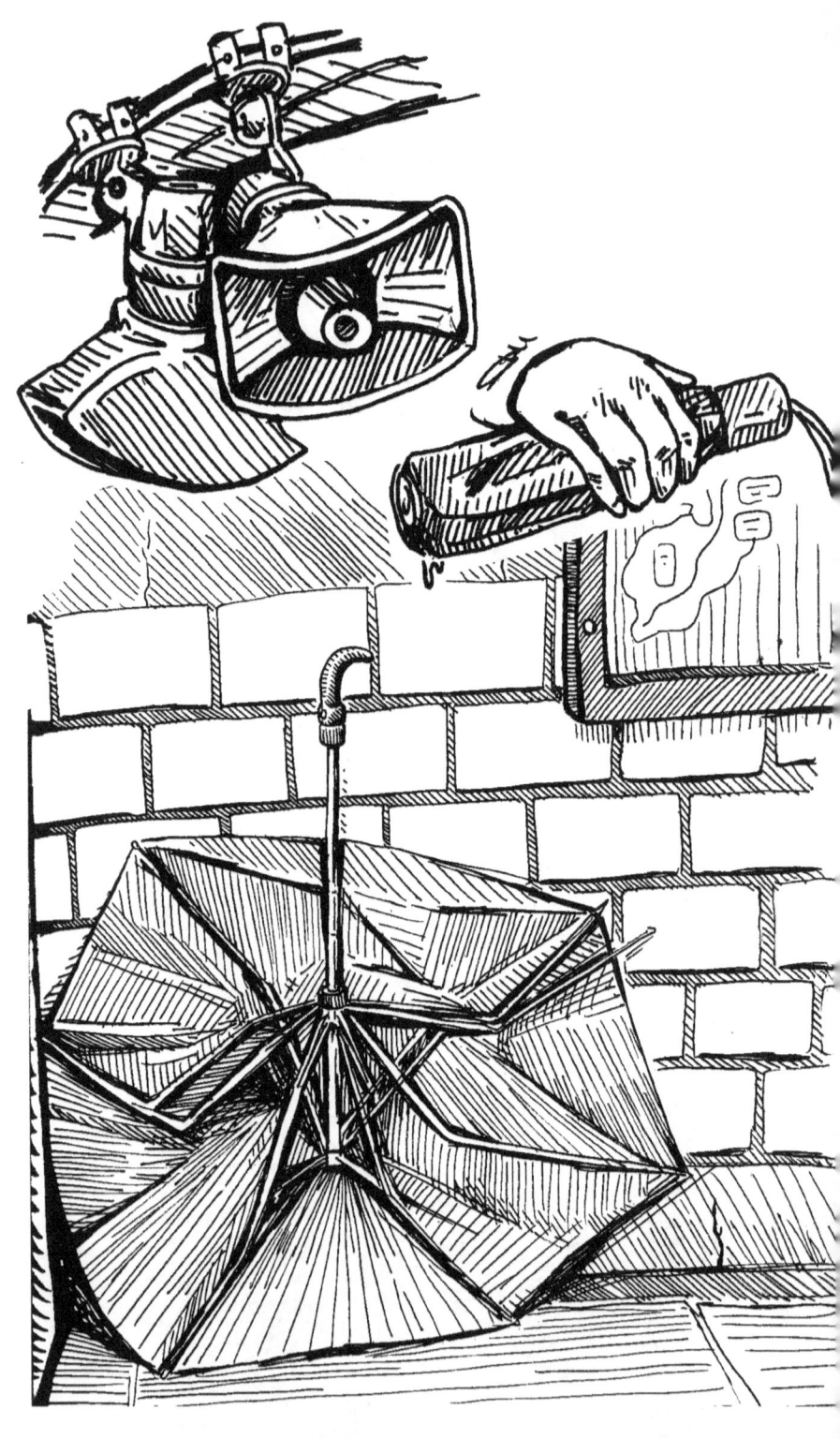

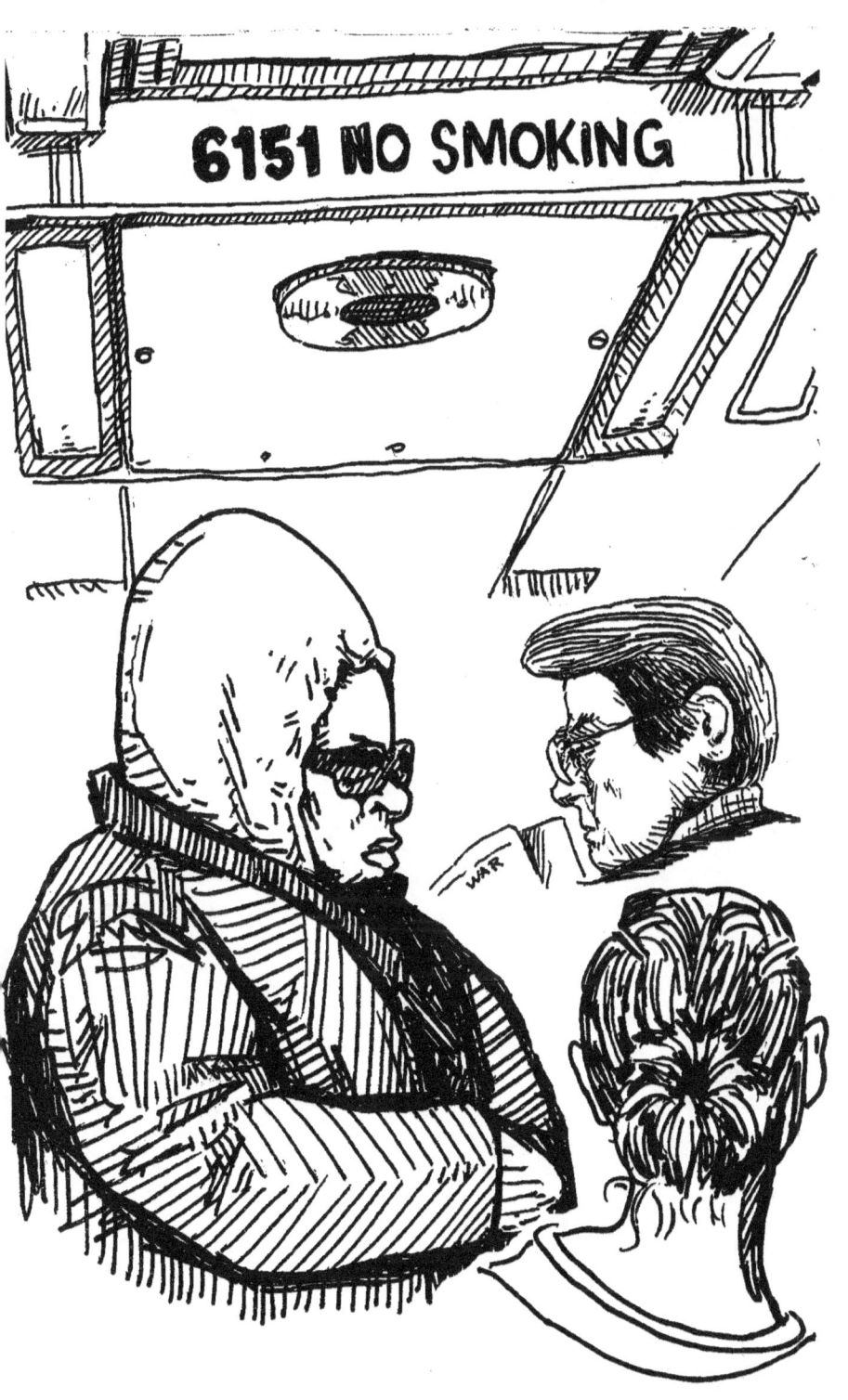

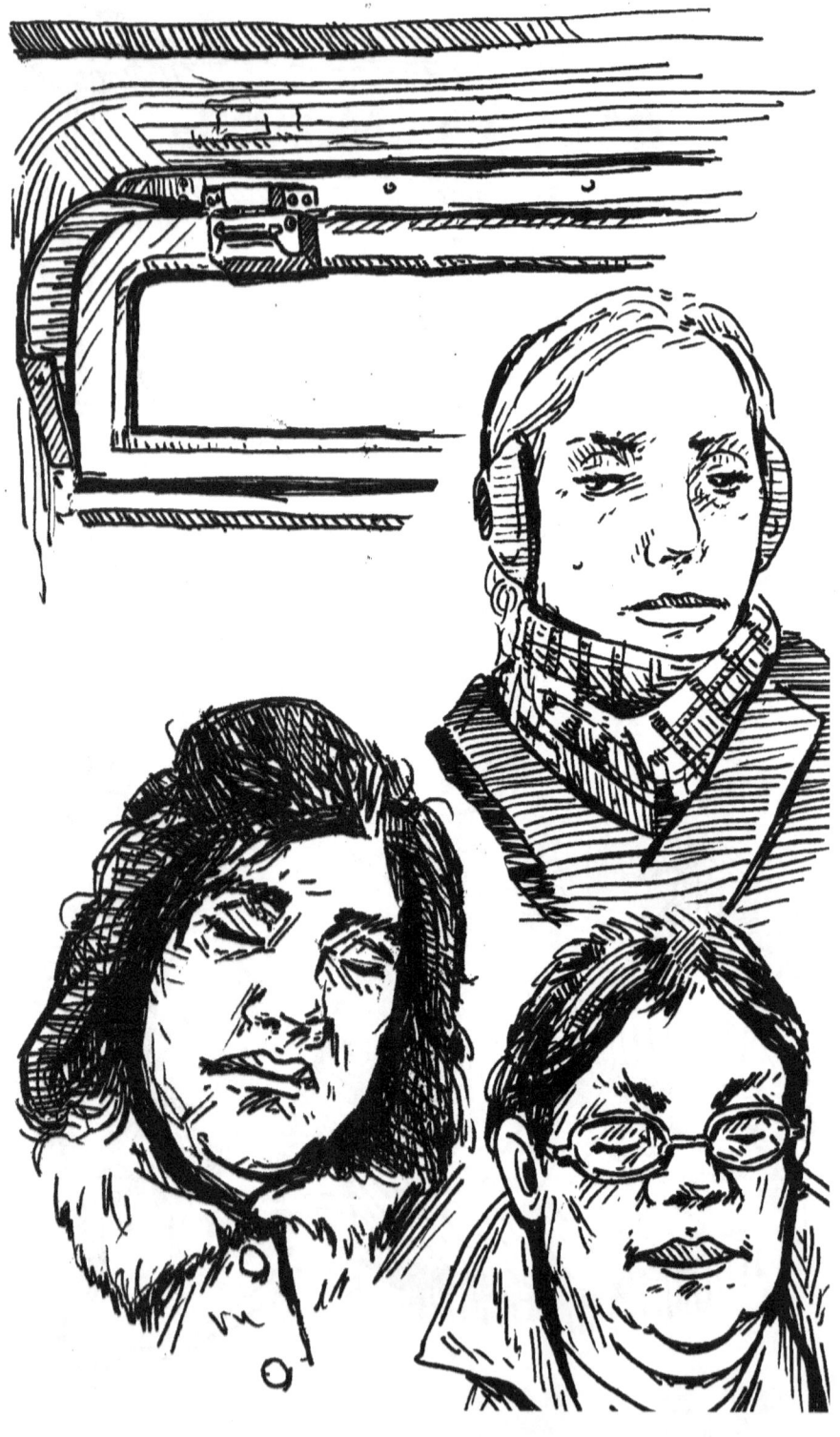

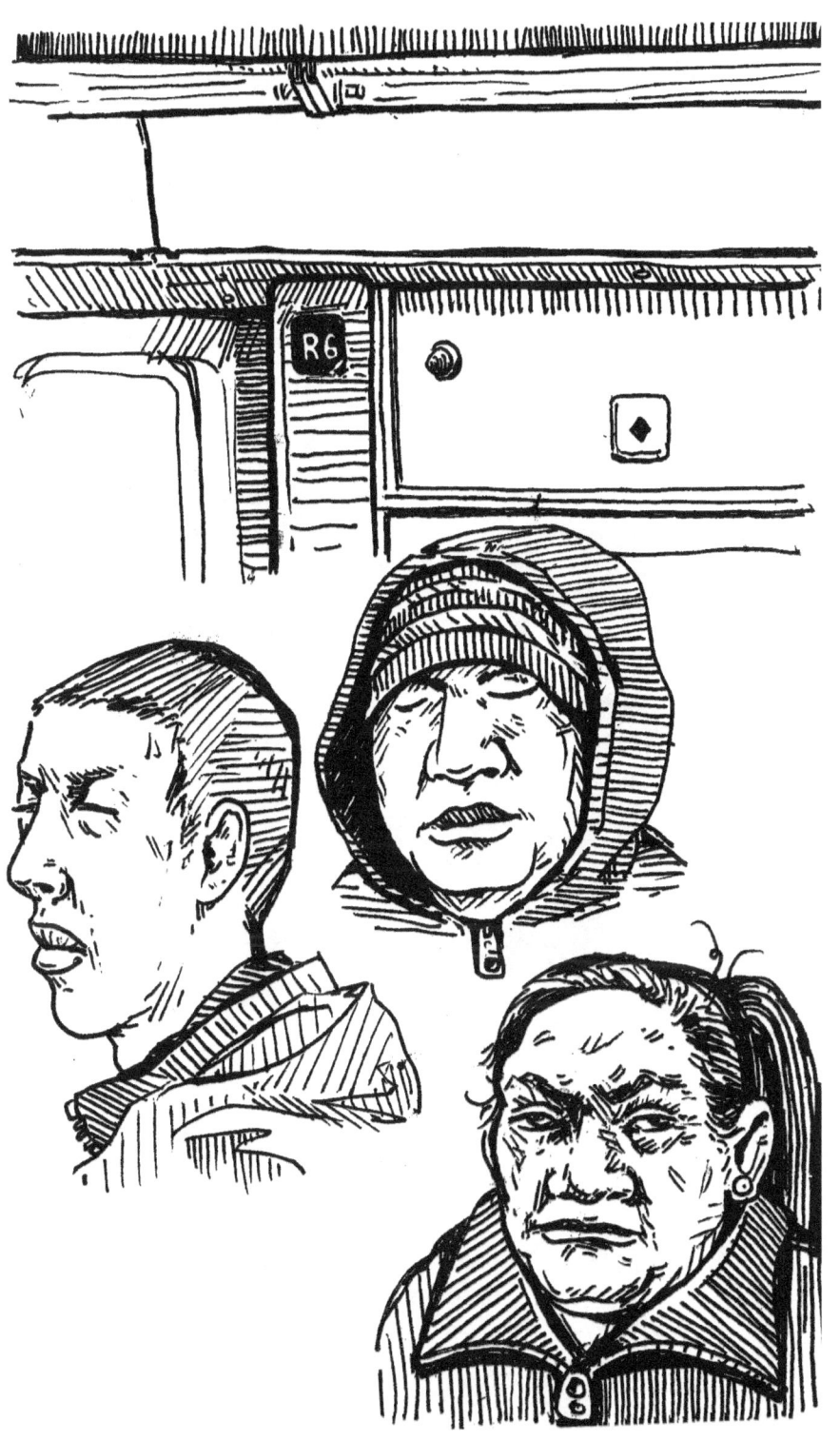

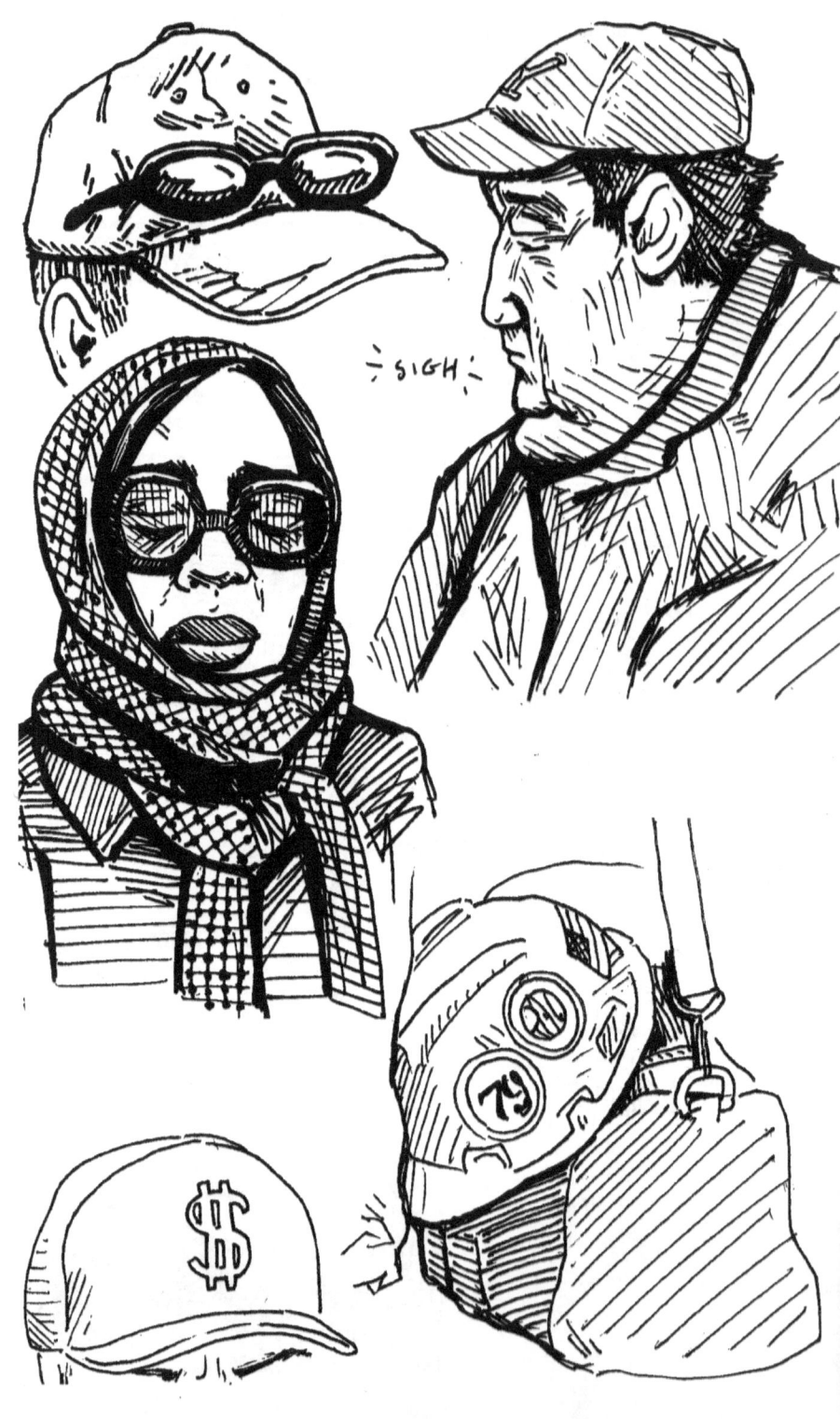

SIGH

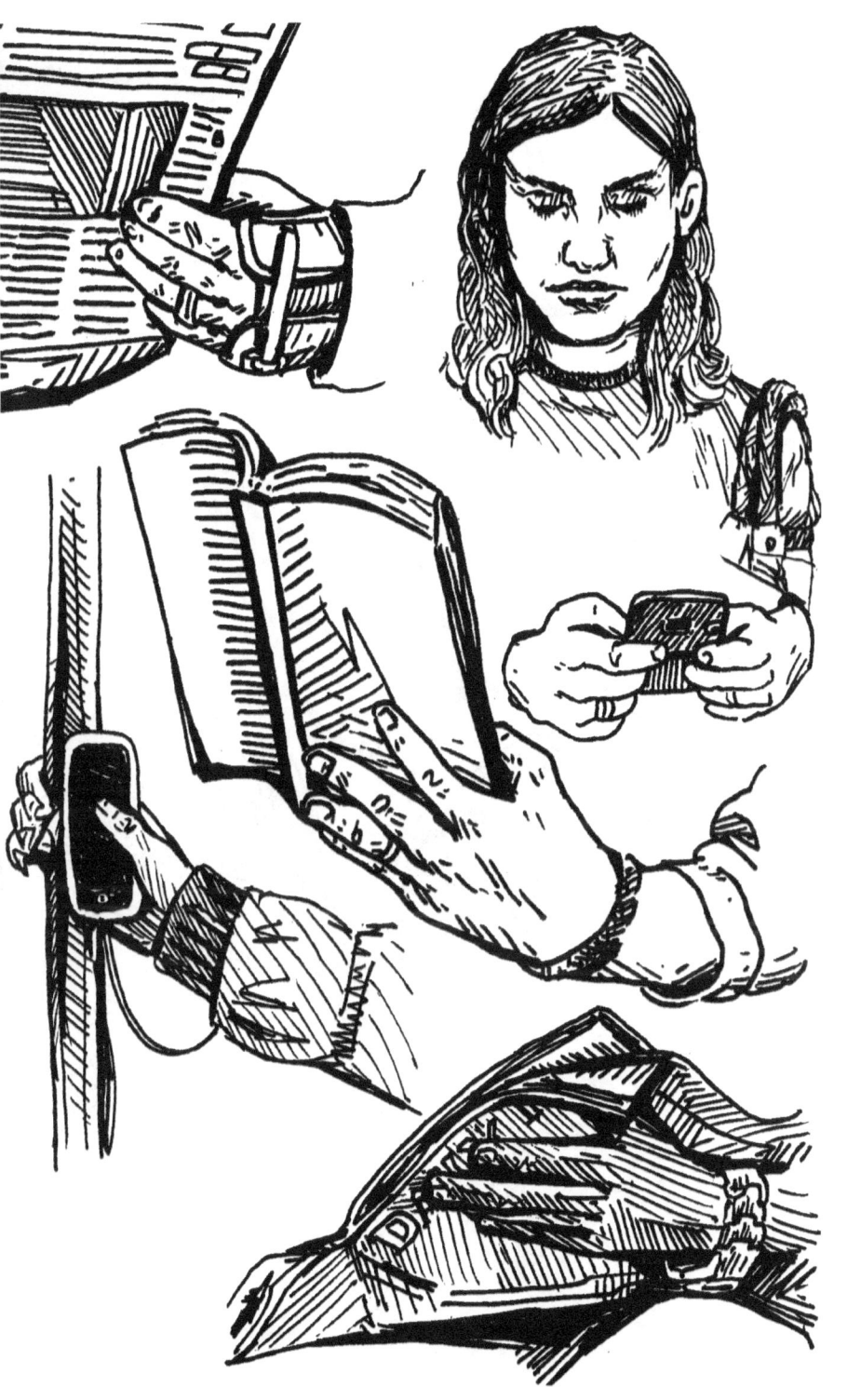

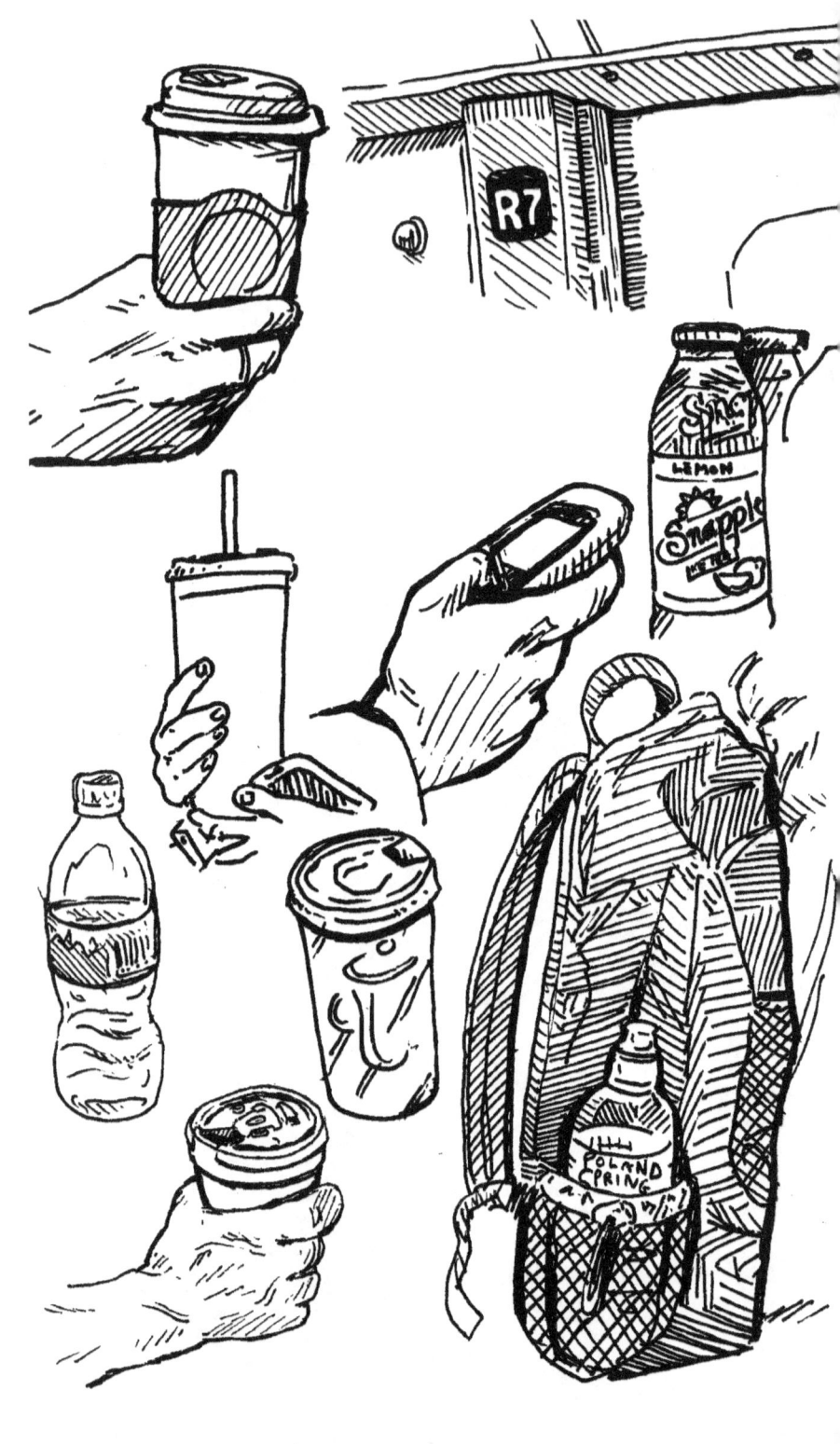

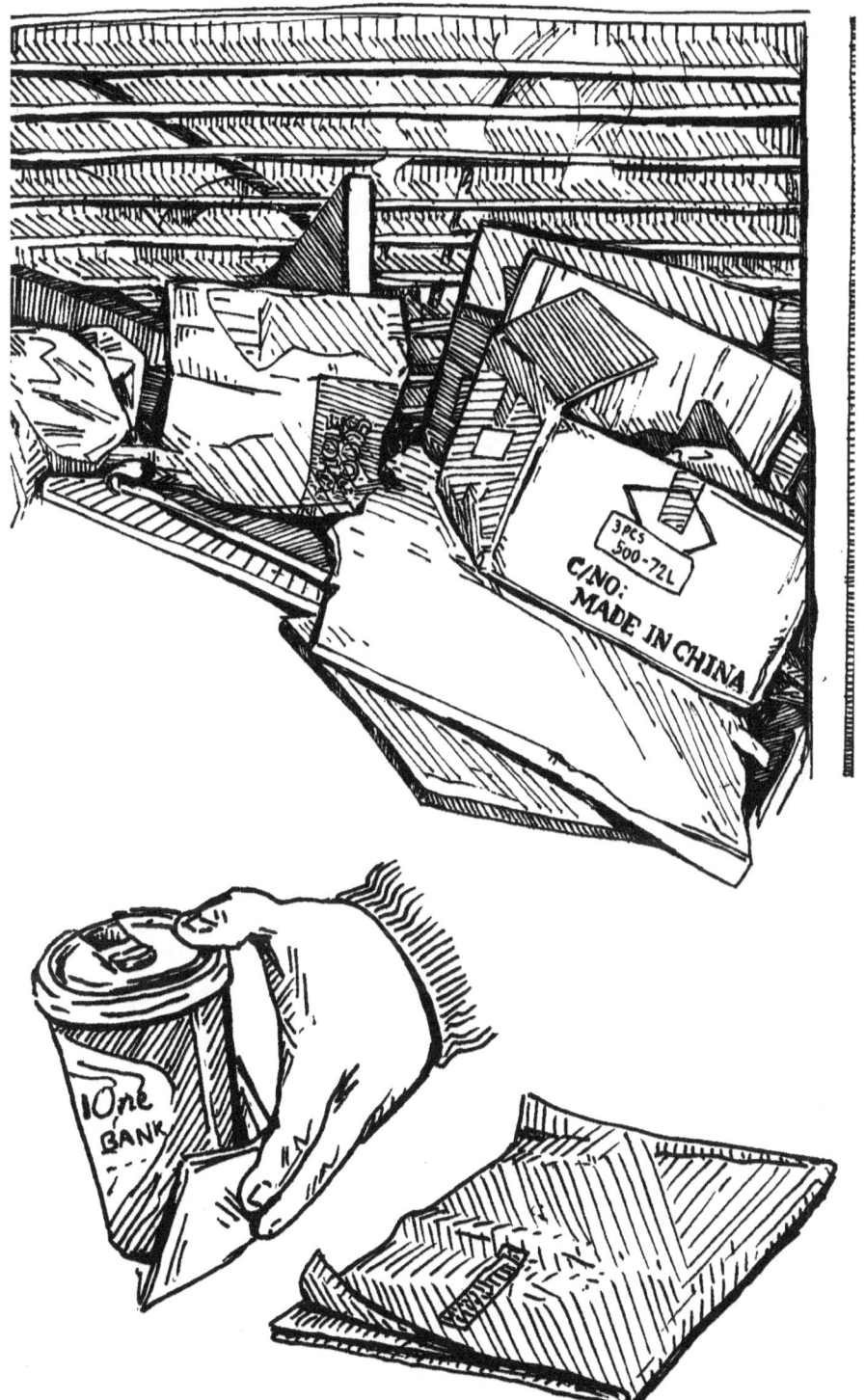

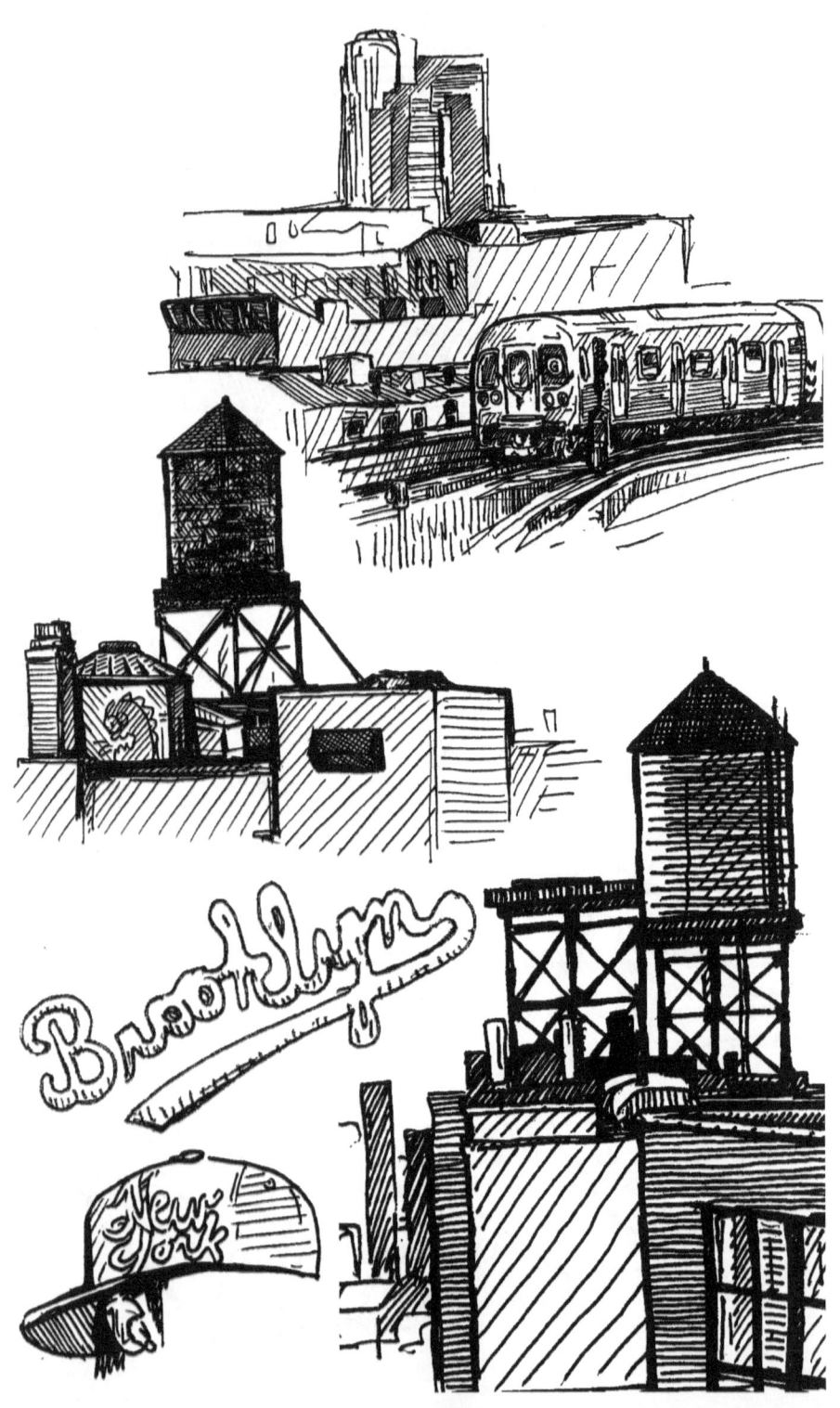

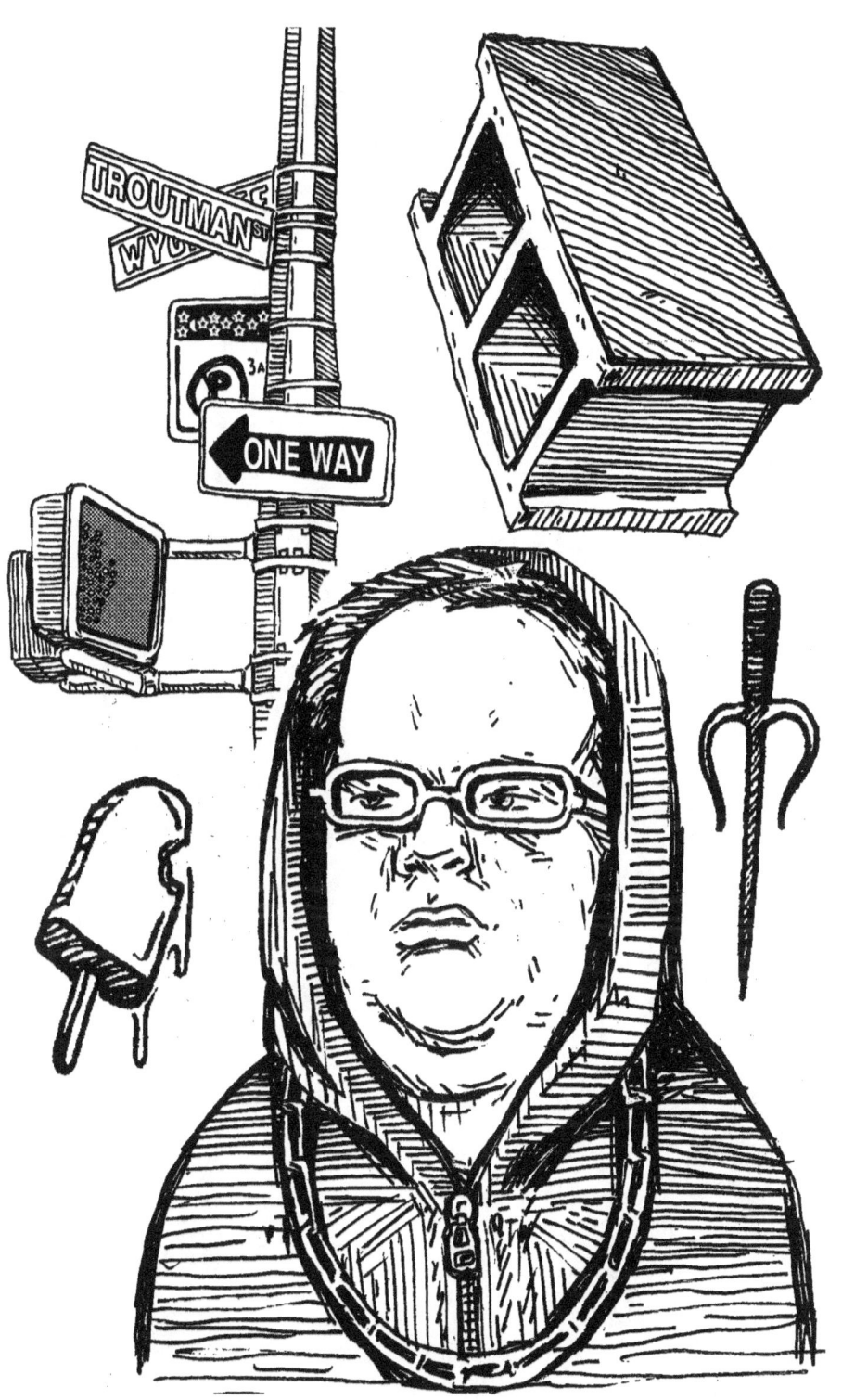

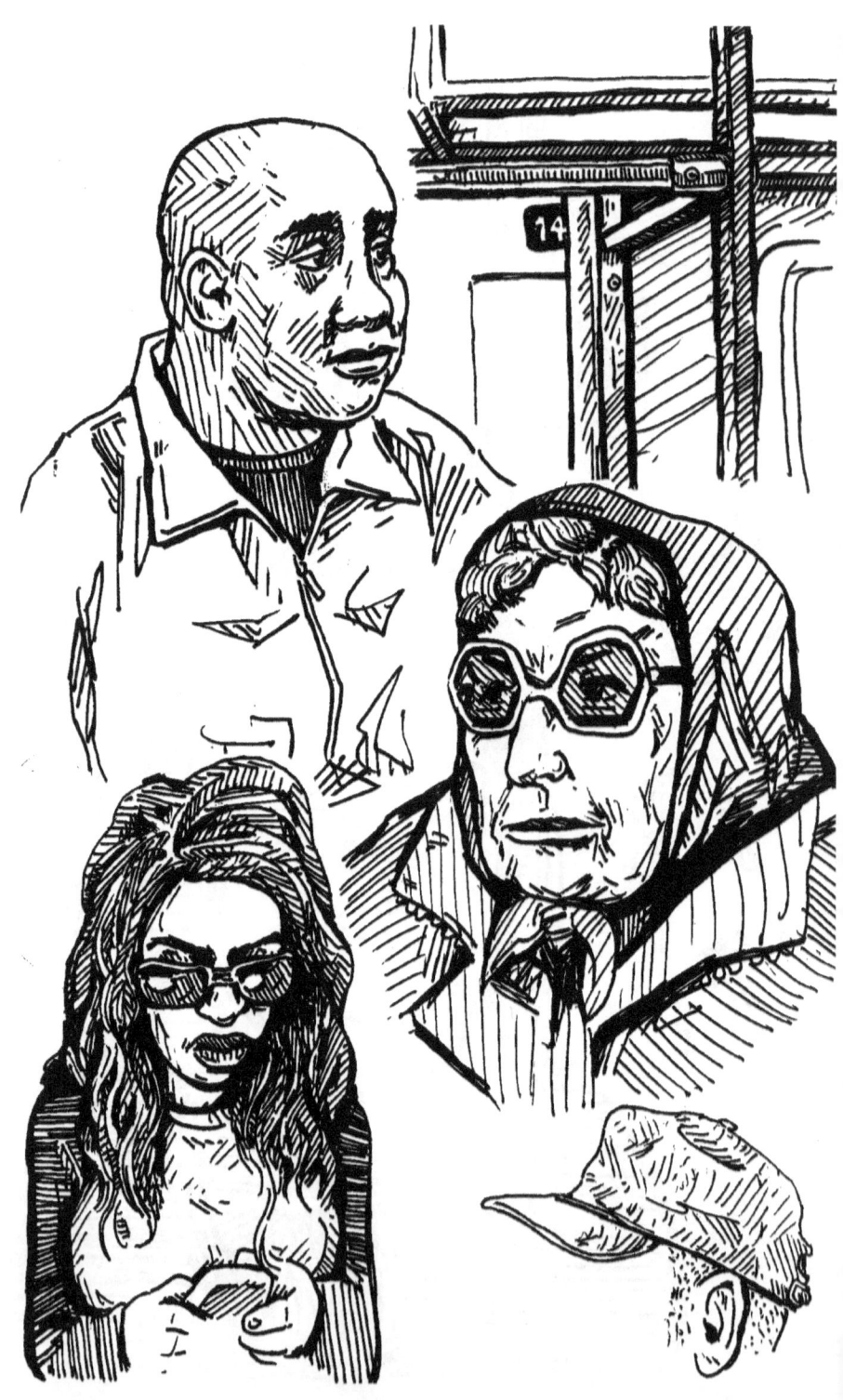

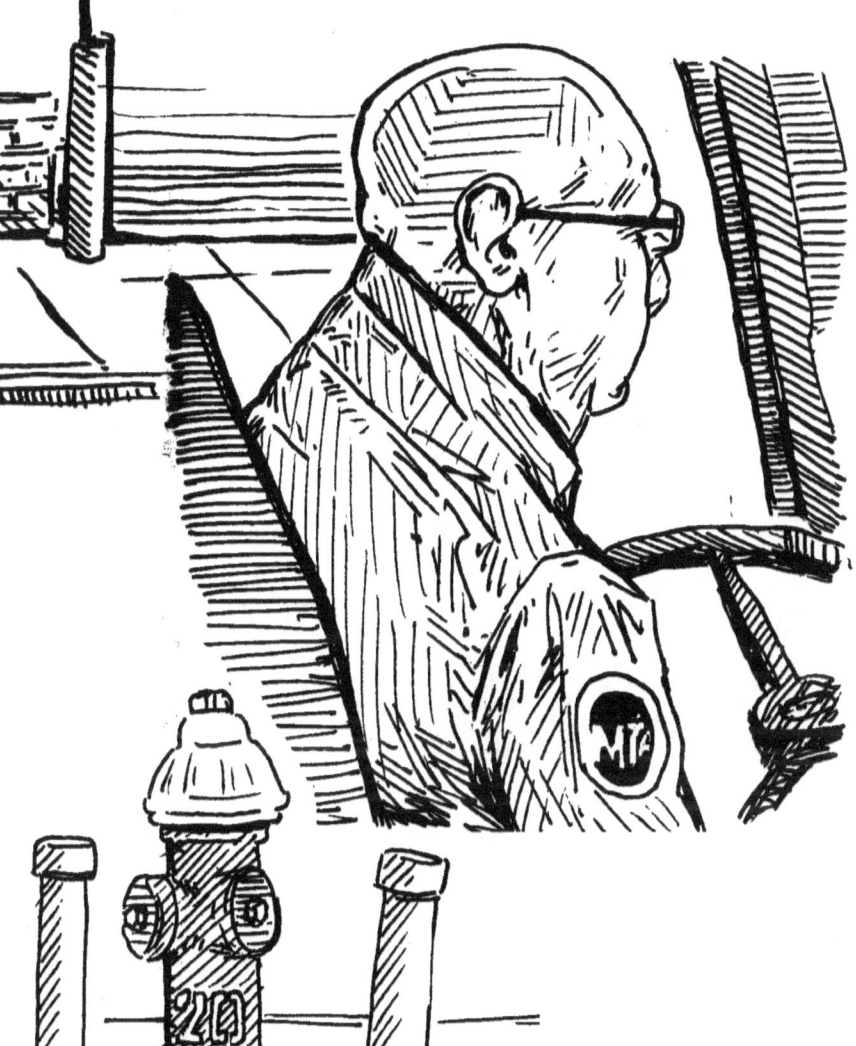

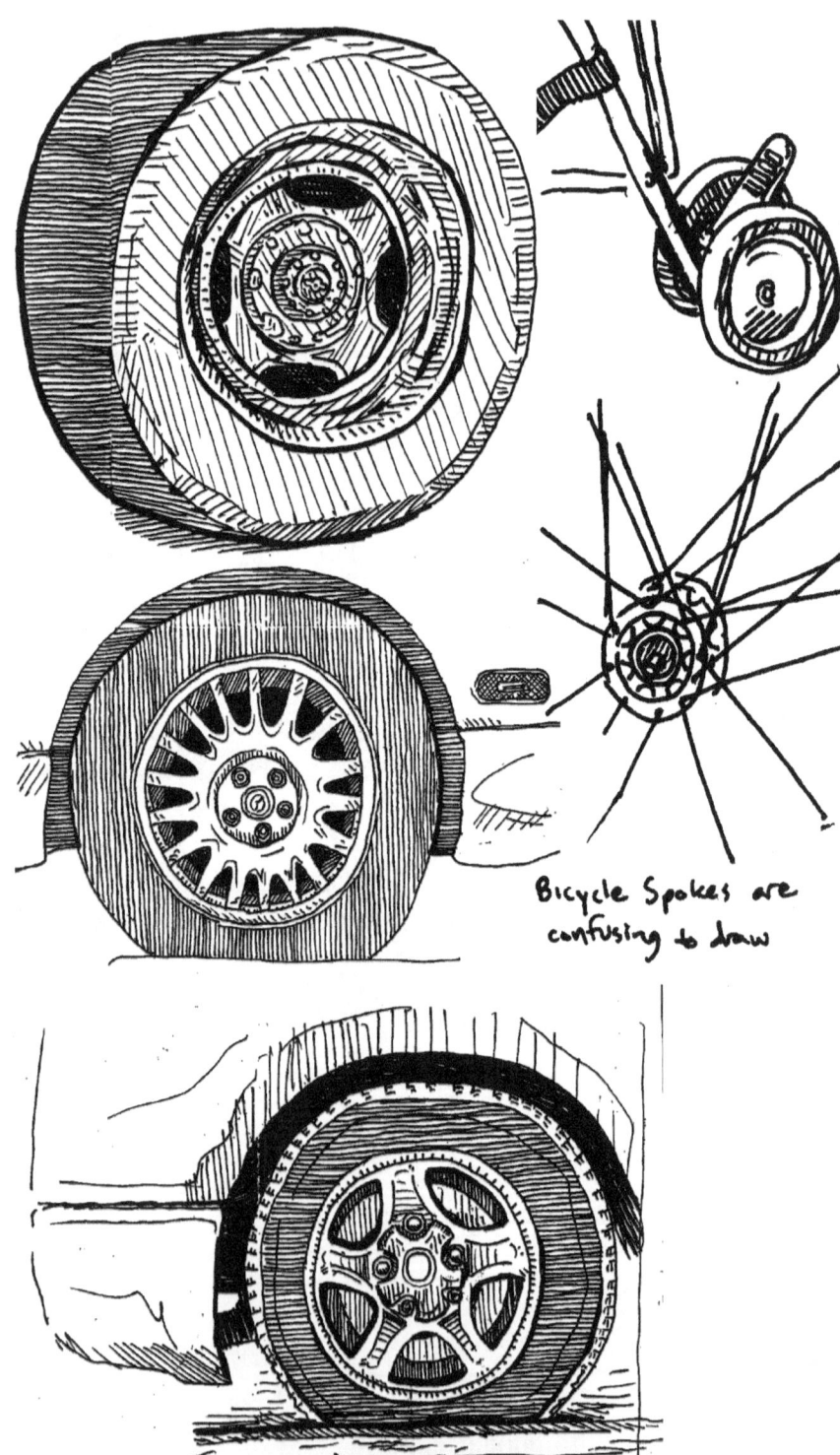

Bicycle Spokes are confusing to draw

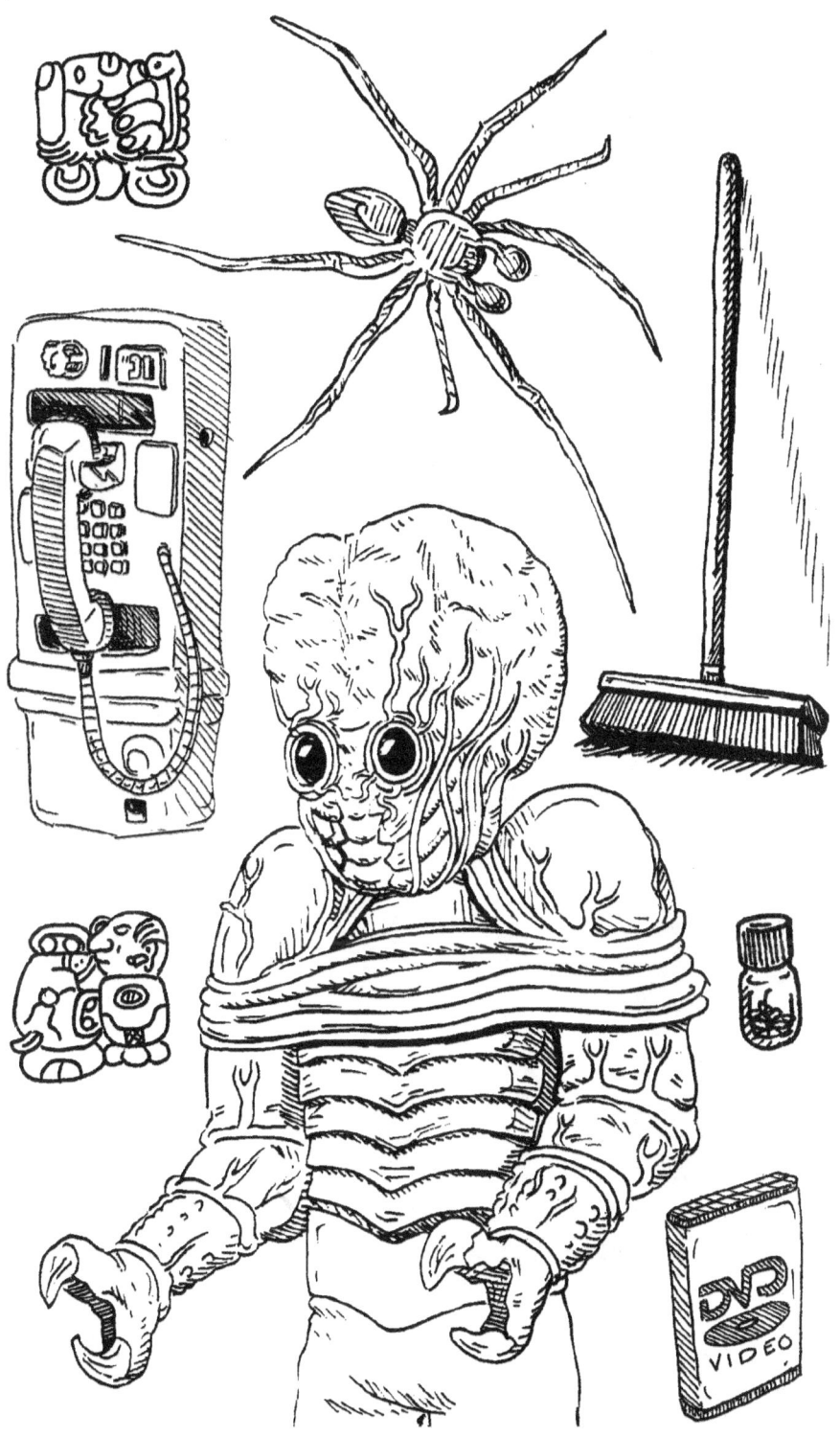

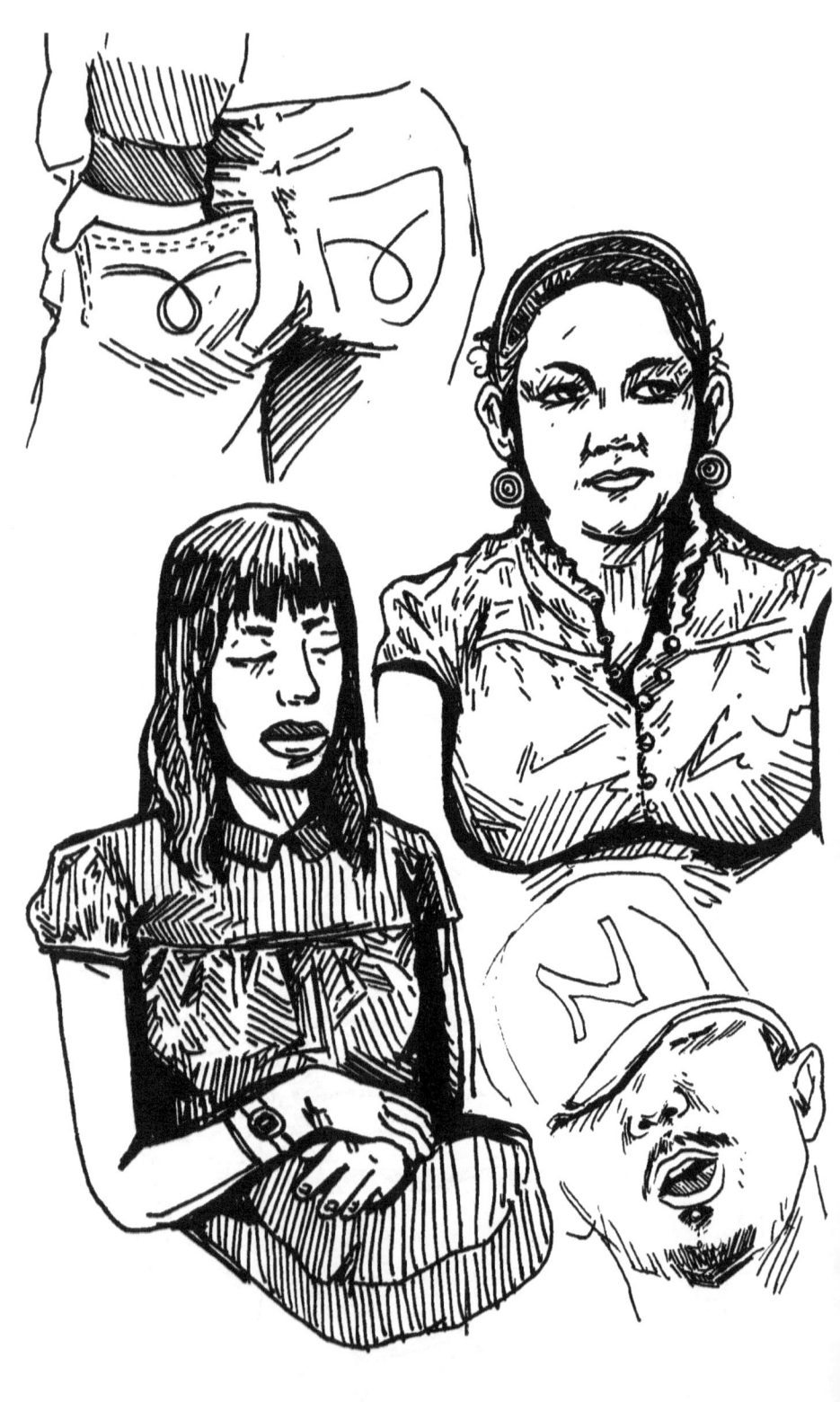

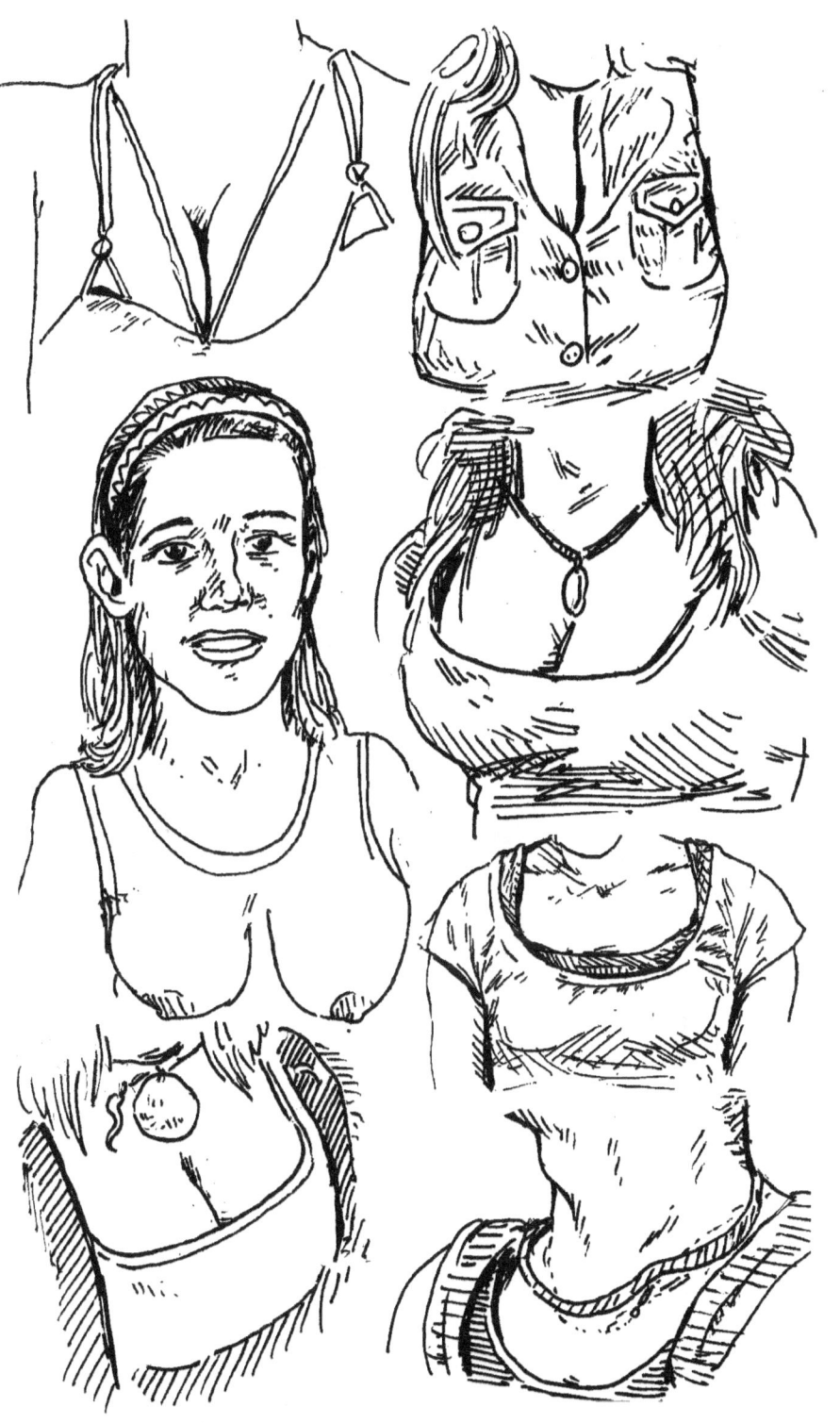

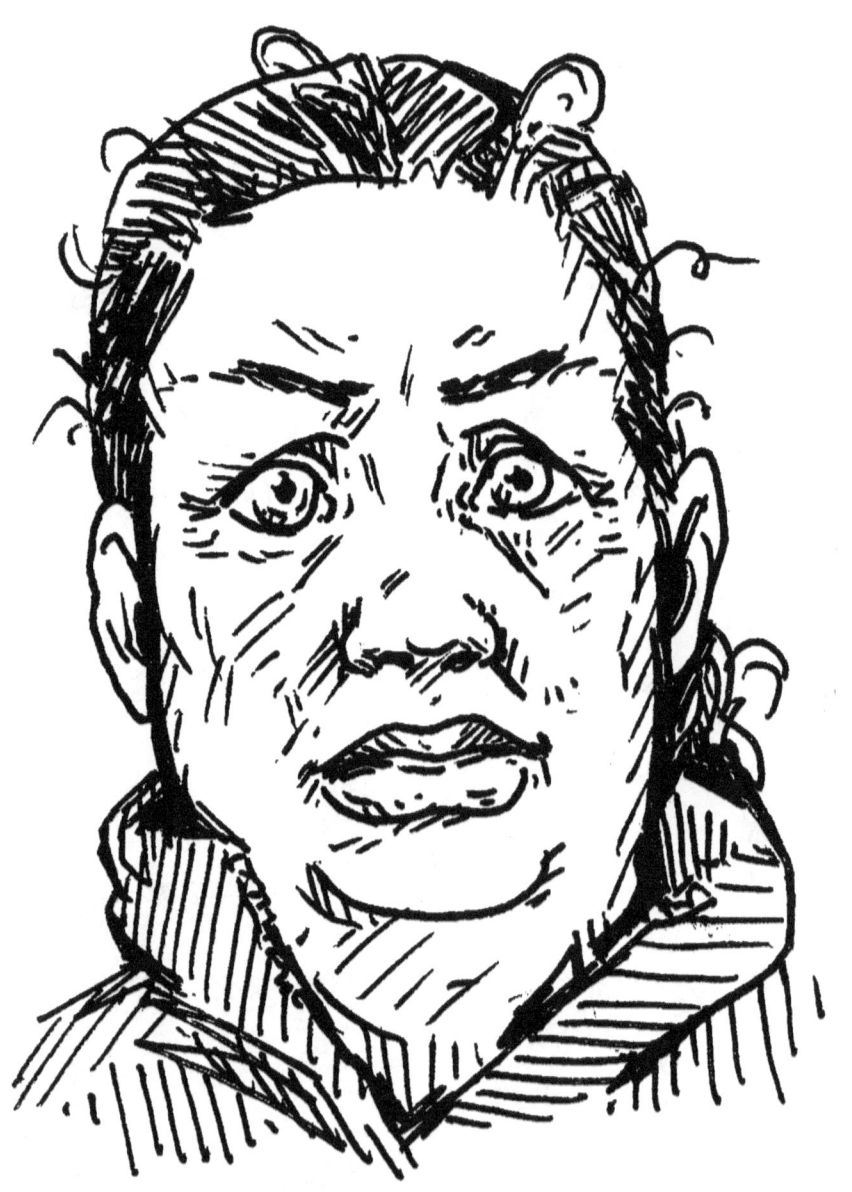

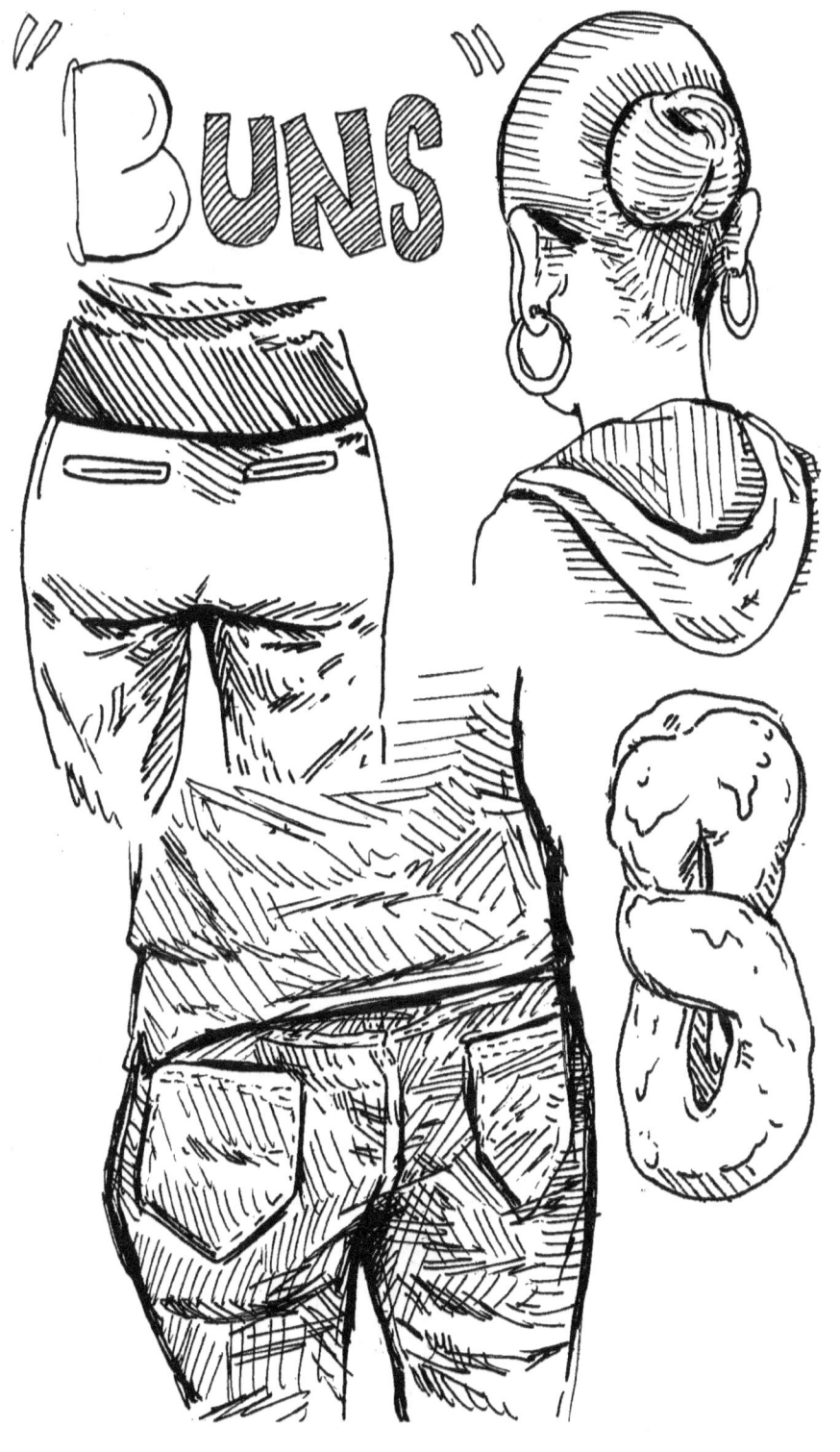

"BUNS"

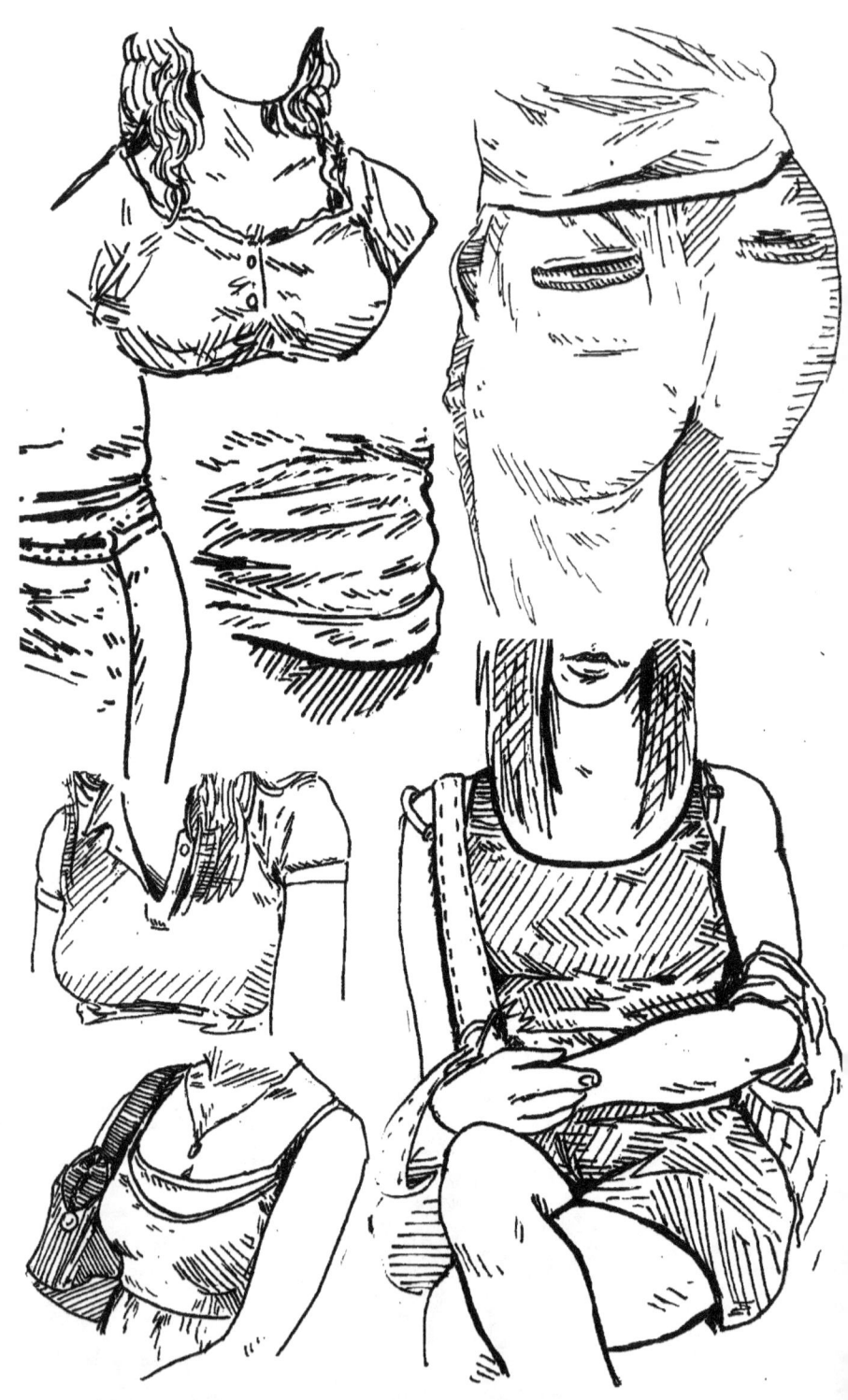

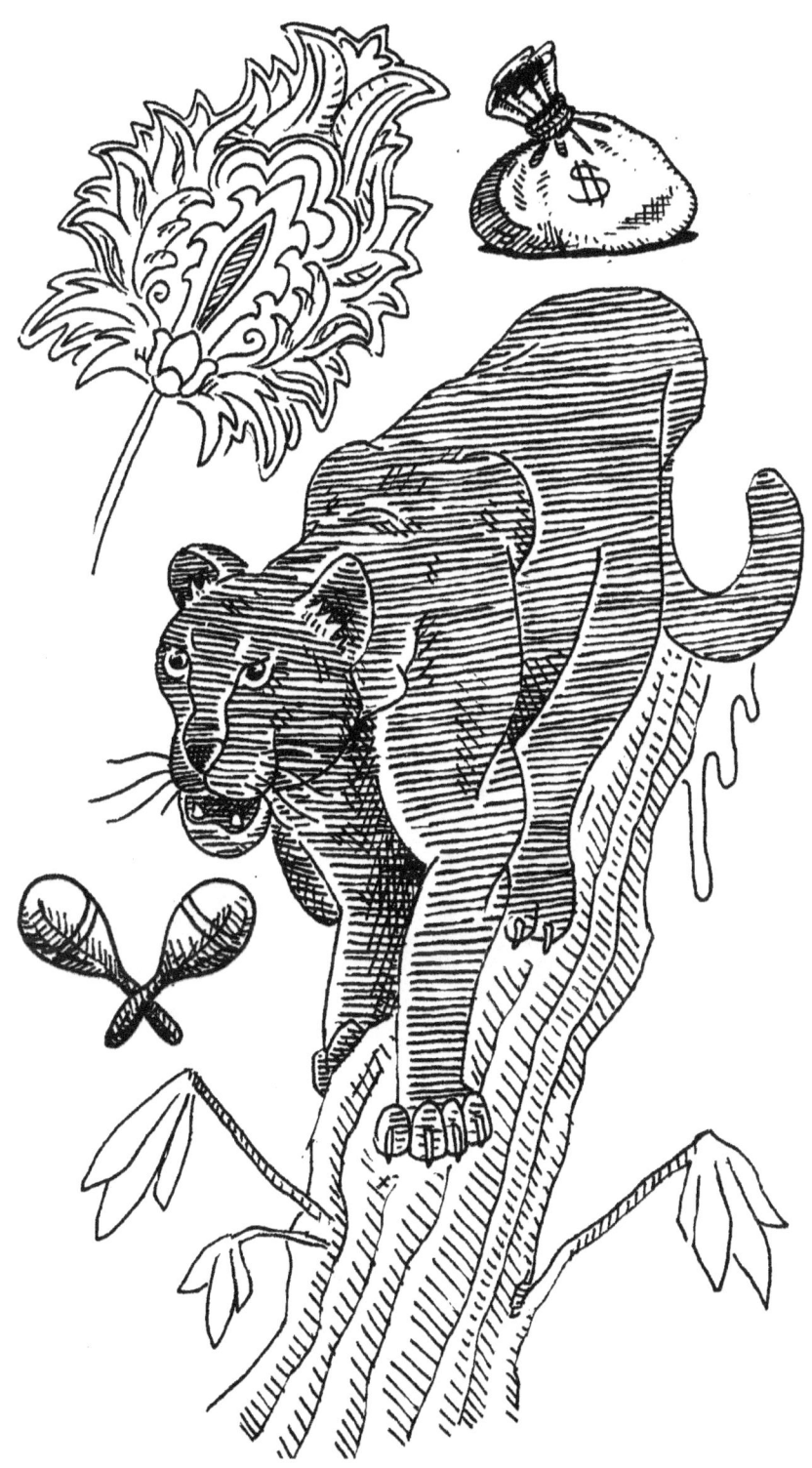

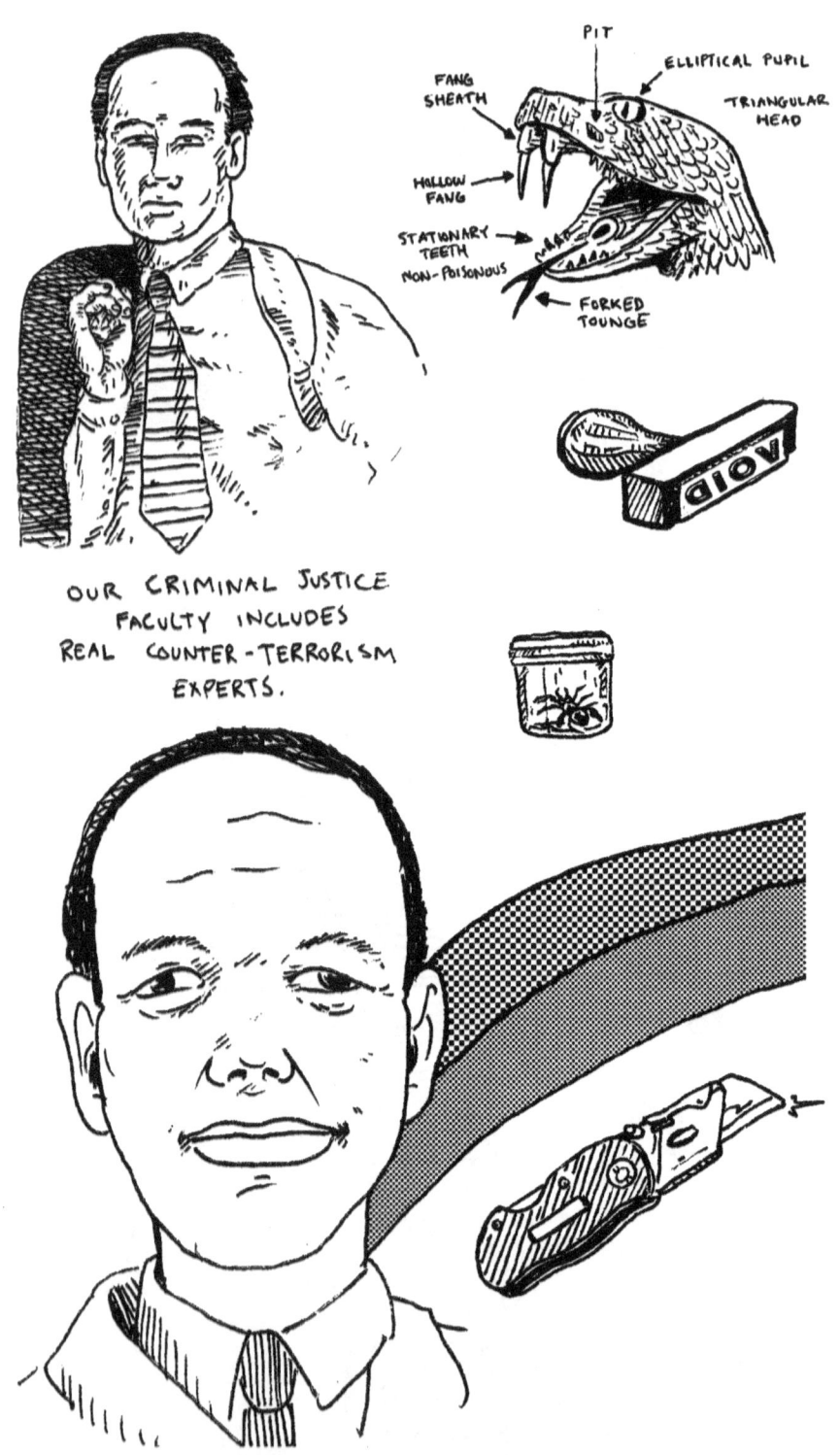

OUR CRIMINAL JUSTICE
FACULTY INCLUDES
REAL COUNTER-TERRORISM
EXPERTS.

PIT

FANG
SHEATH

ELLIPTICAL PUPIL

TRIANGULAR
HEAD

HOLLOW
FANG

STATIONARY
TEETH
NON-POISONOUS

FORKED
TOUNGE

VOID

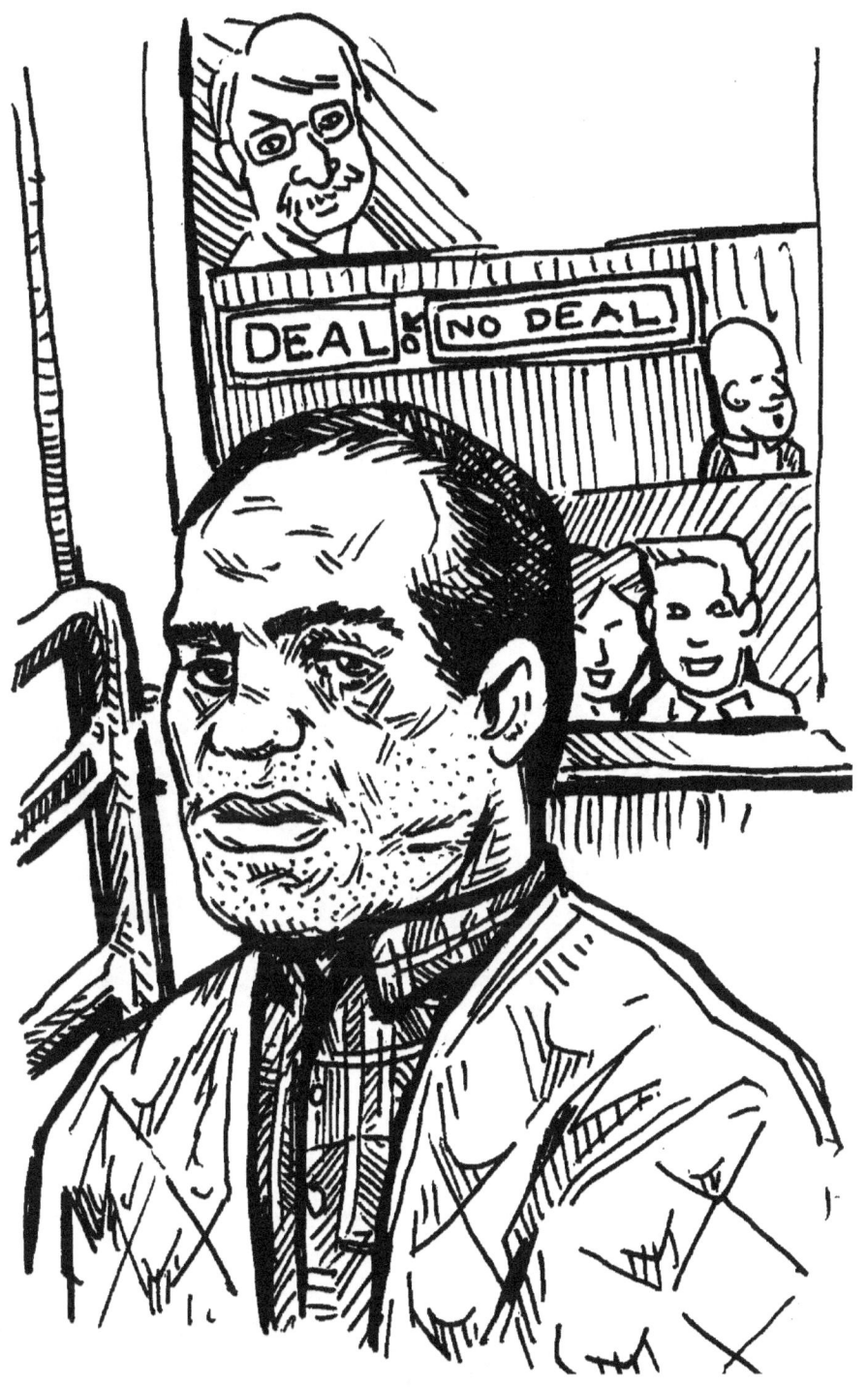

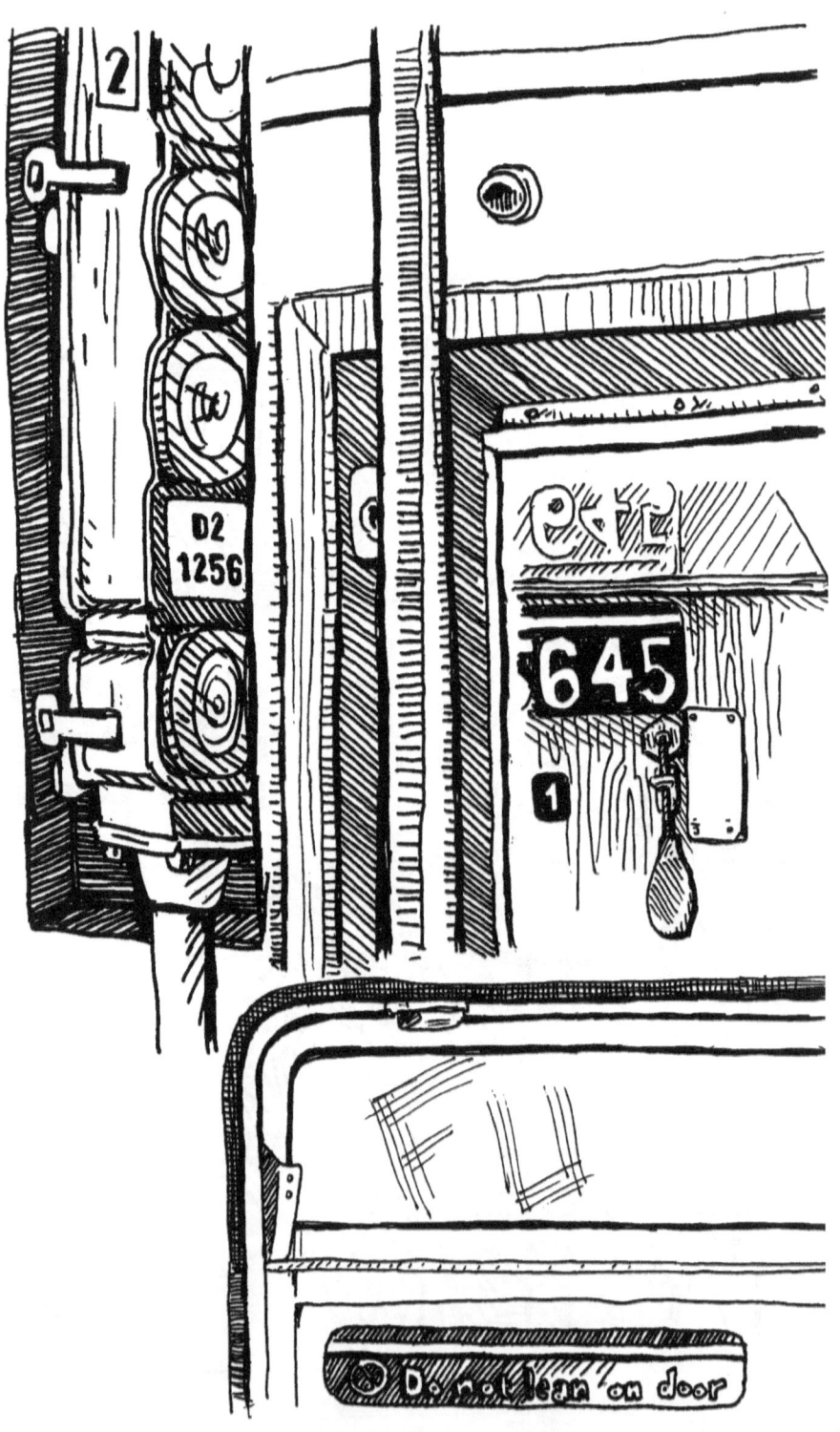

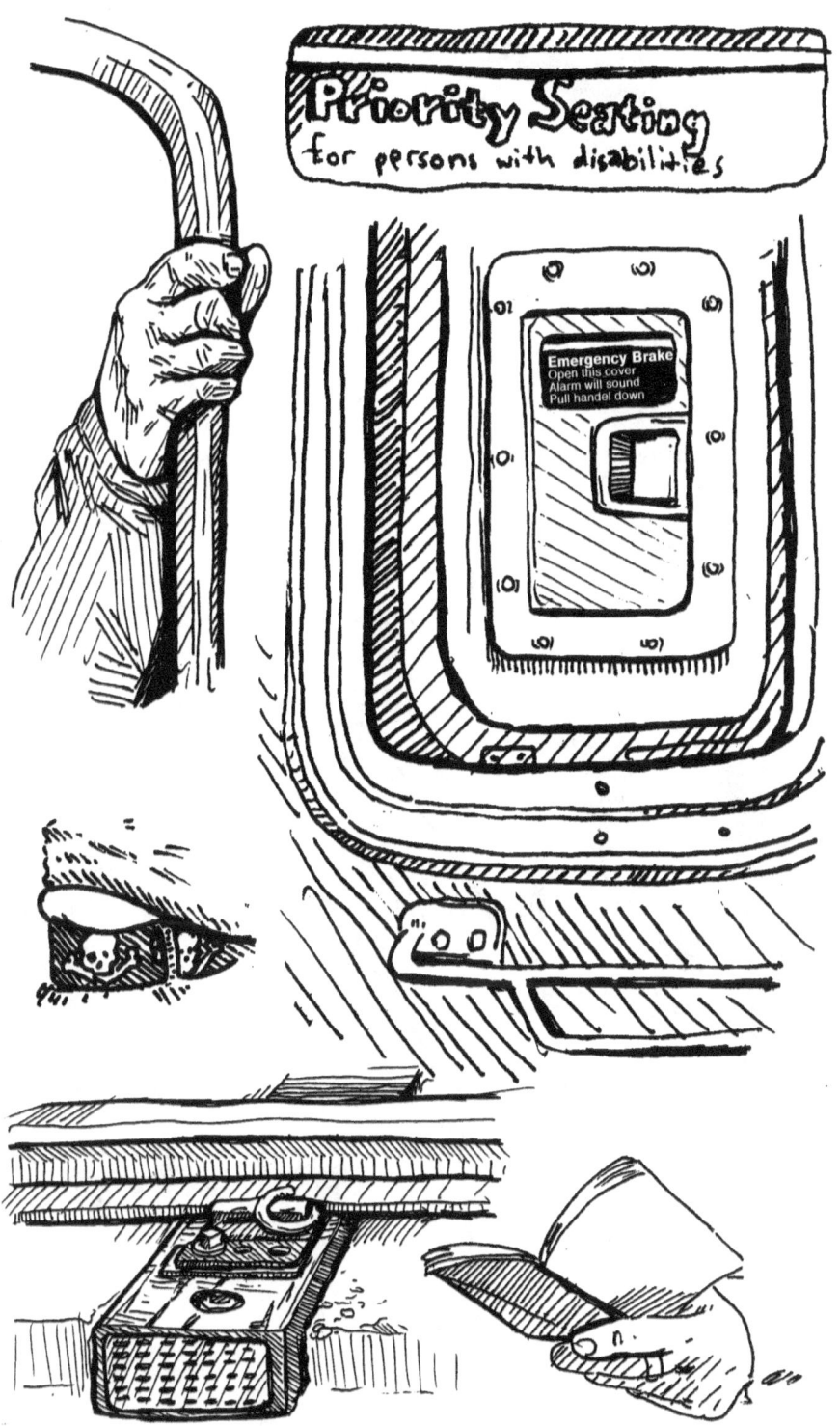

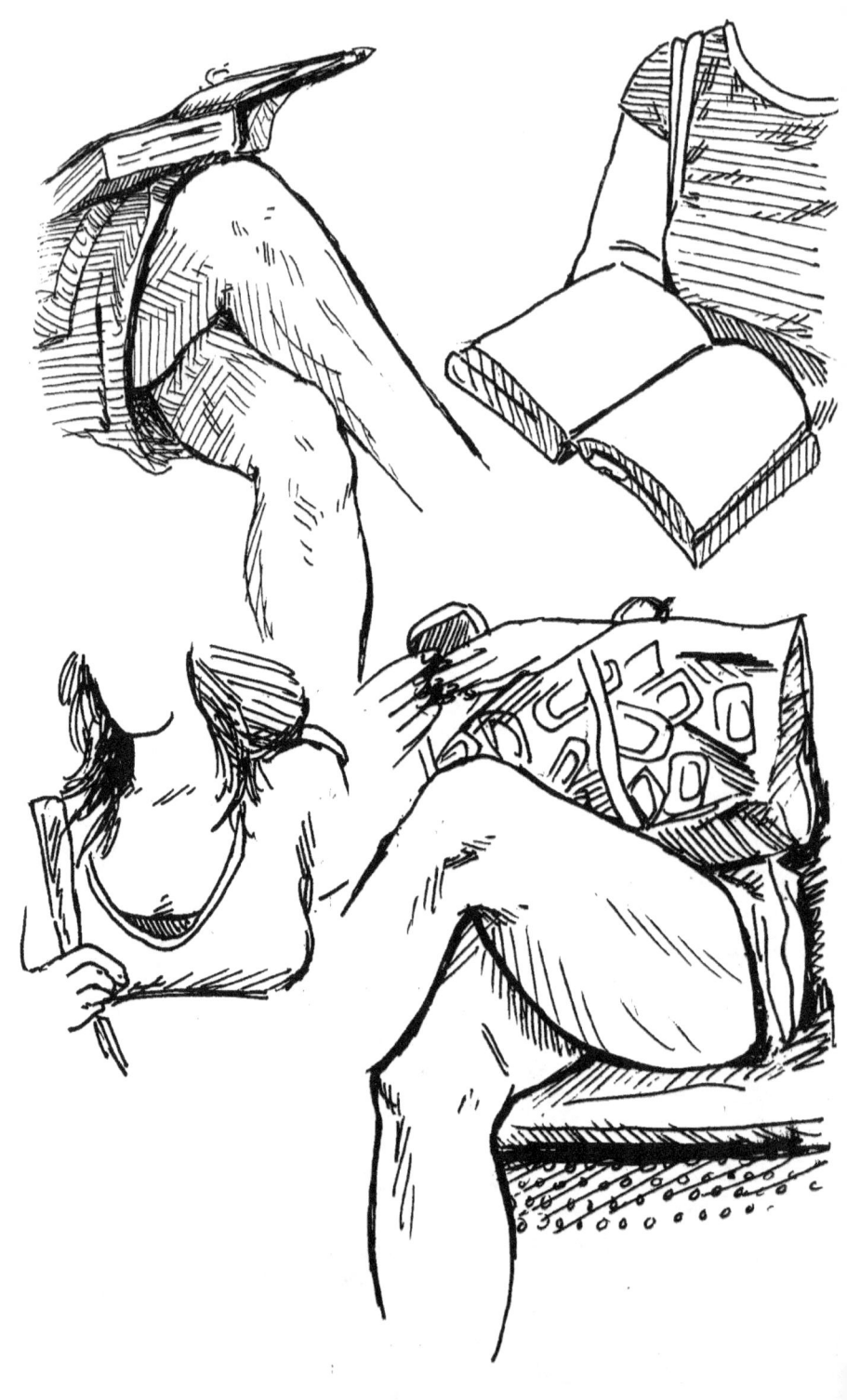

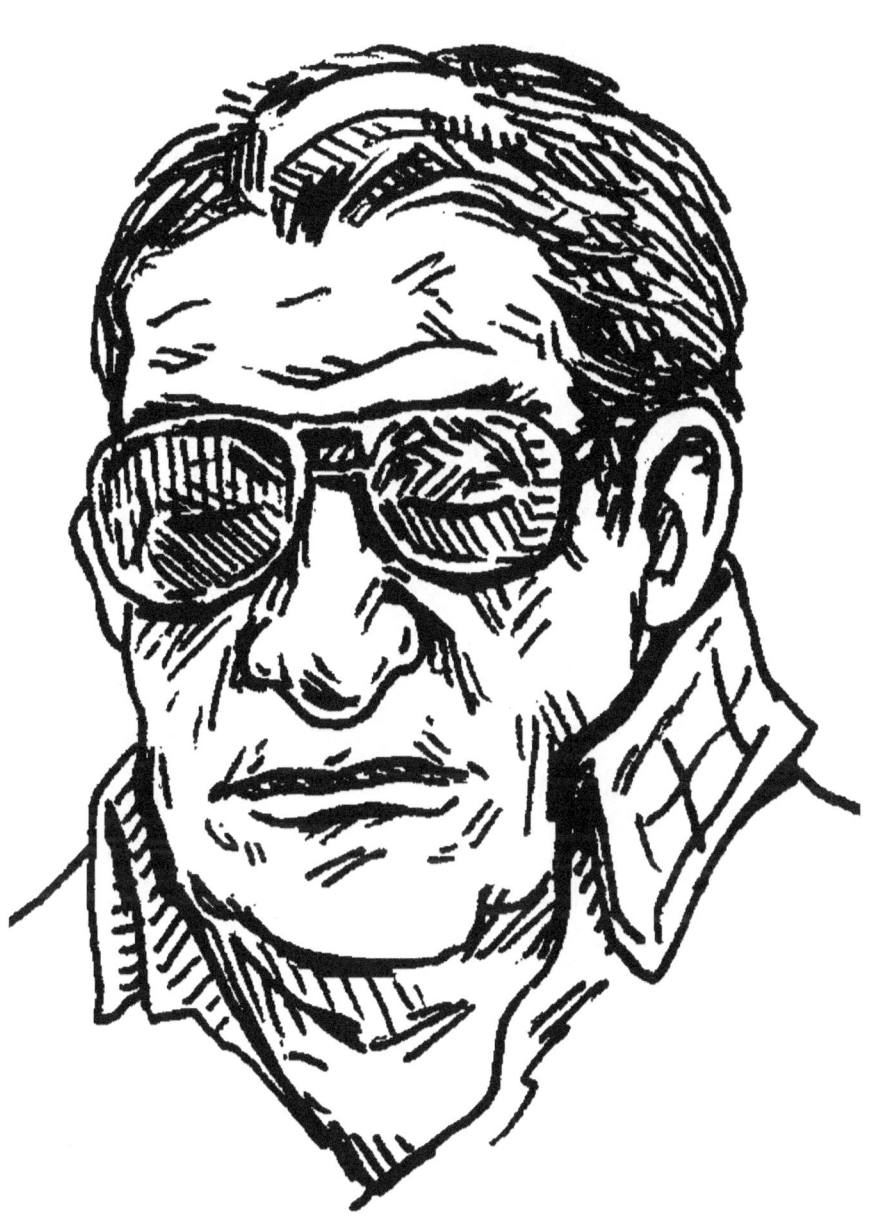

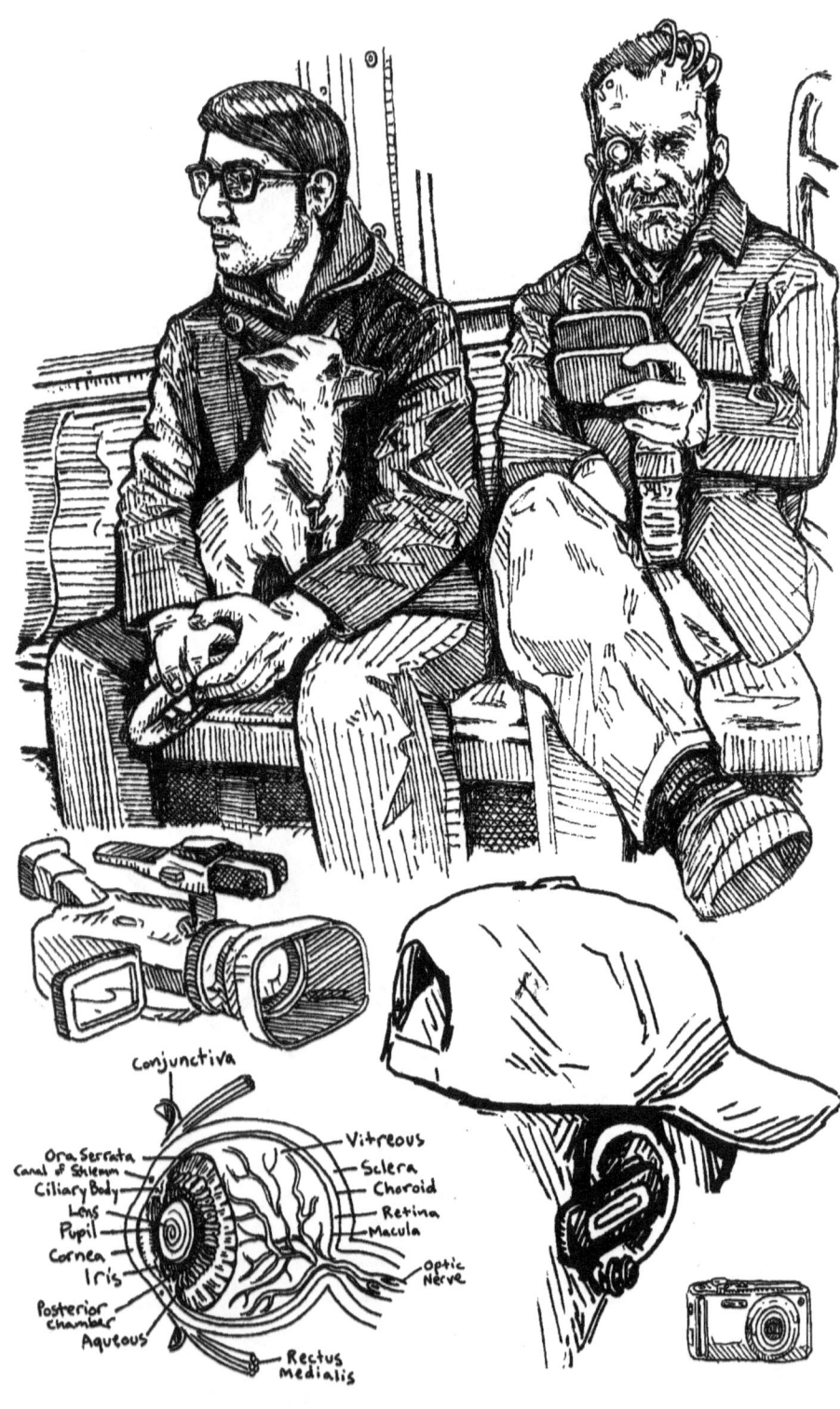

Conjunctiva

Vitreous

Ora Serrata
Canal of Schlemm
Ciliary Body
Lens
Pupil
Cornea
Iris

Sclera
Choroid
Retina
Macula

Optic
Nerve

Posterior
chamber
Aqueous

Rectus
Medialis

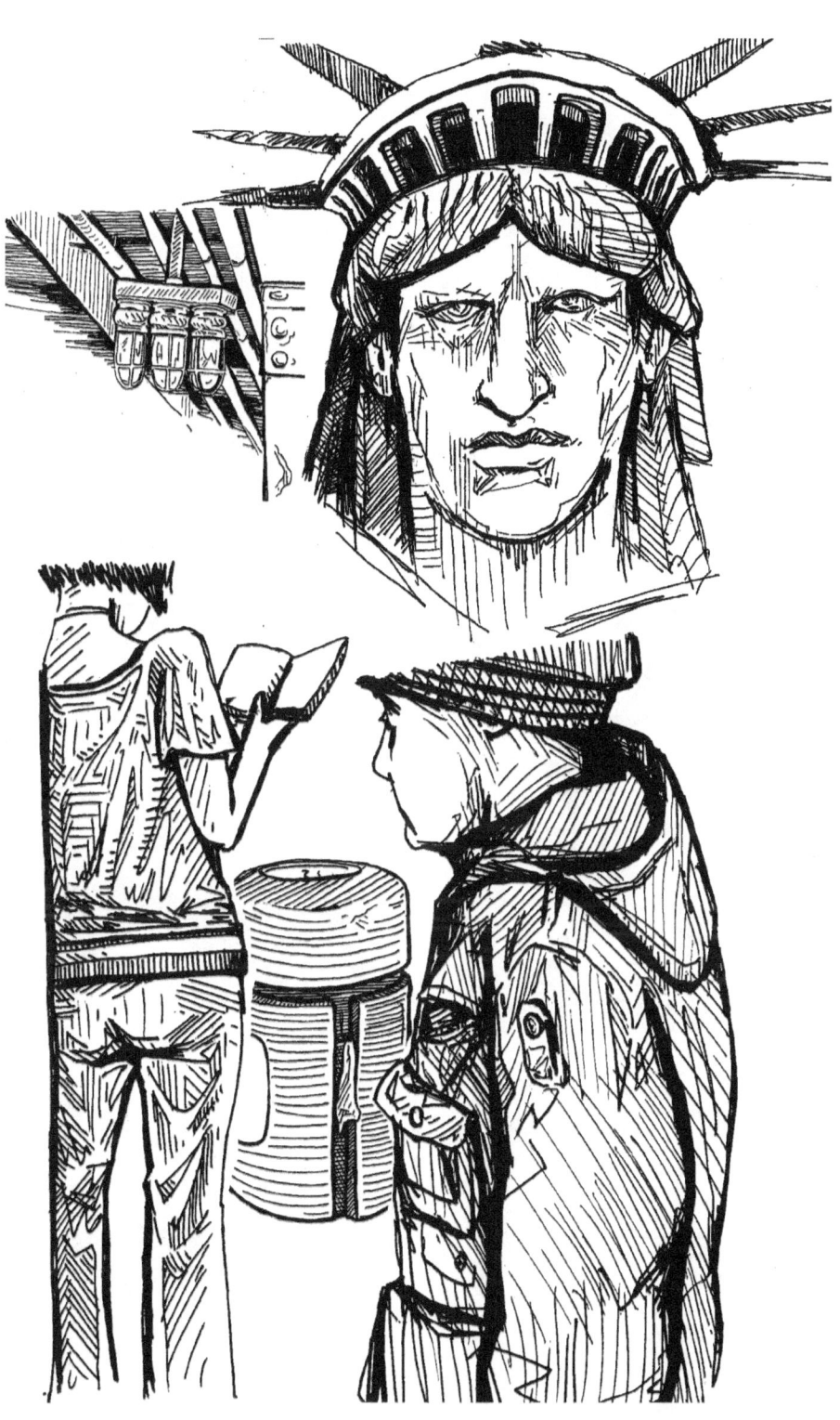

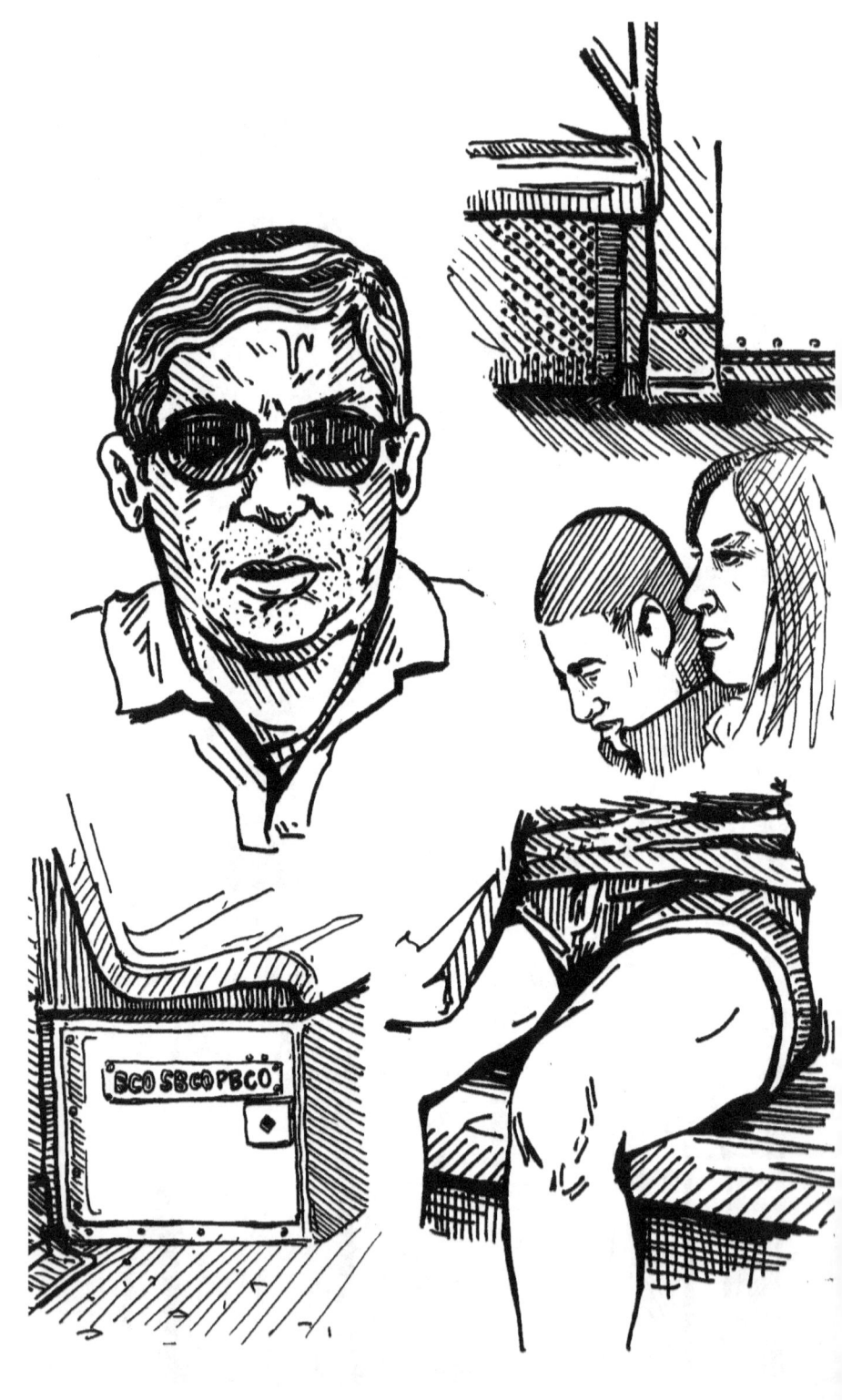

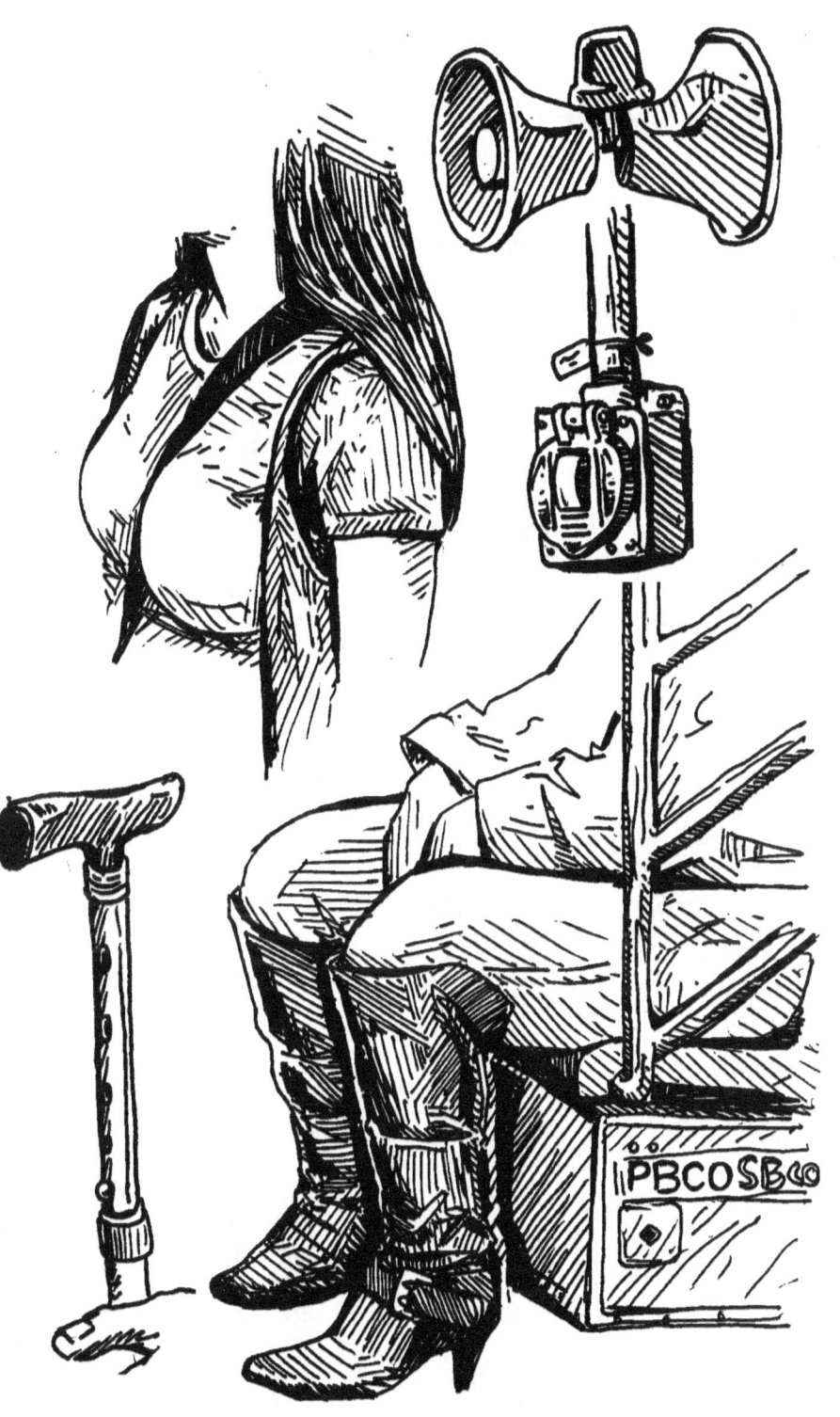

PBCOSB℗

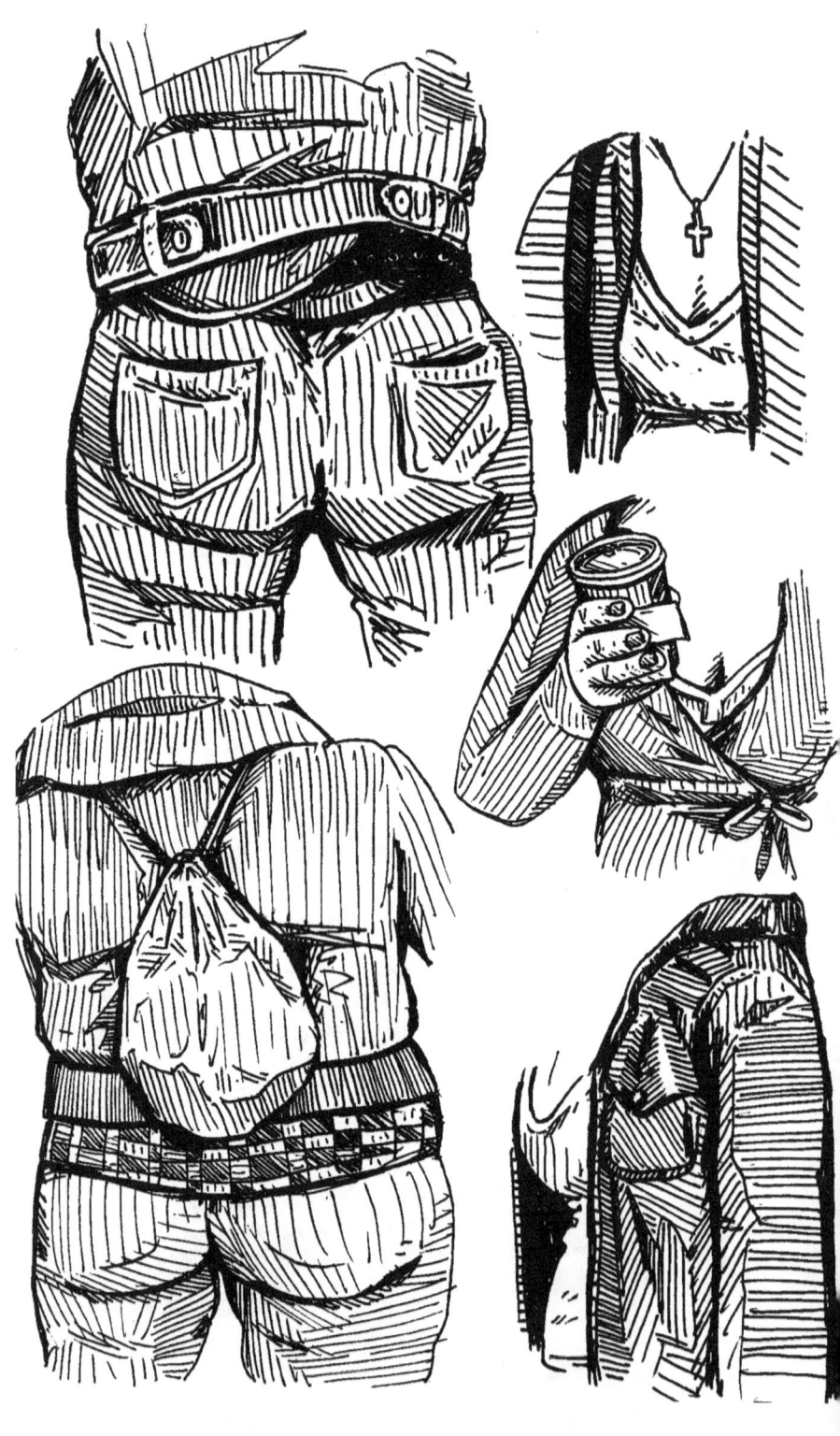

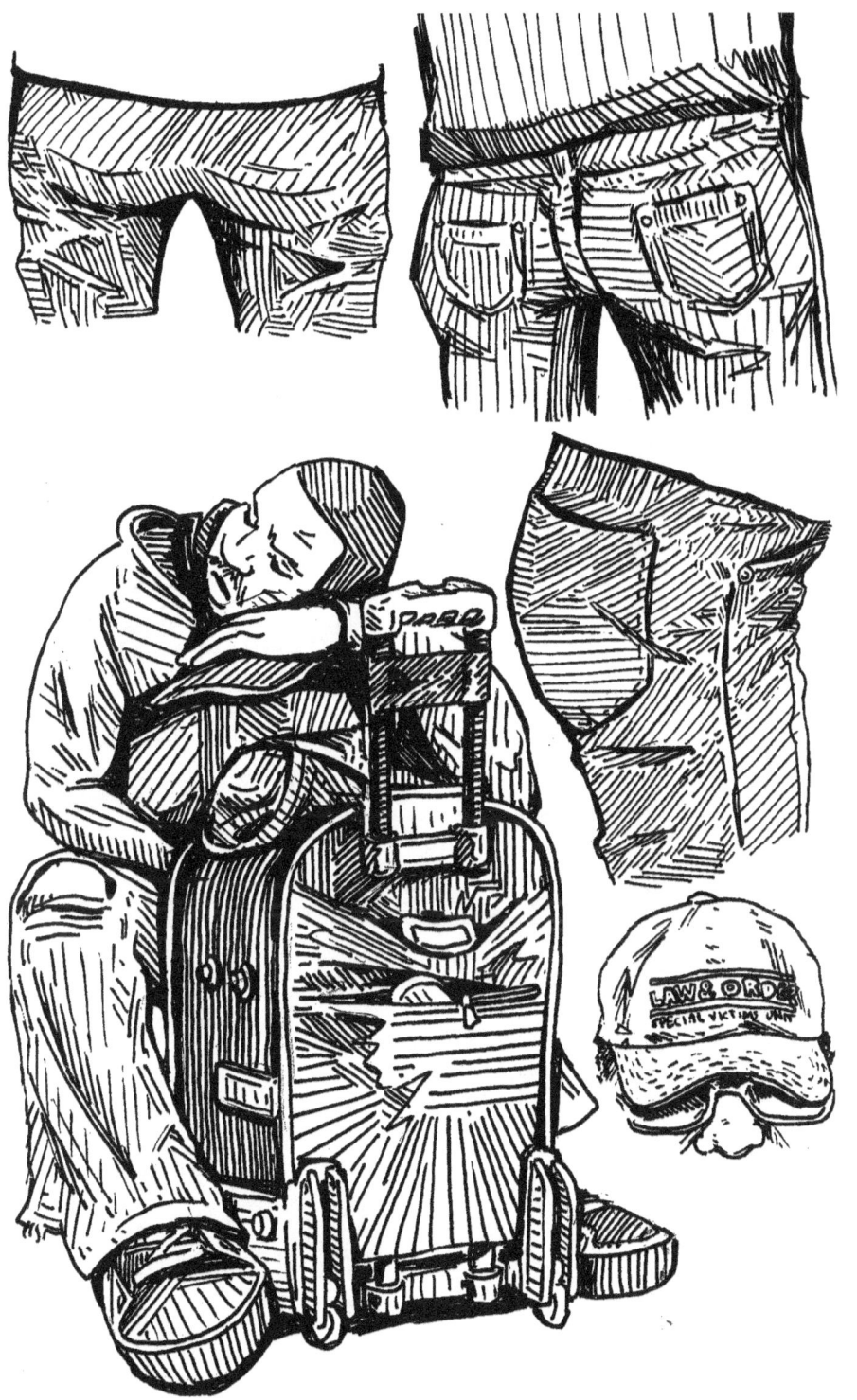

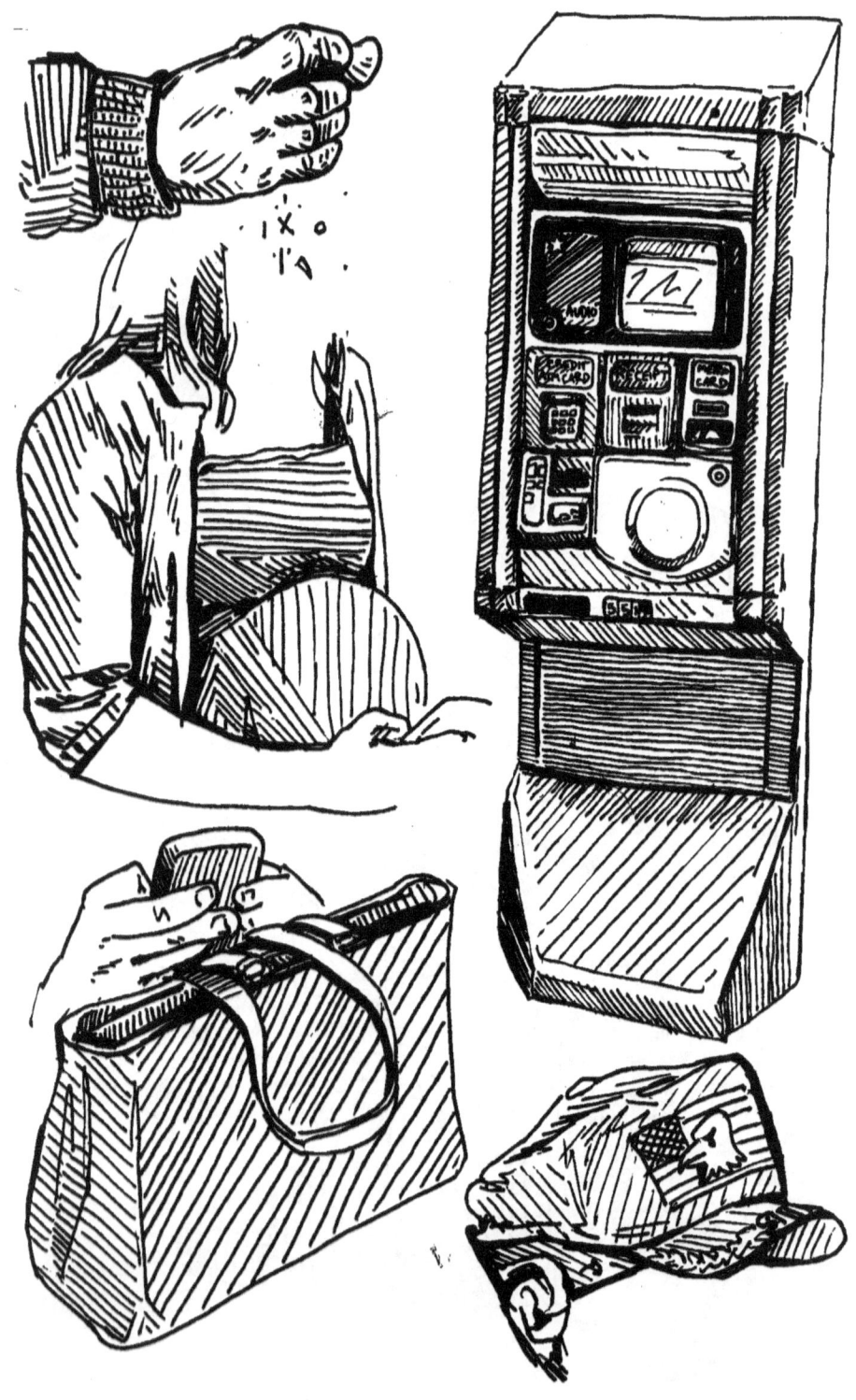

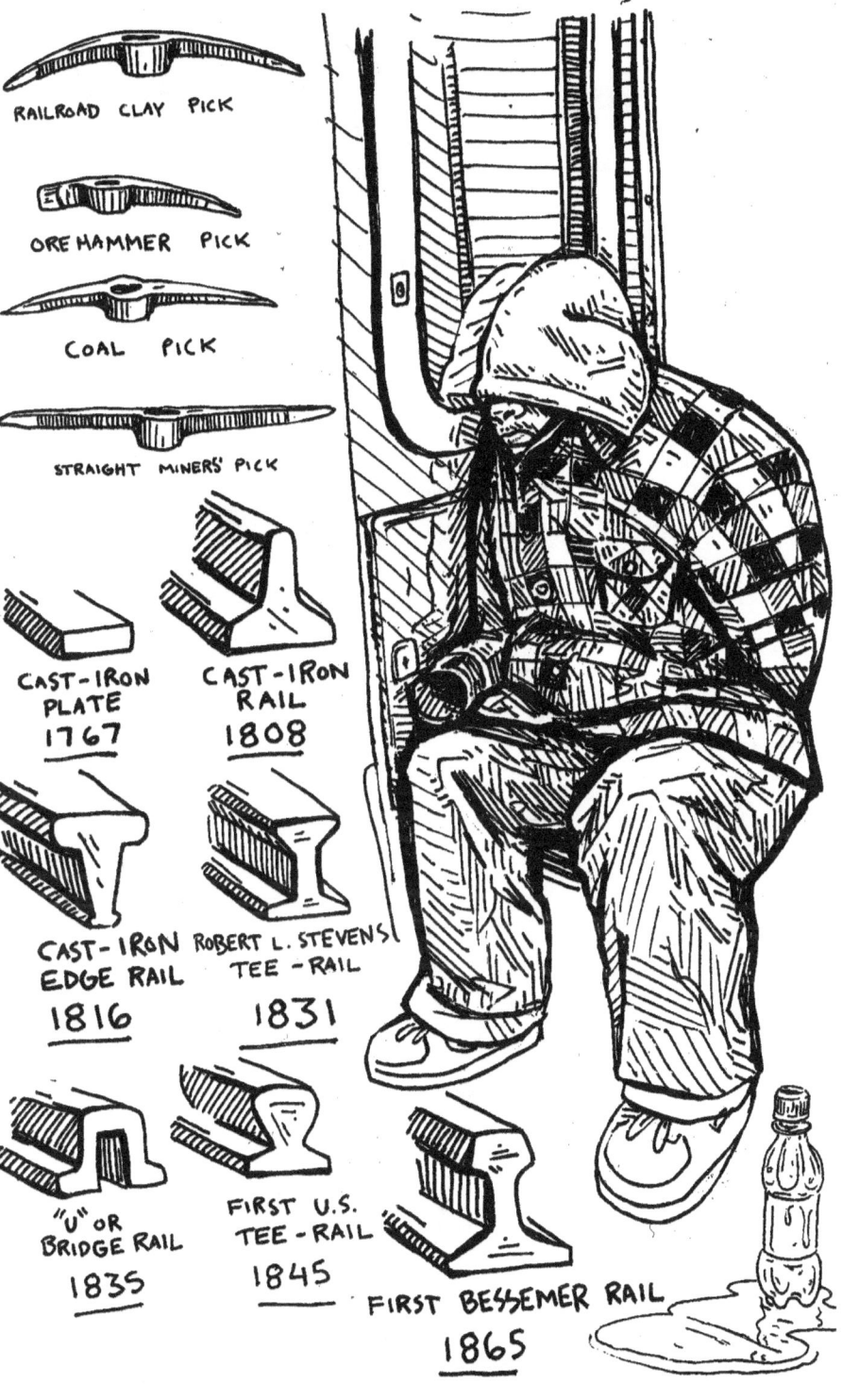

RAILROAD CLAY PICK

ORE HAMMER PICK

COAL PICK

STRAIGHT MINERS' PICK

CAST-IRON PLATE 1767

CAST-IRON RAIL 1808

CAST-IRON EDGE RAIL 1816

ROBERT L. STEVENS TEE-RAIL 1831

"U" OR BRIDGE RAIL 1835

FIRST U.S. TEE-RAIL 1845

FIRST BESSEMER RAIL 1865

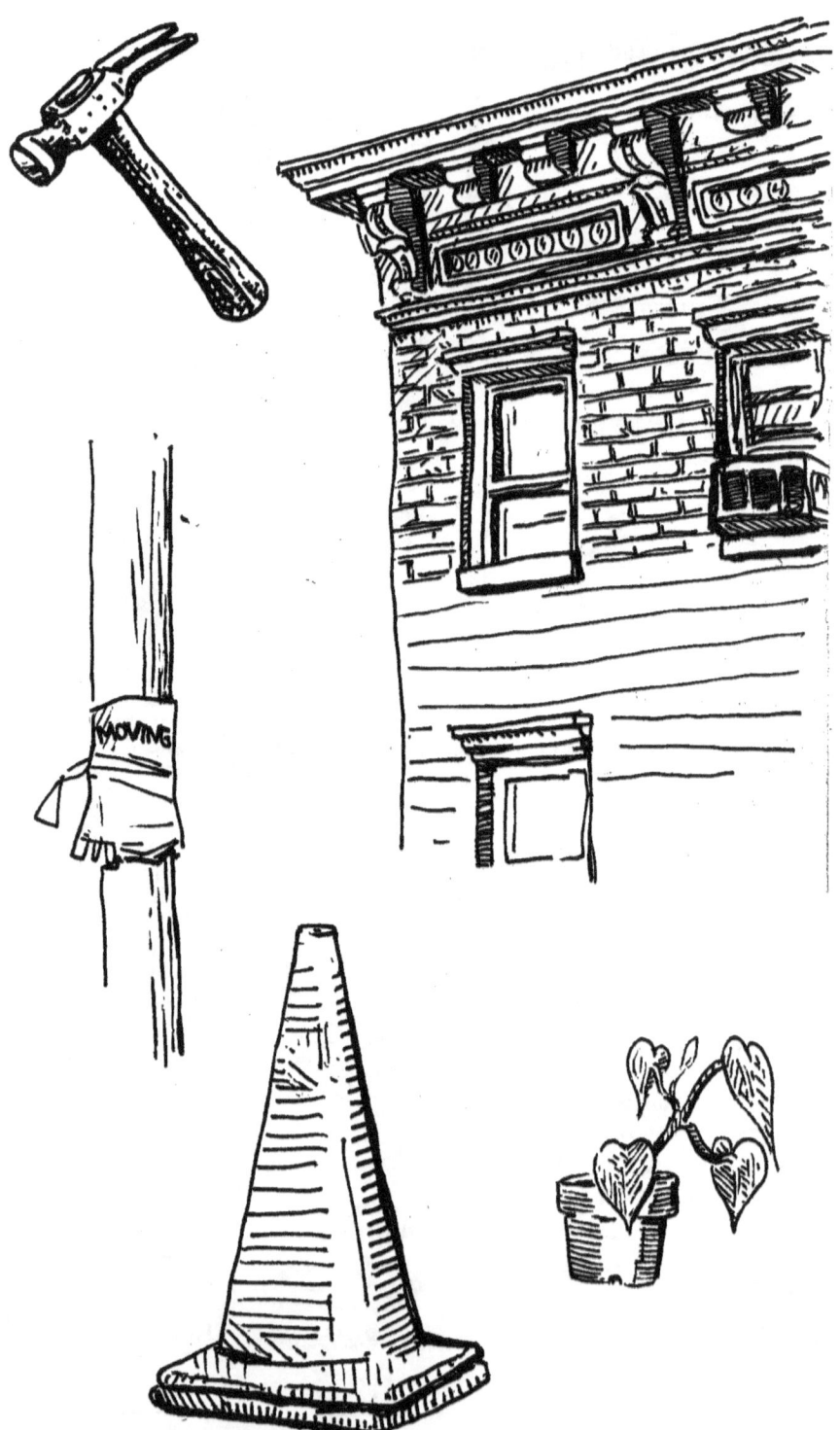

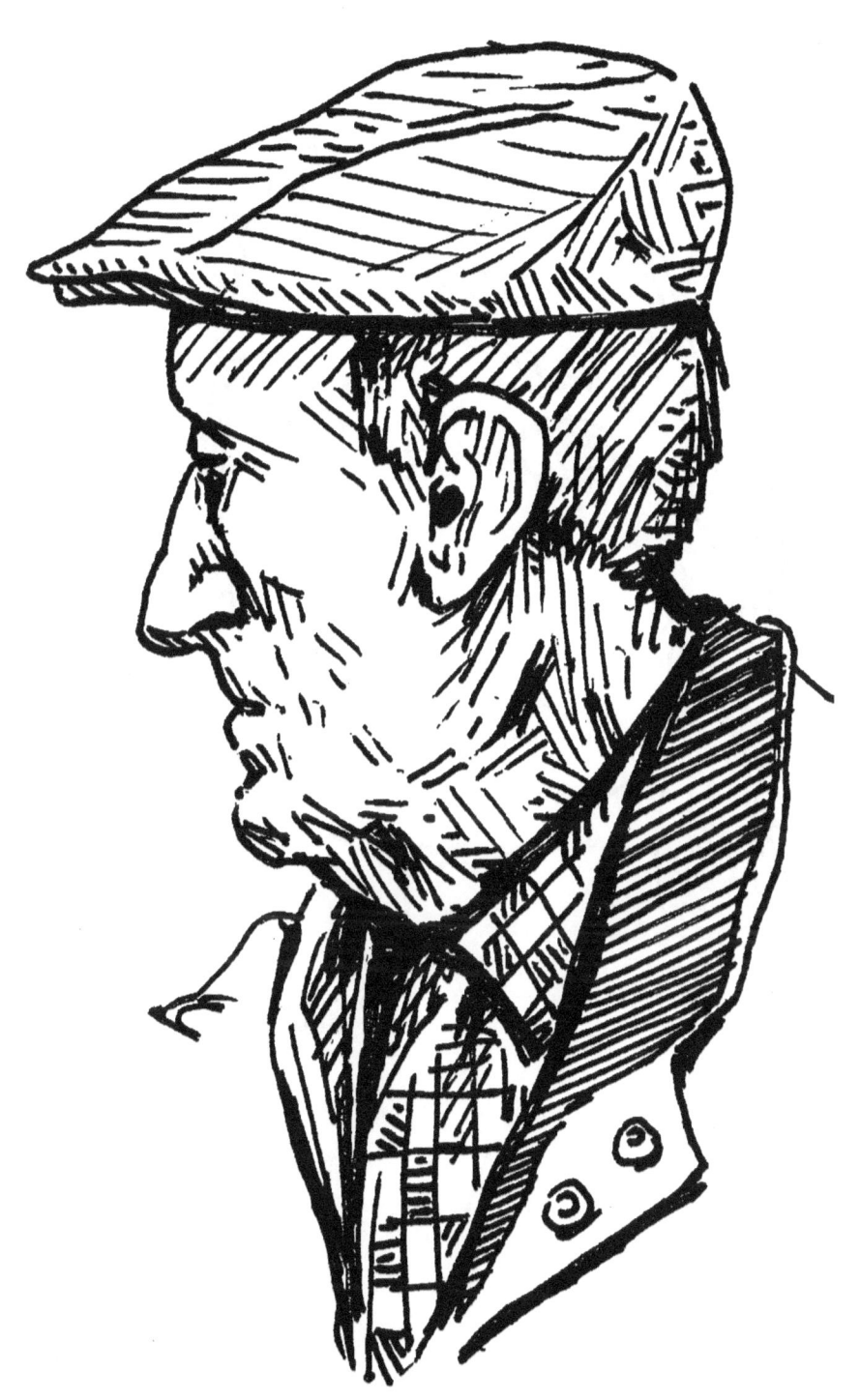

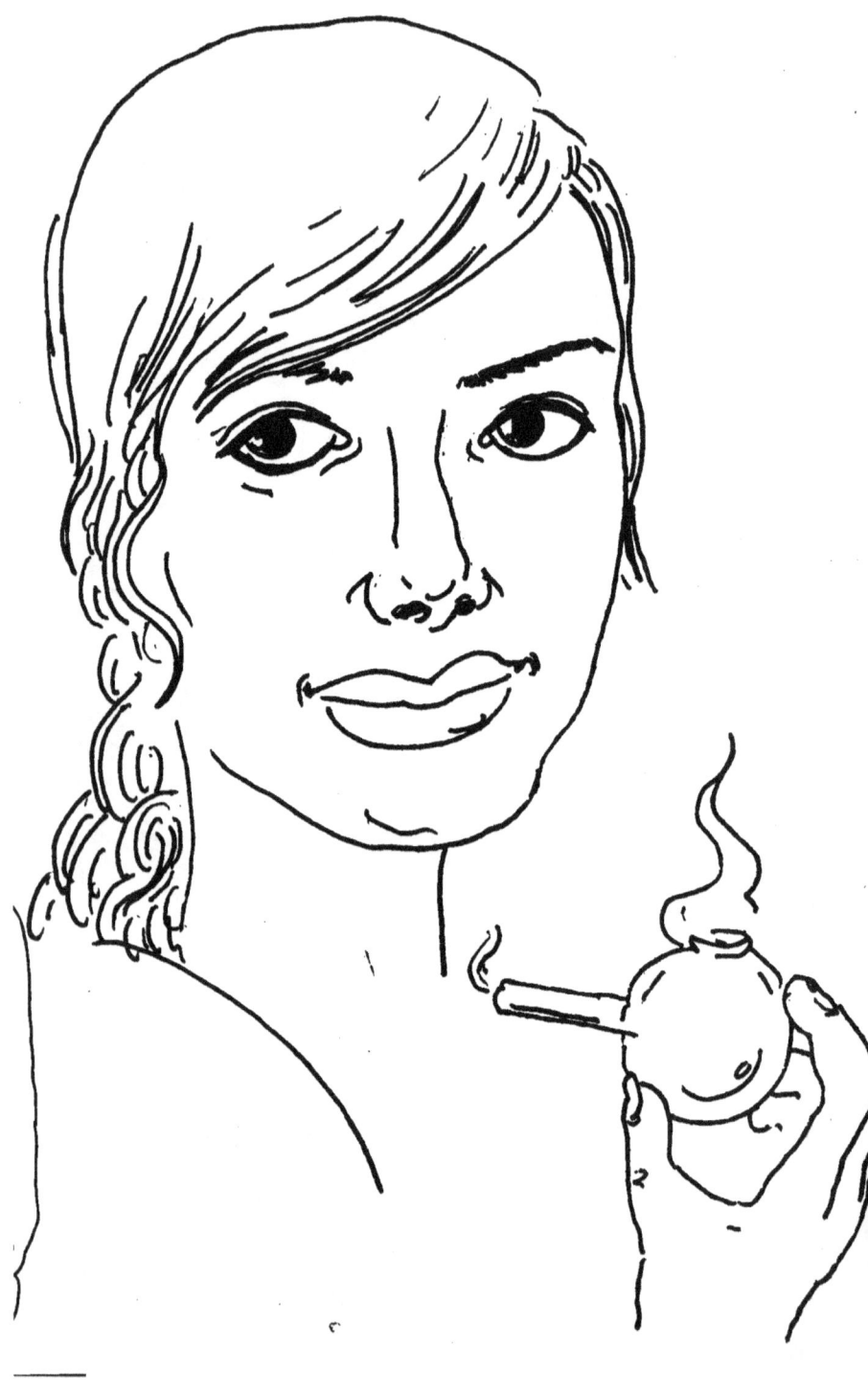

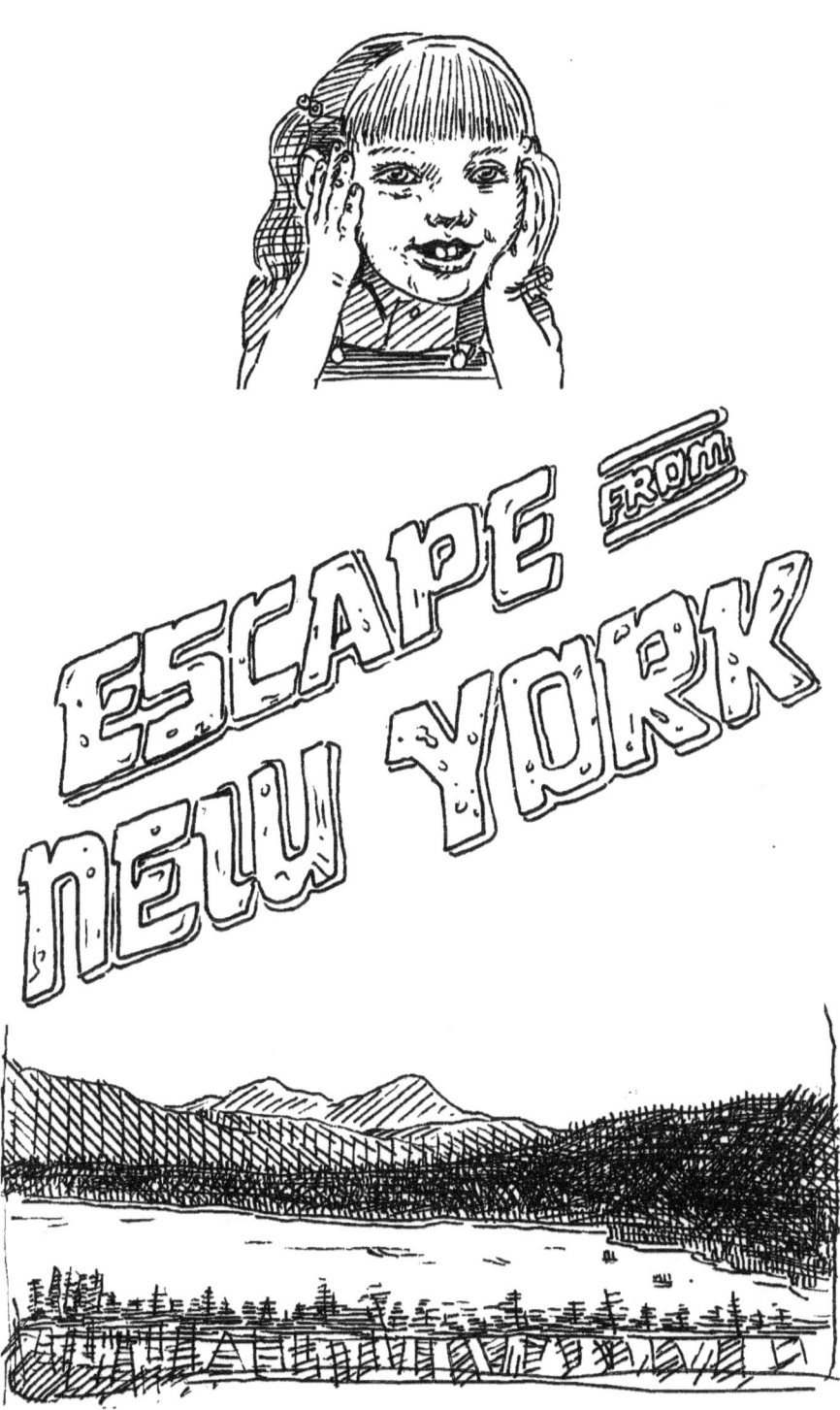

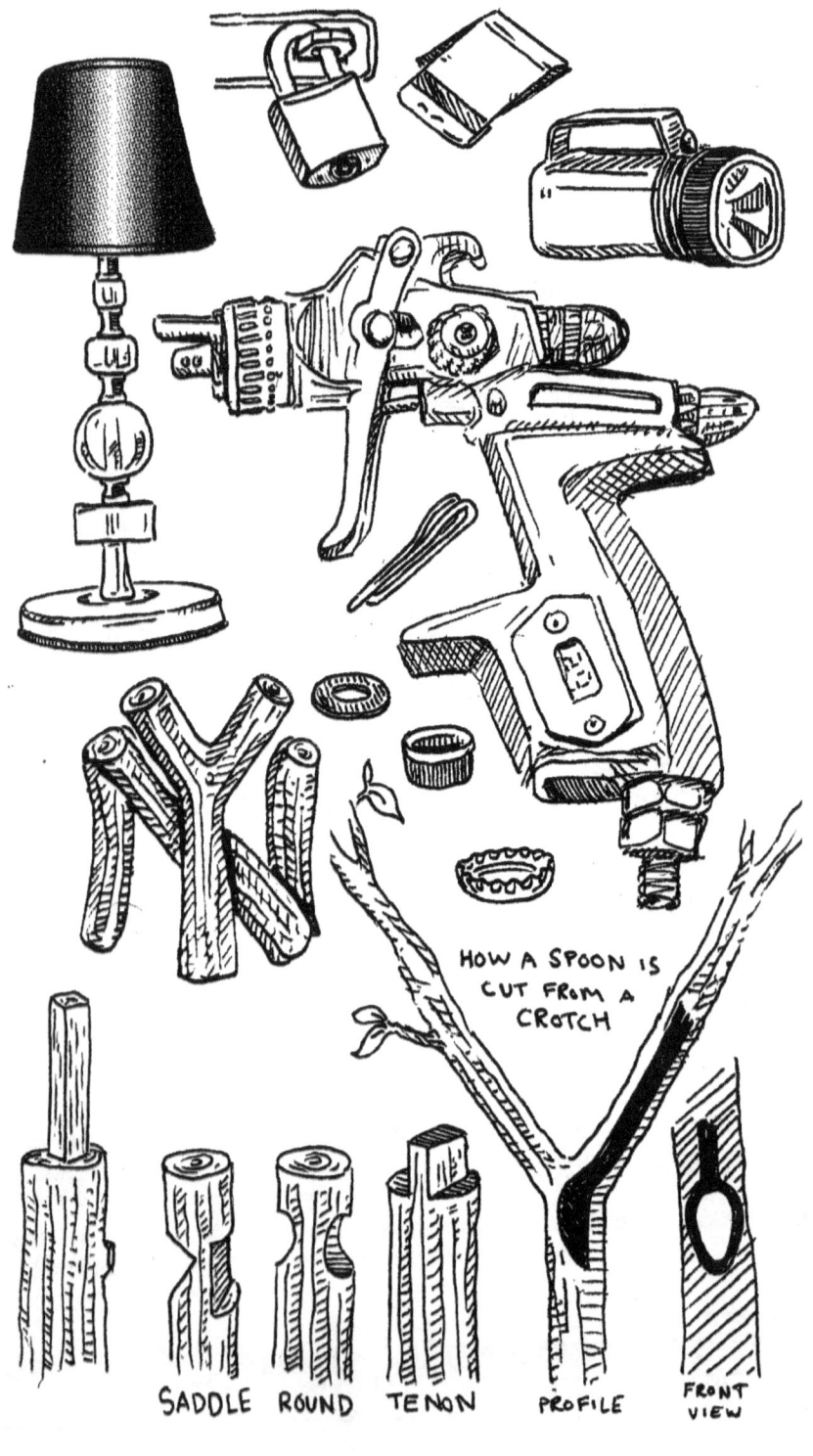

HOW A SPOON IS
CUT FROM A
CROTCH

SADDLE   ROUND   TENON   PROFILE   FRONT
VIEW

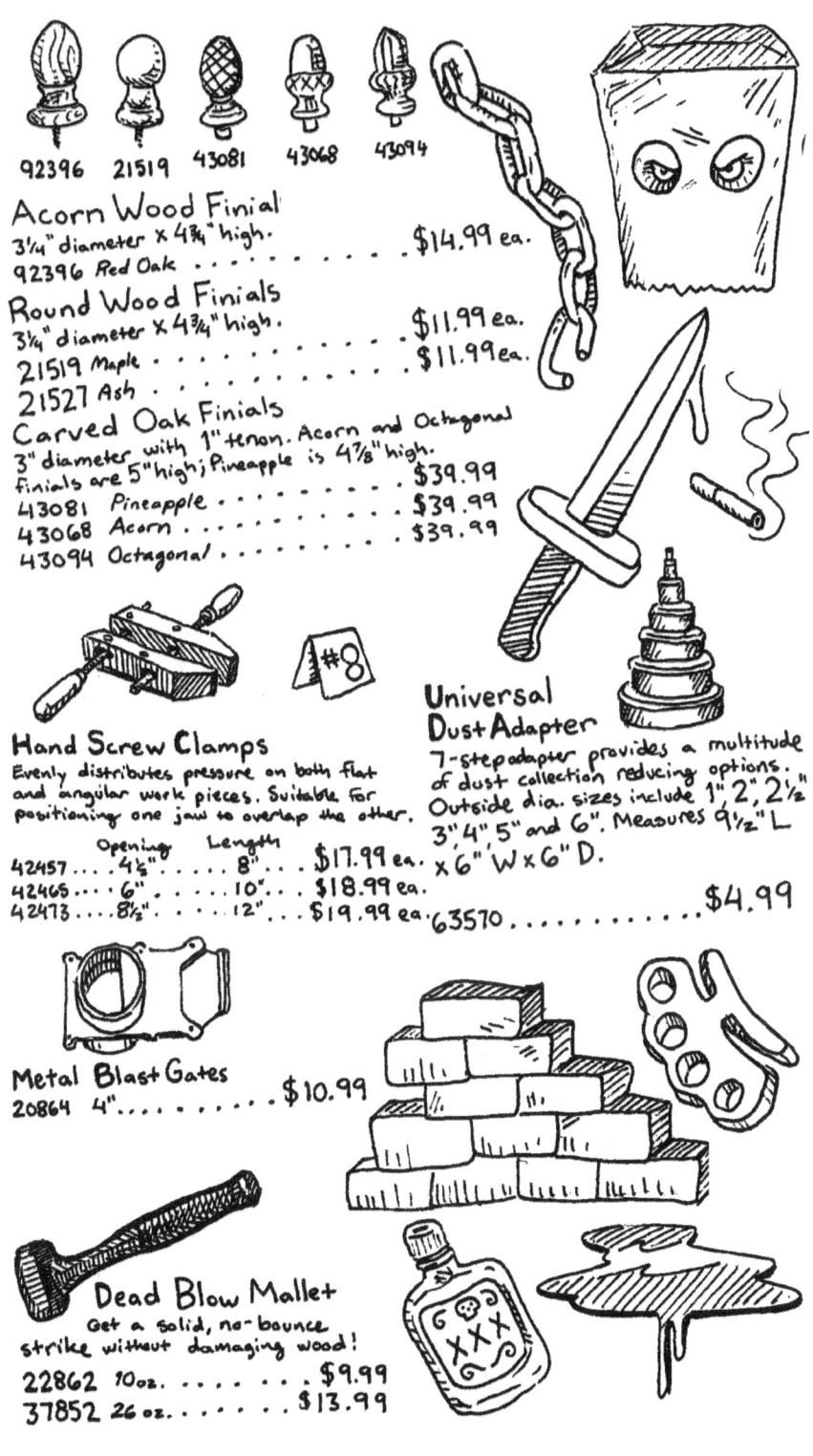

92396 21519 43081 43068 43094

Acorn Wood Finial
3¼" diameter × 4¾" high.
92396 Red Oak . . . . $14.99 ea.

Round Wood Finials
3¼" diameter × 4¾" high.
21519 Maple . . . . $11.99 ea.
21527 Ash . . . . $11.99 ea.

Carved Oak Finials
3" diameter with 1" tenon. Acorn and Octagonal
Finials are 5" high; Pineapple is 4⅞" high.
43081 Pineapple $39.99
43068 Acorn $39.99
43094 Octagonal $39.99

Hand Screw Clamps
Evenly distributes pressure on both flat
and angular work pieces. Suitable for
positioning one jaw to overlap the other.

	Opening	Length	
42457	4½"	8"	$17.99 ea.
42465	6"	10"	$18.99 ea.
42473	8½"	12"	$19.99 ea.

Universal Dust Adapter
7-step adapter provides a multitude
of dust collection reducing options.
Outside dia. sizes include 1", 2", 2½"
3" 4" 5" and 6". Measures 9½" L
× 6" W × 6" D.
63570 . . . . $4.99

Metal Blast Gates
20864 4" $10.99

Dead Blow Mallet
Get a solid, no-bounce
strike without damaging wood!
22862 10 oz. $9.99
37852 26 oz. $13.99

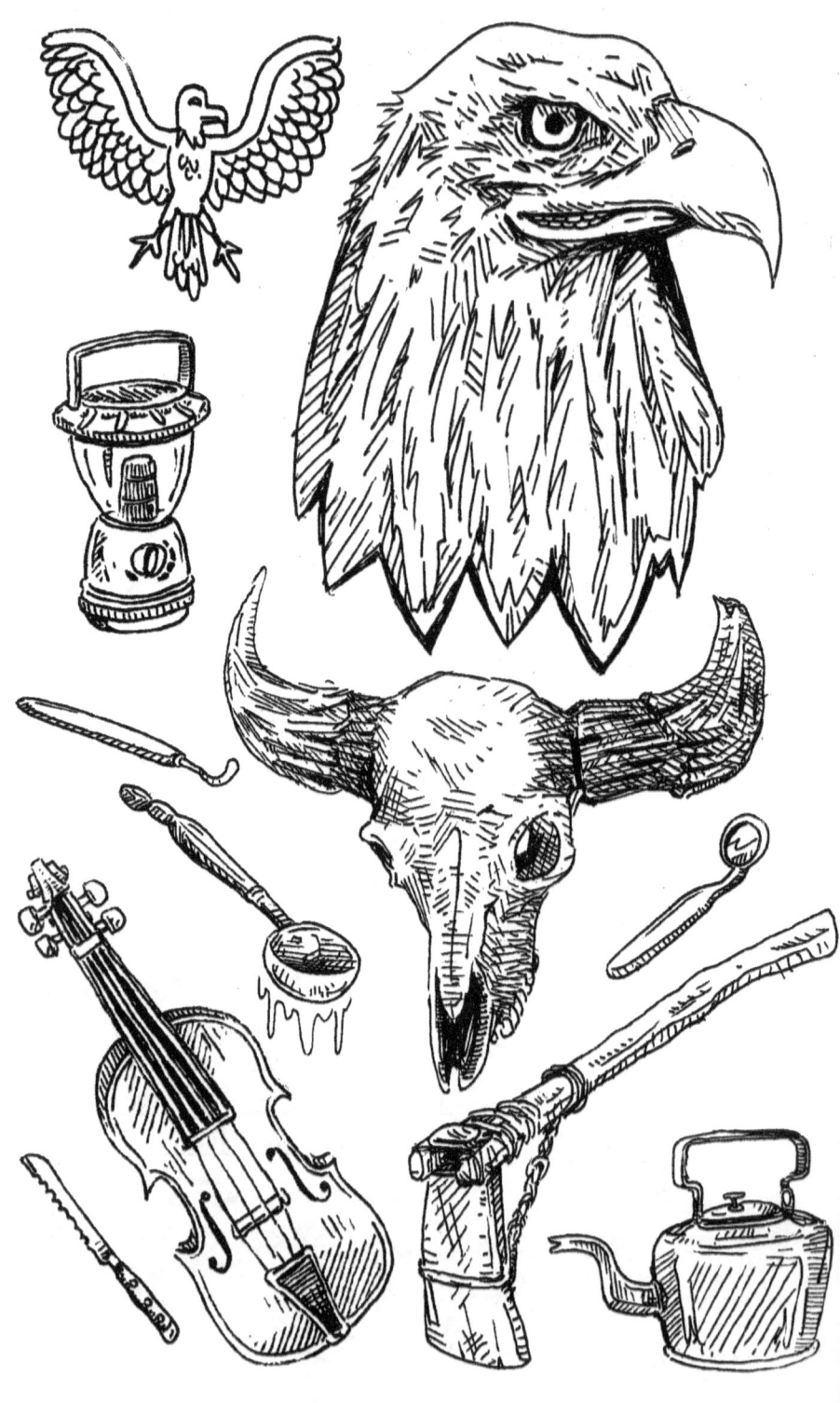

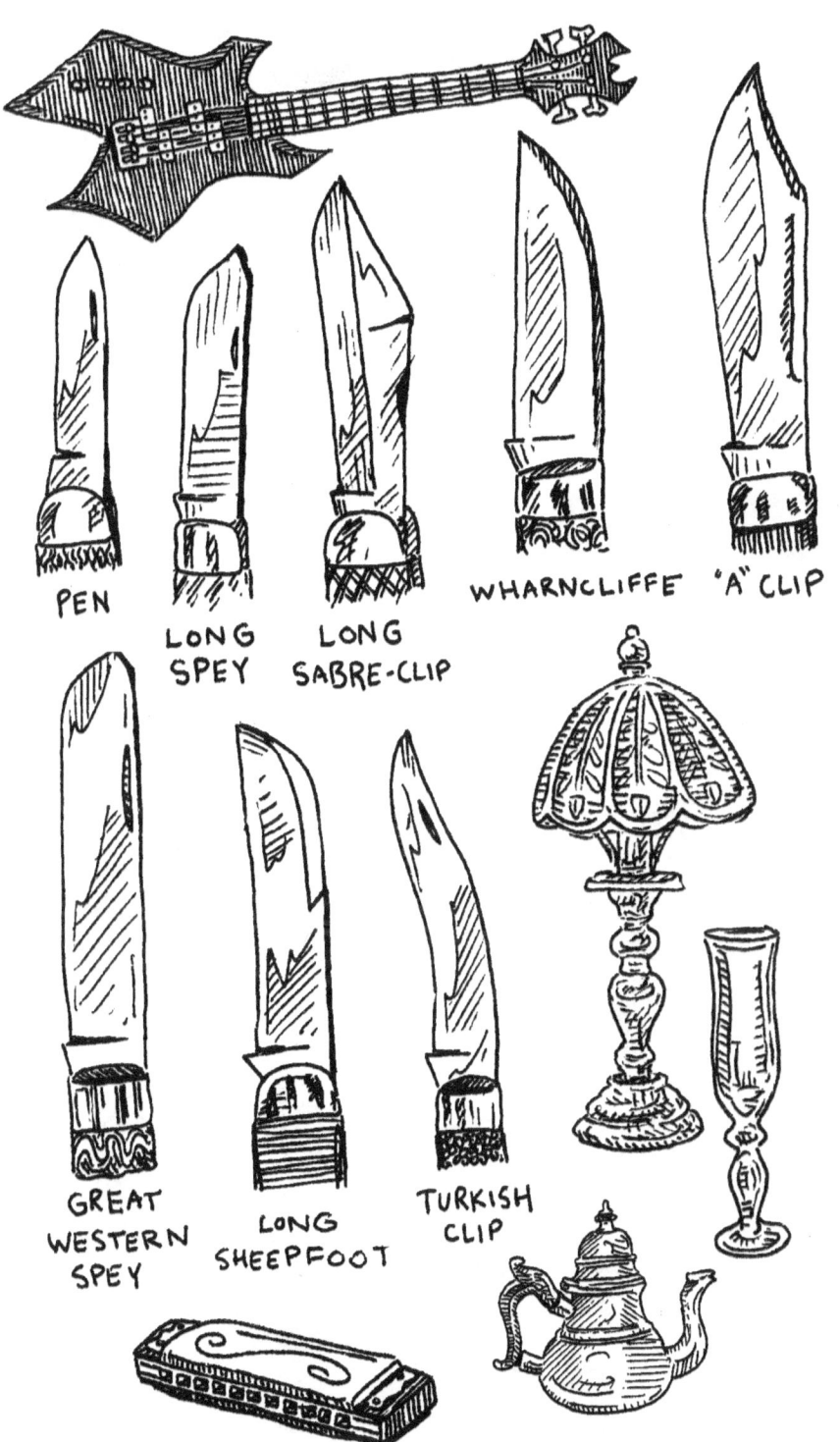

PEN

LONG
SPEY

LONG
SABRE-CLIP

WHARNCLIFFE

"A" CLIP

GREAT
WESTERN
SPEY

LONG
SHEEPFOOT

TURKISH
CLIP

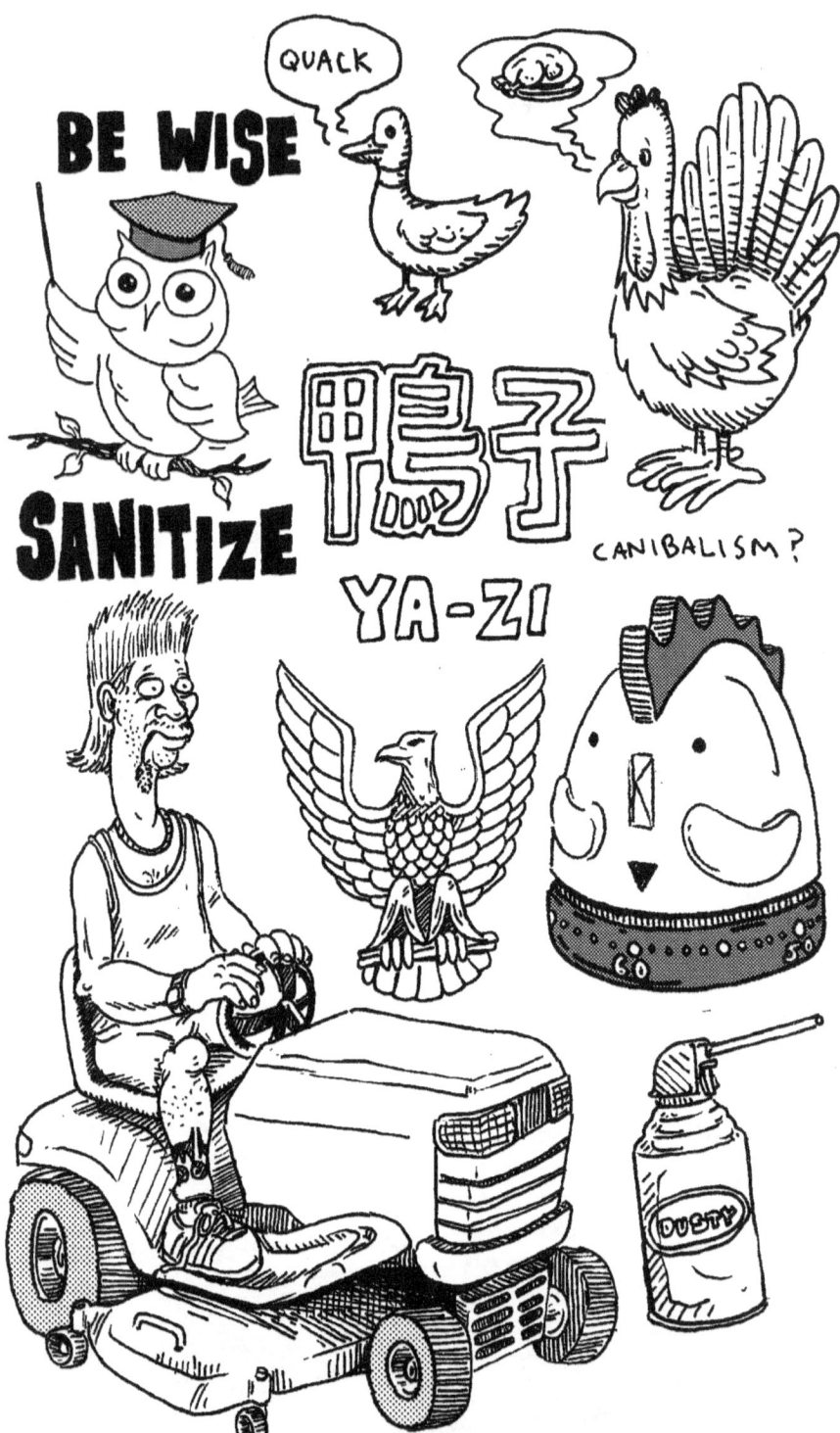

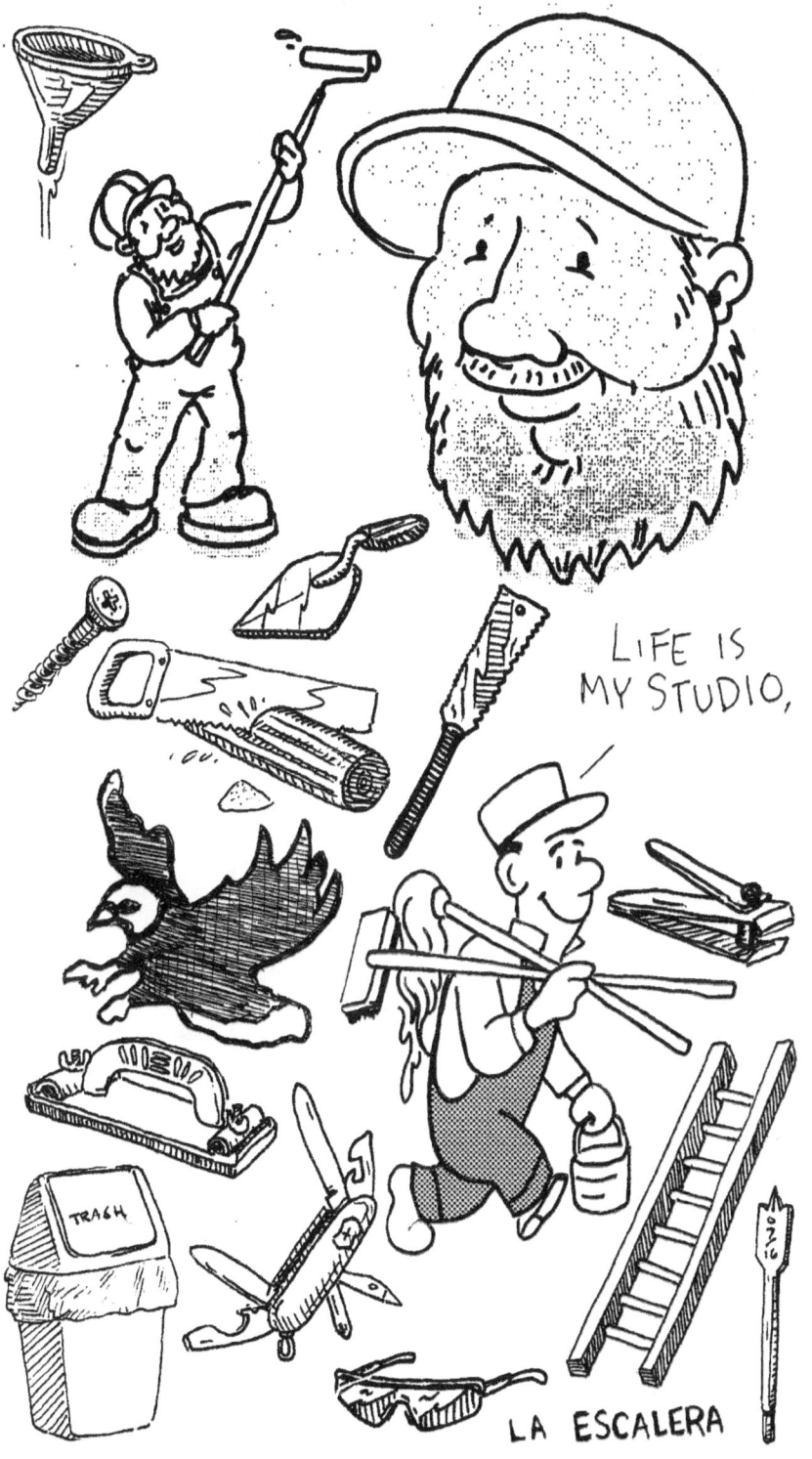

LIFE IS
MY STUDIO.

TRASH

LA ESCALERA

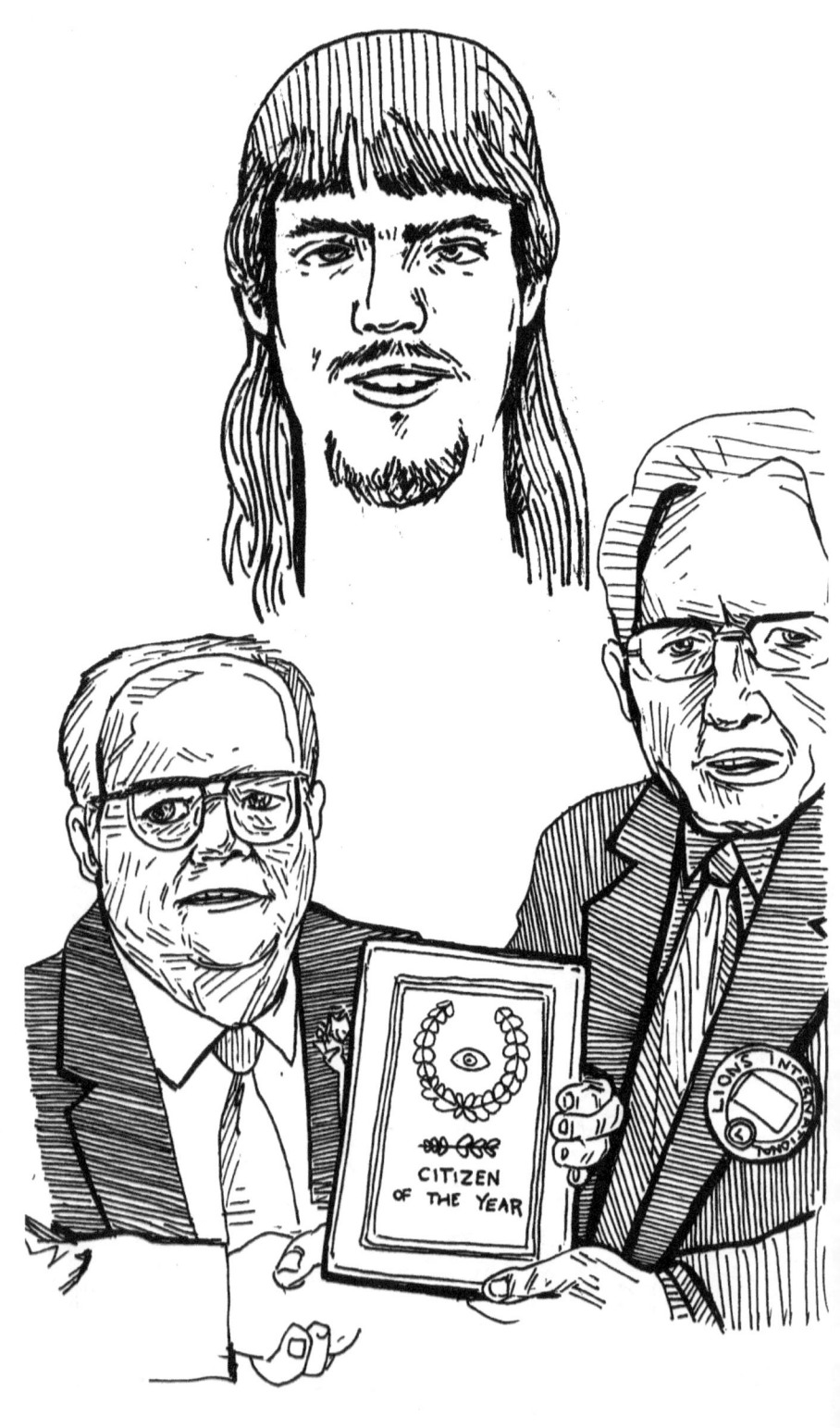

CITIZEN
OF THE YEAR

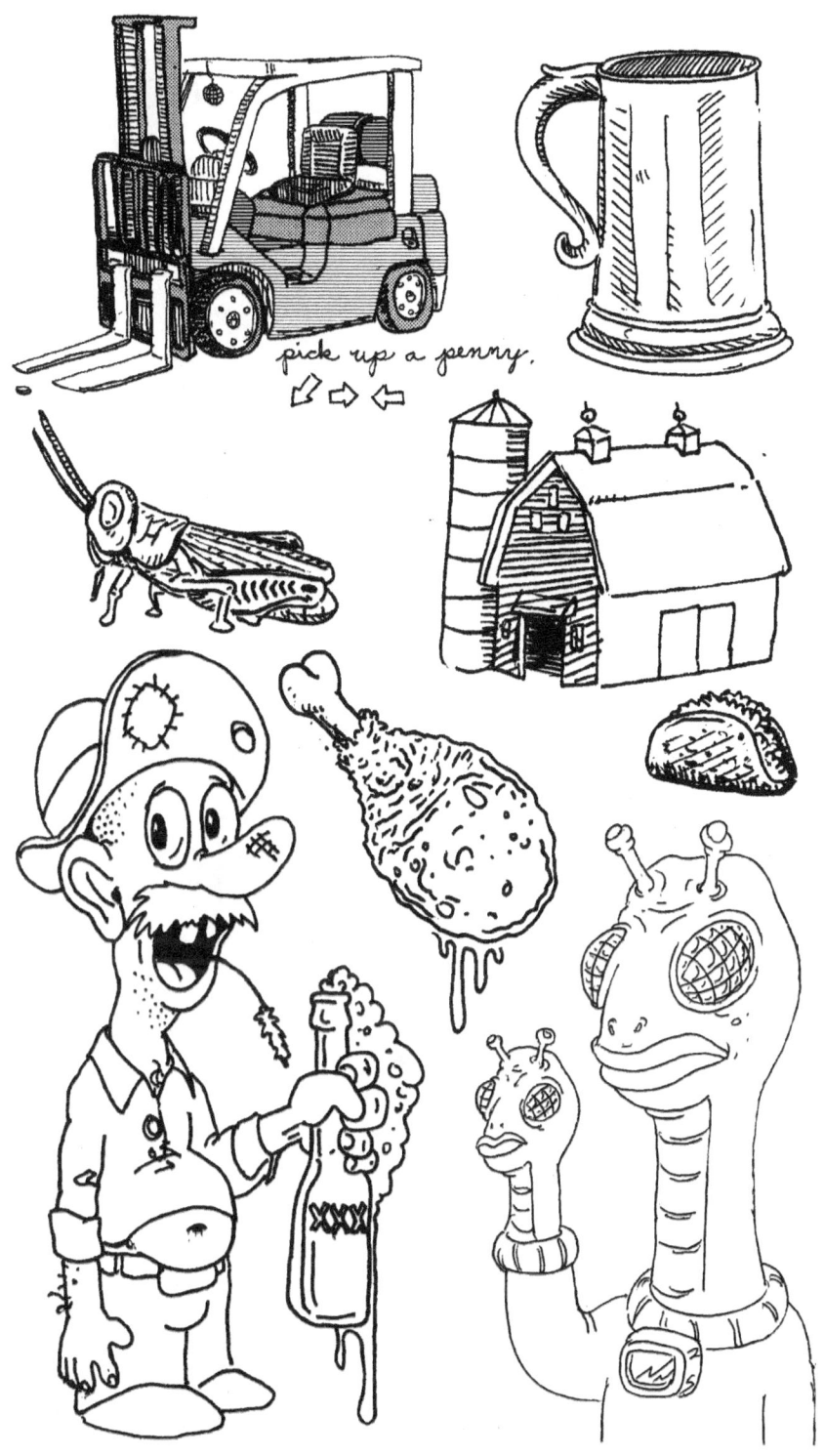

pick up a penny.

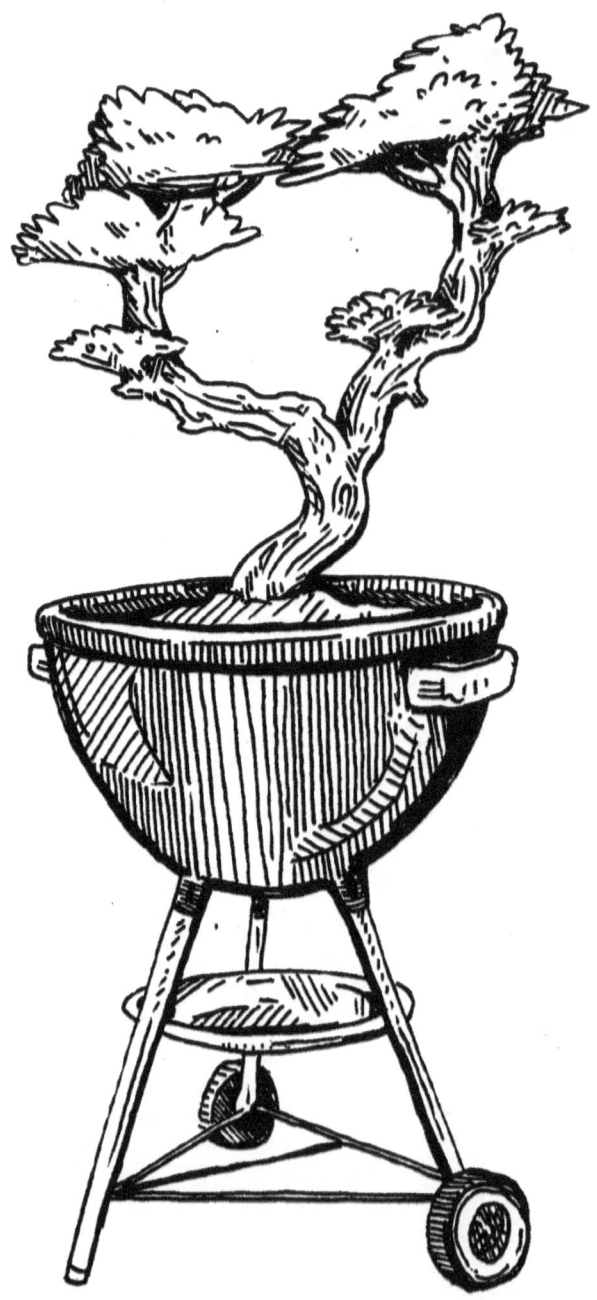

East by Midwest

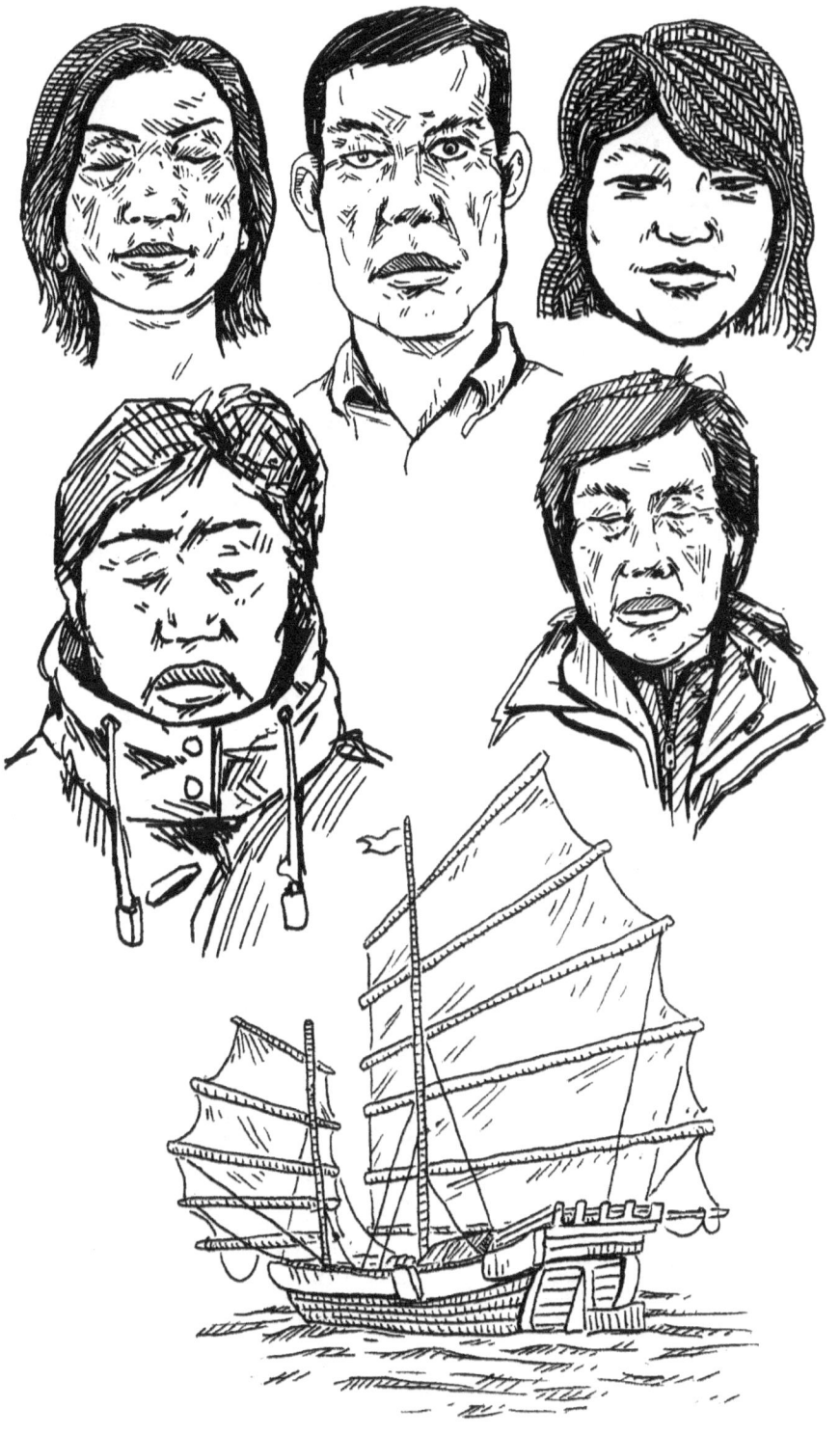

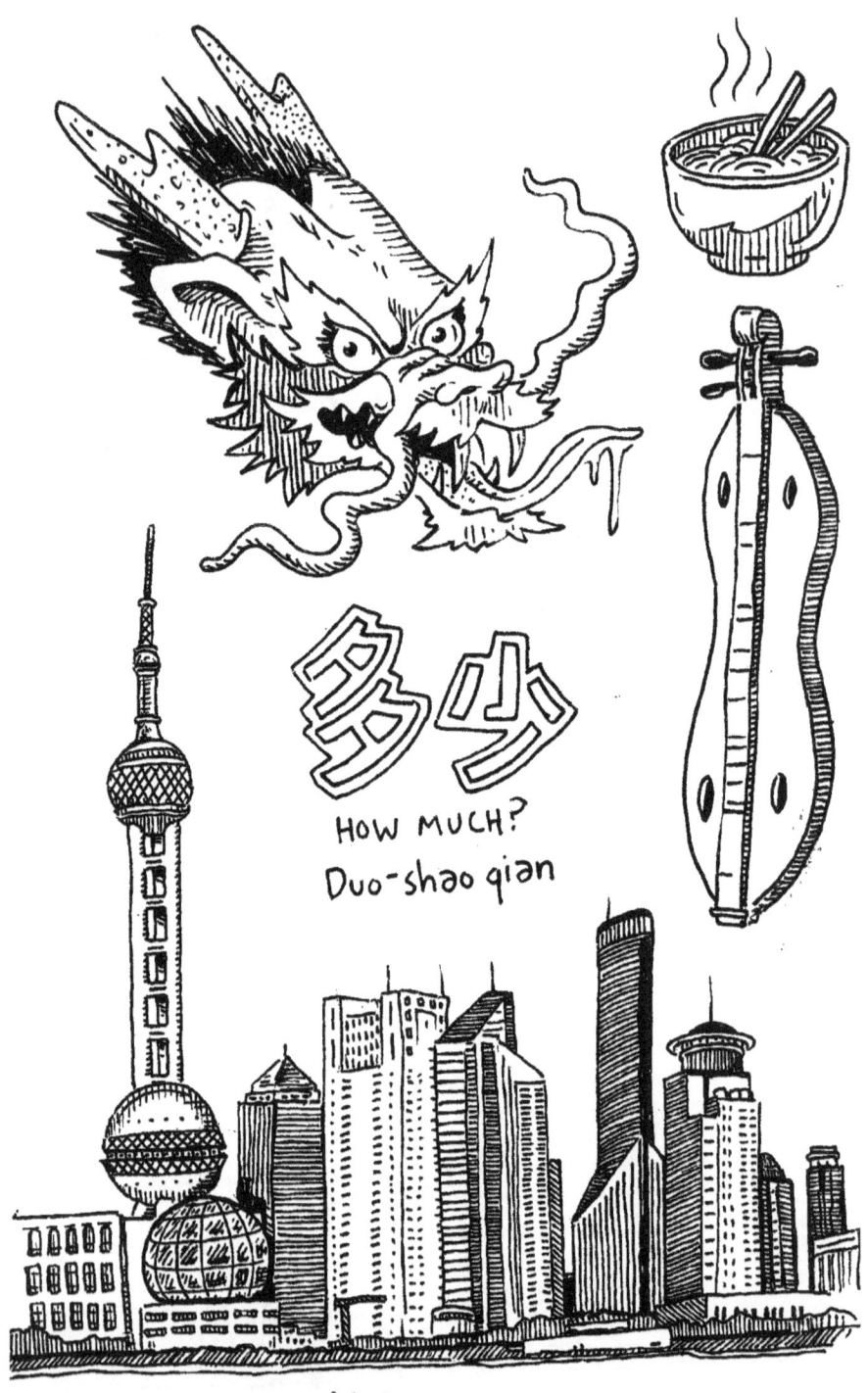

多少

HOW MUCH?
Duo-shao qian

Shanghai

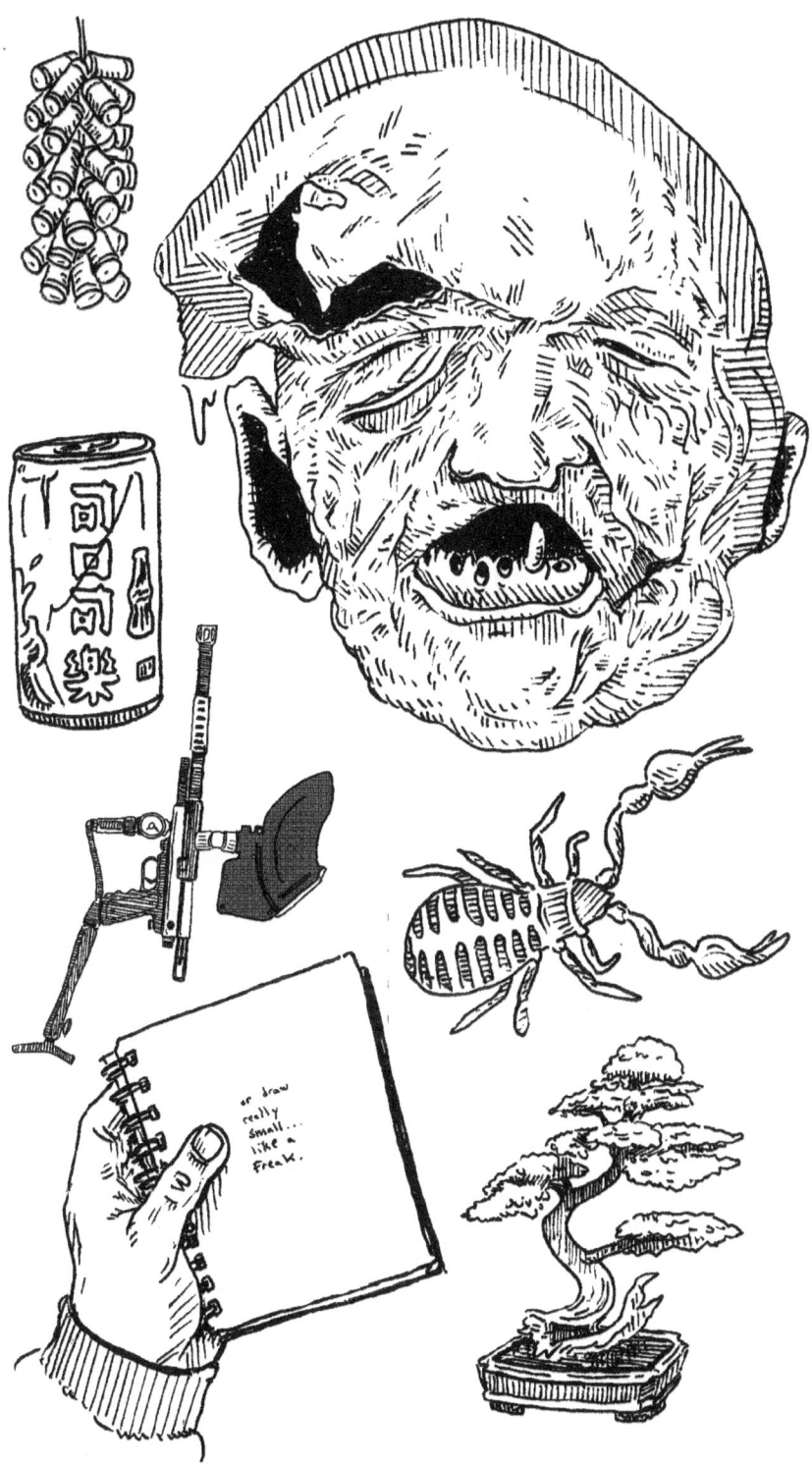

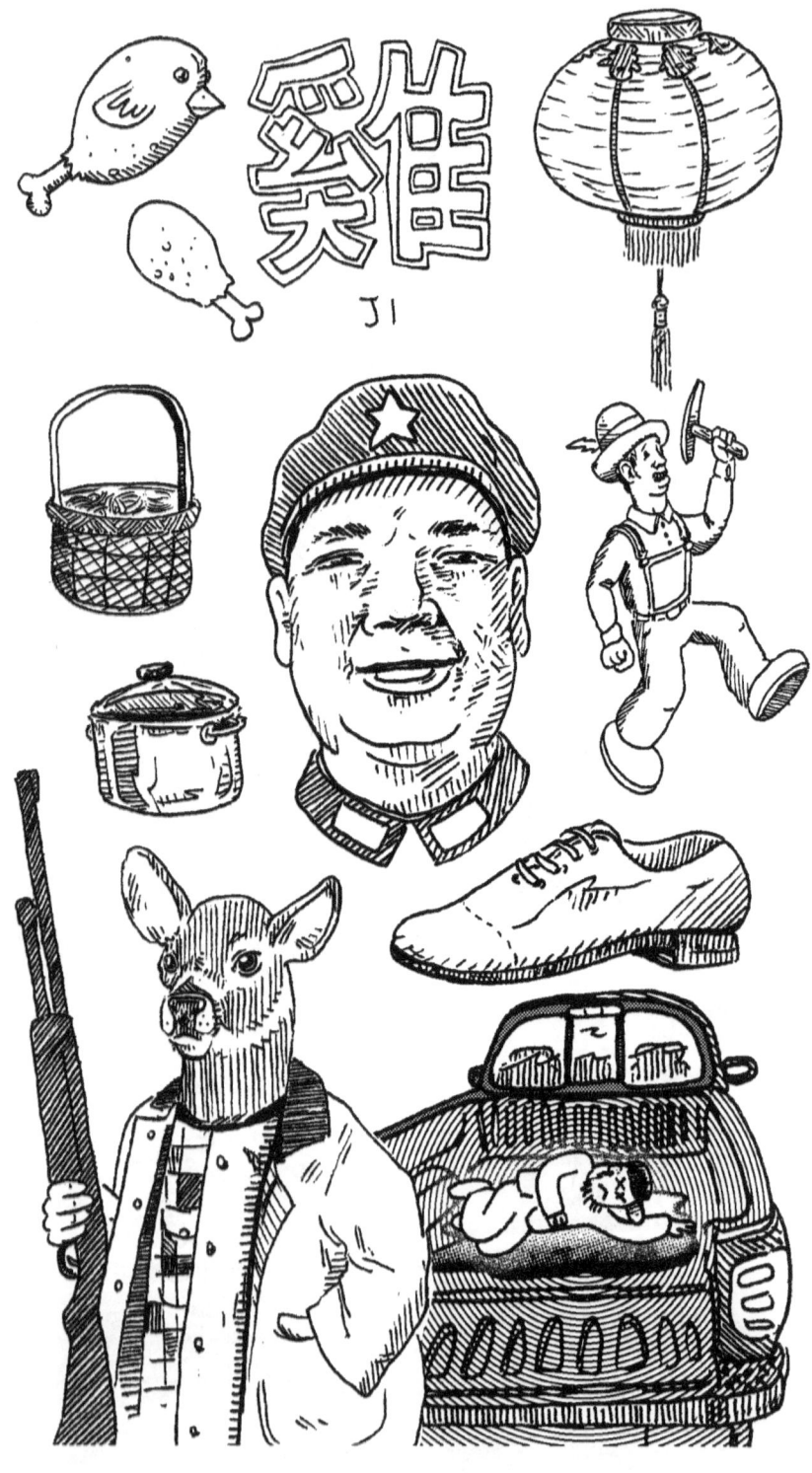

雞

JI

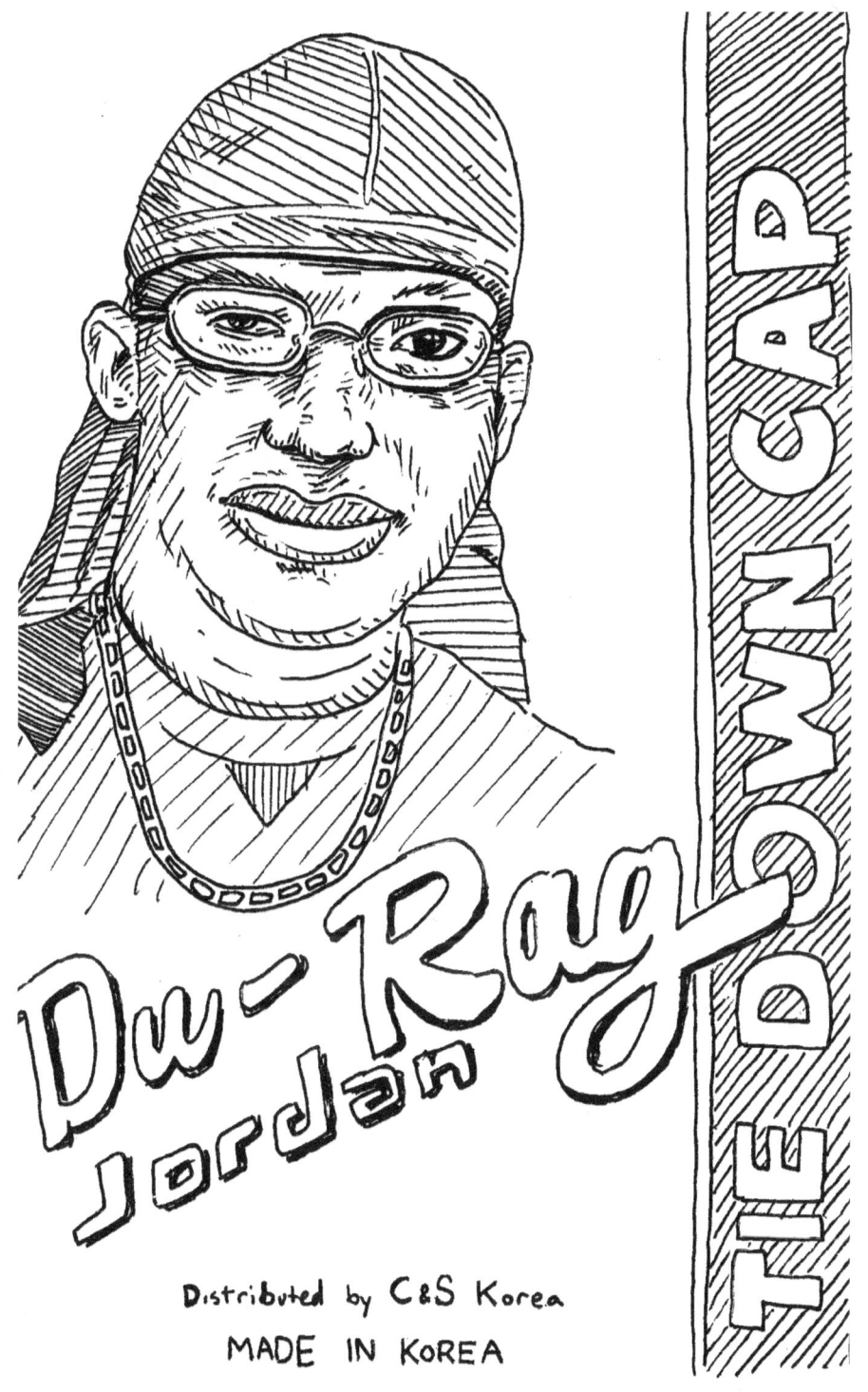

COUPON #17972

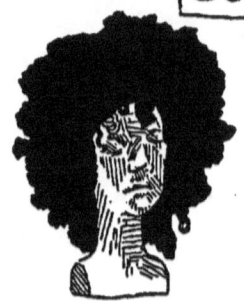

Halloween Wigs
Asst. Colors.
Afro Style.
5.99 Value. (169)

2⁹⁹

CASH VALUE OF 1/20TH OF A CENT. SELECTION MAY VARY.

SEE STORE OR COVER FOR EXPIRATION DATE. GOOD WHILE QUANTITIES LAST.   5-30

COUPON #16619

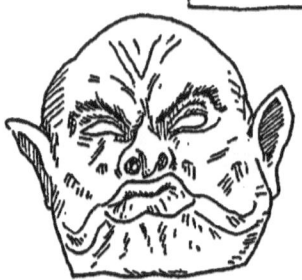

Full Masks
Asst.
6.99 Value. (327)

3⁹⁹

CASH VALUE OF 1/20TH OF A CENT. SELECTION MAY VARY.

SEE STORE OR COVER FOR EXPIRATION DATE. GOOD WHILE QUANTITIES LAST.   5-30

COUPON #17918

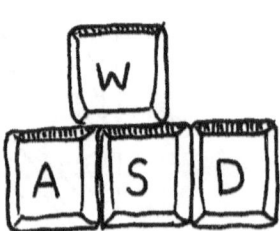

Figure Inside. 8".
7.99 Value. (459)

4⁹⁹

CASH VALUE OF 1/20TH OF A CENT. SELECTION MAY VARY.

SEE STORE OR COVER FOR EXPIRATION DATE. GOOD WHILE QUANTITIES LAST.   5-30

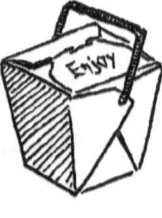

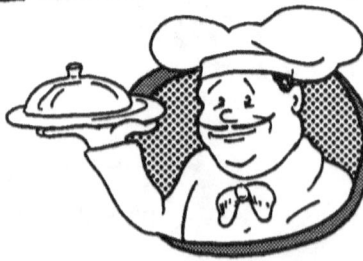

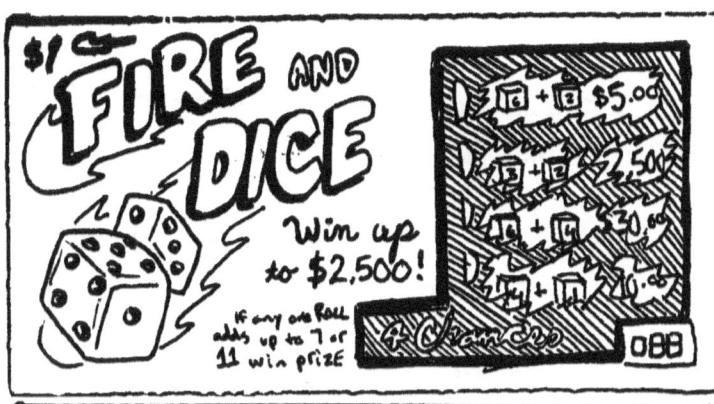

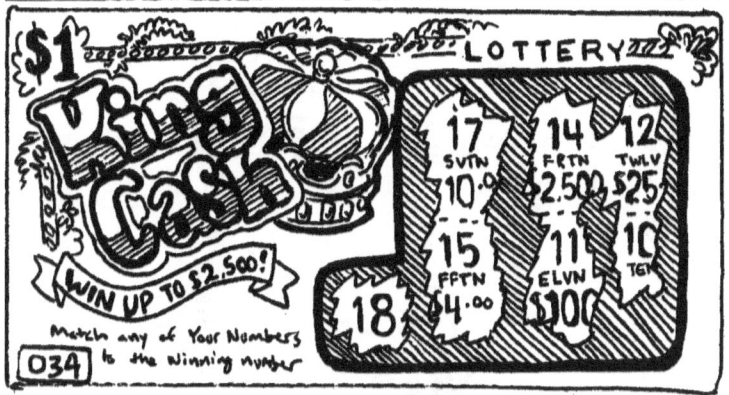

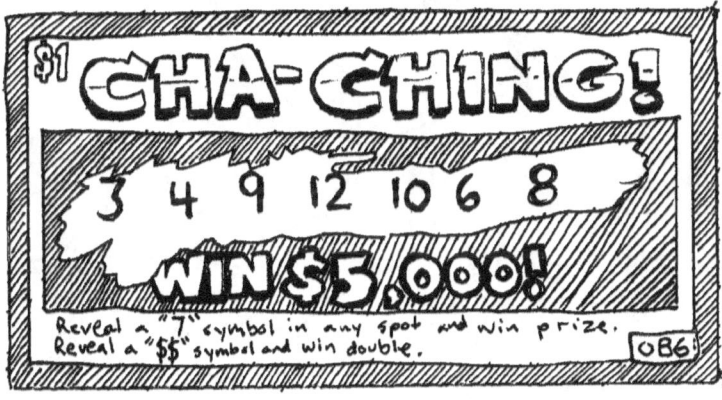

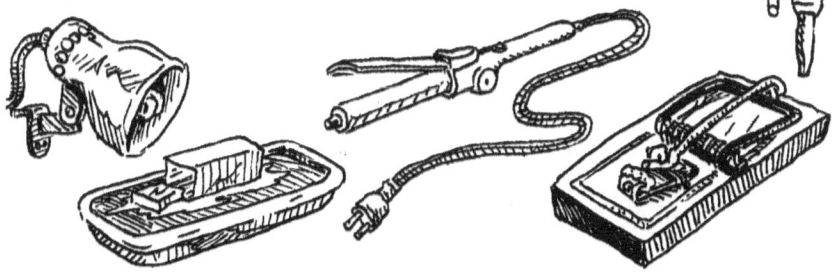

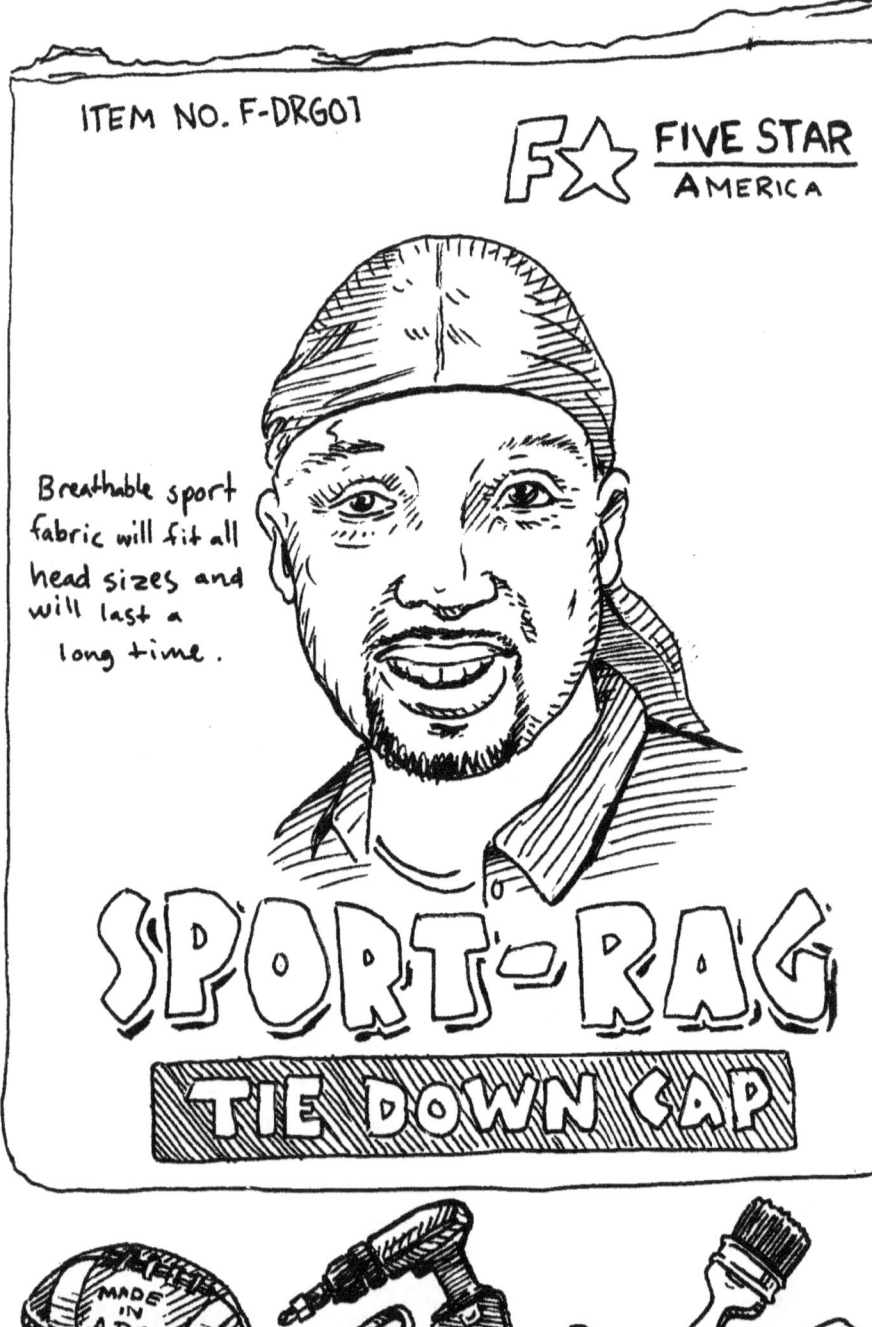

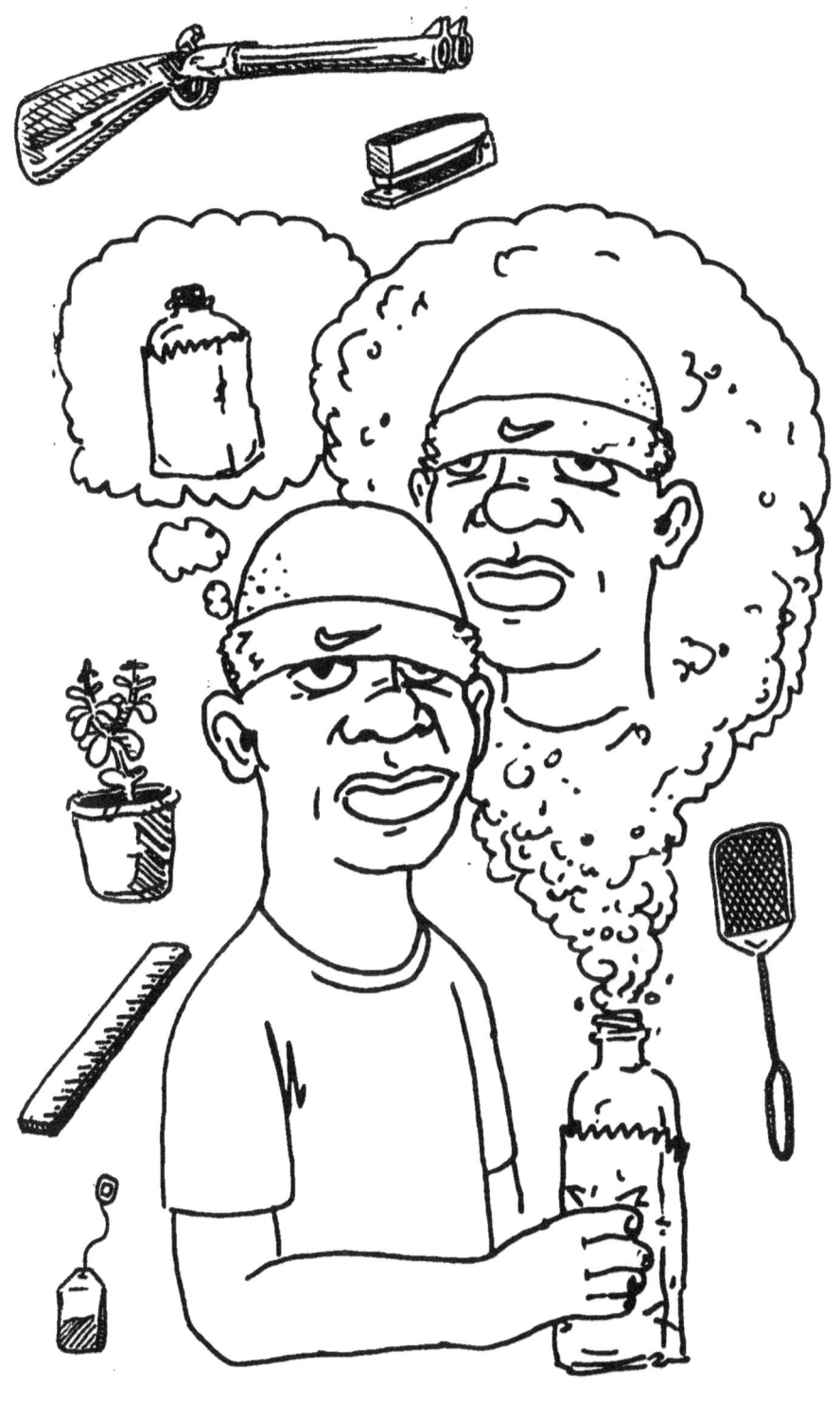

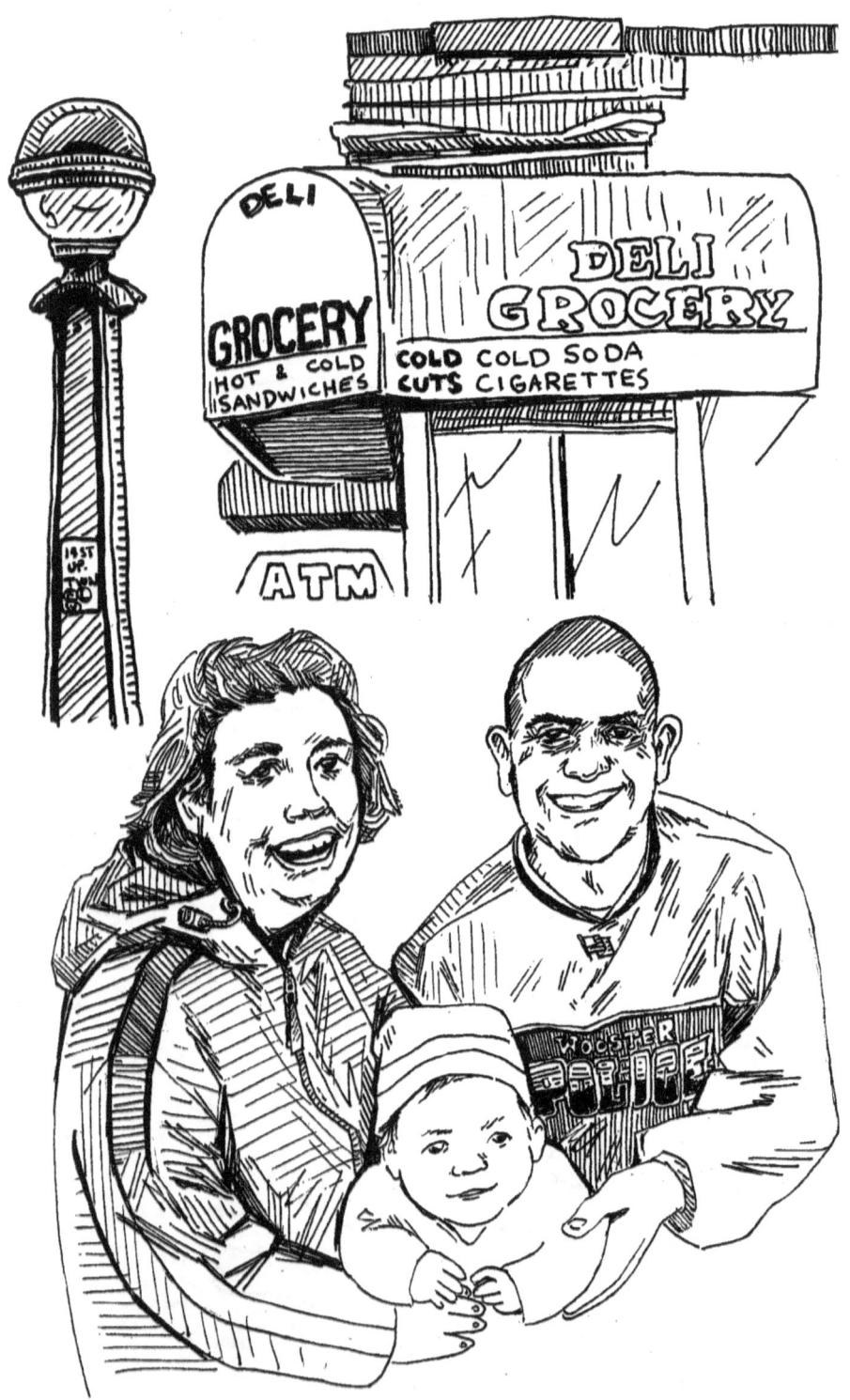

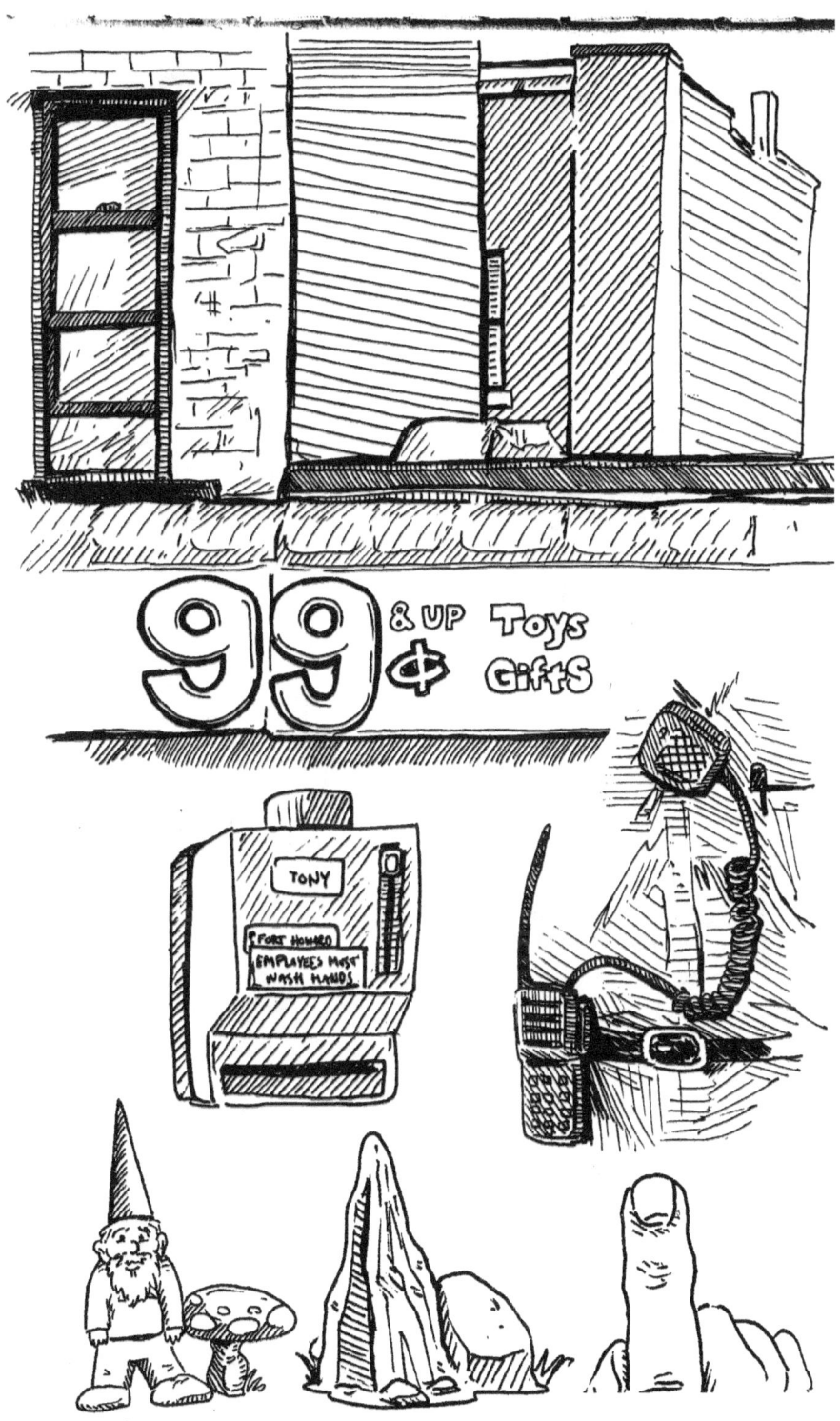

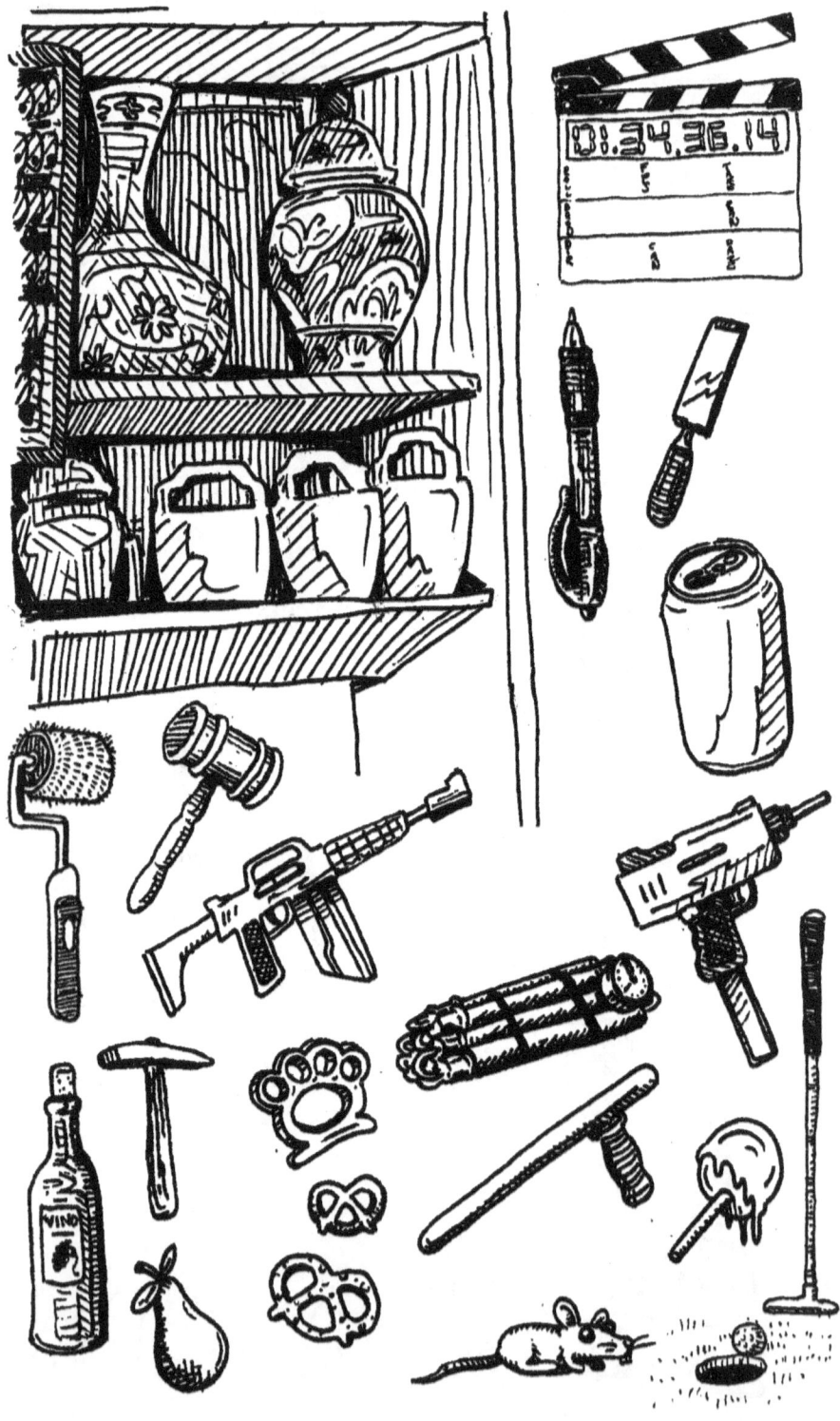

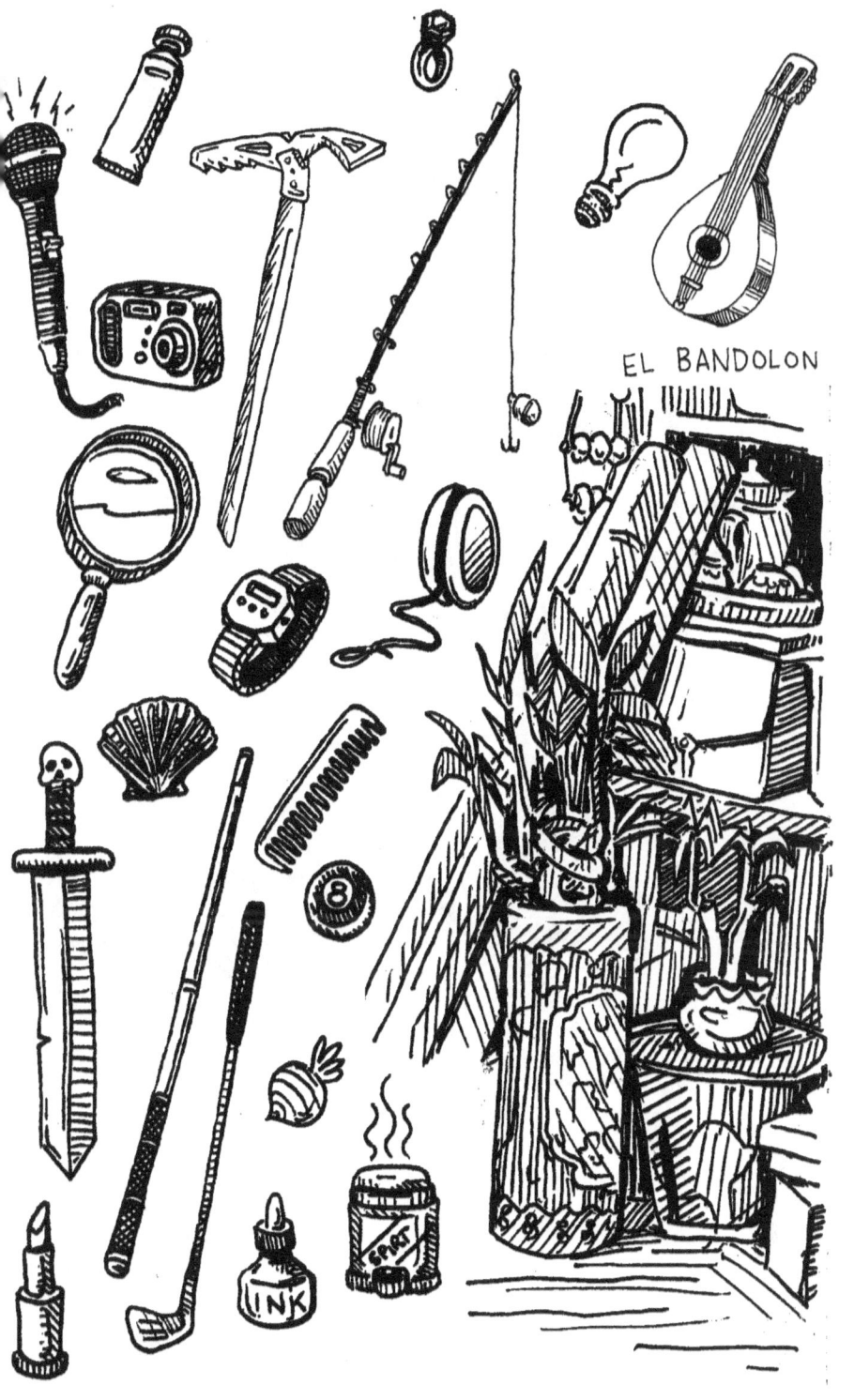

EL BANDOLON

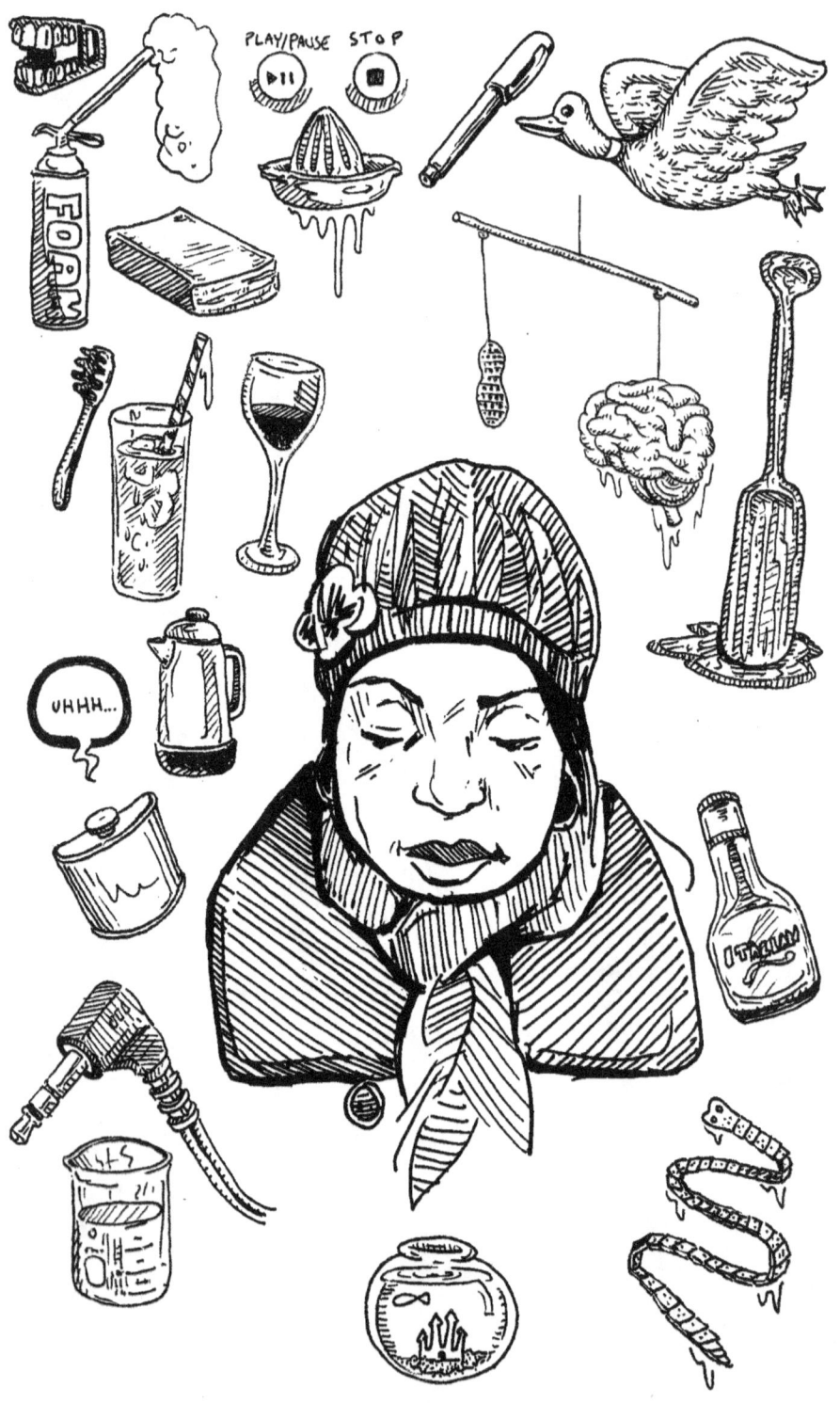

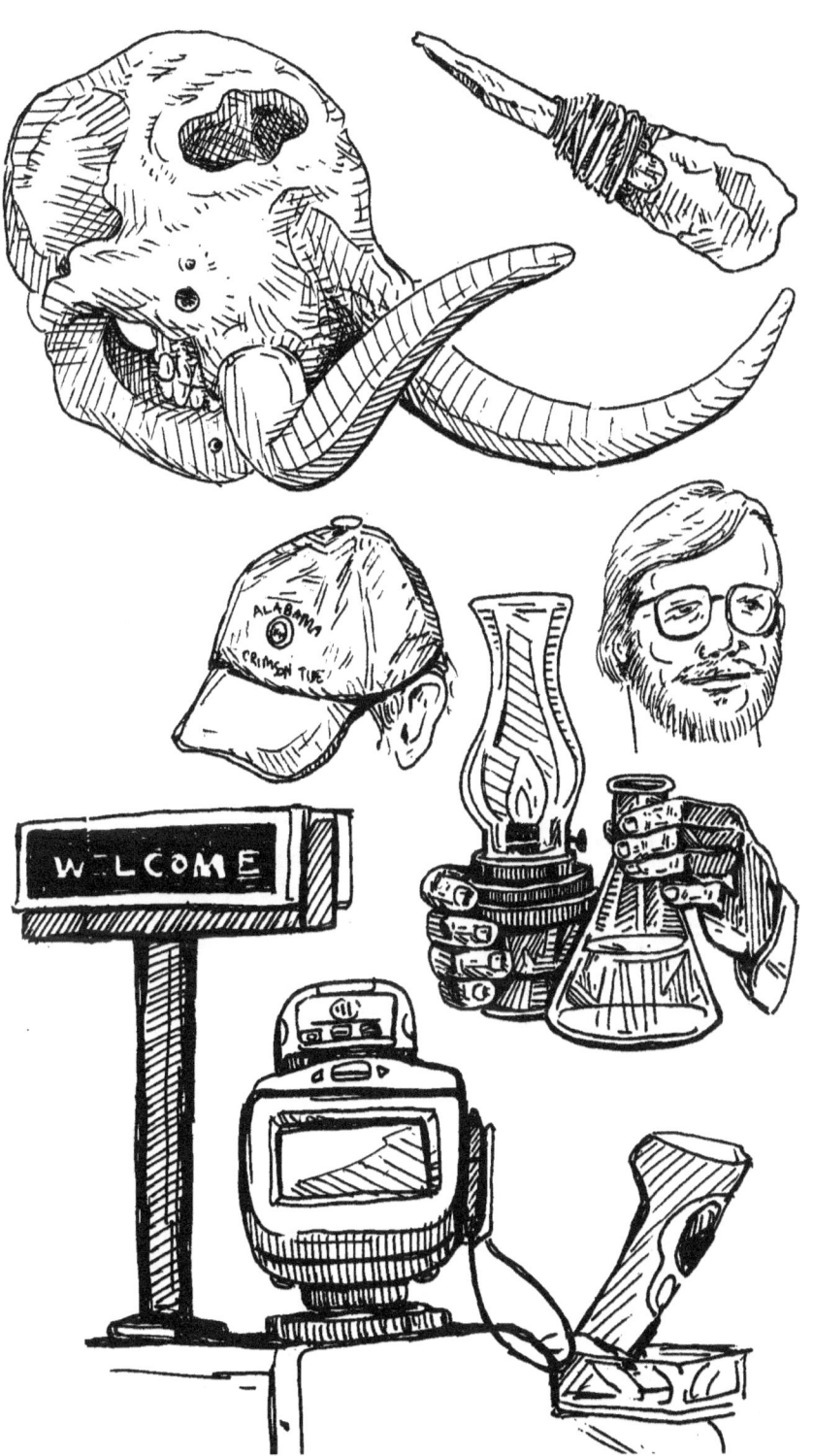

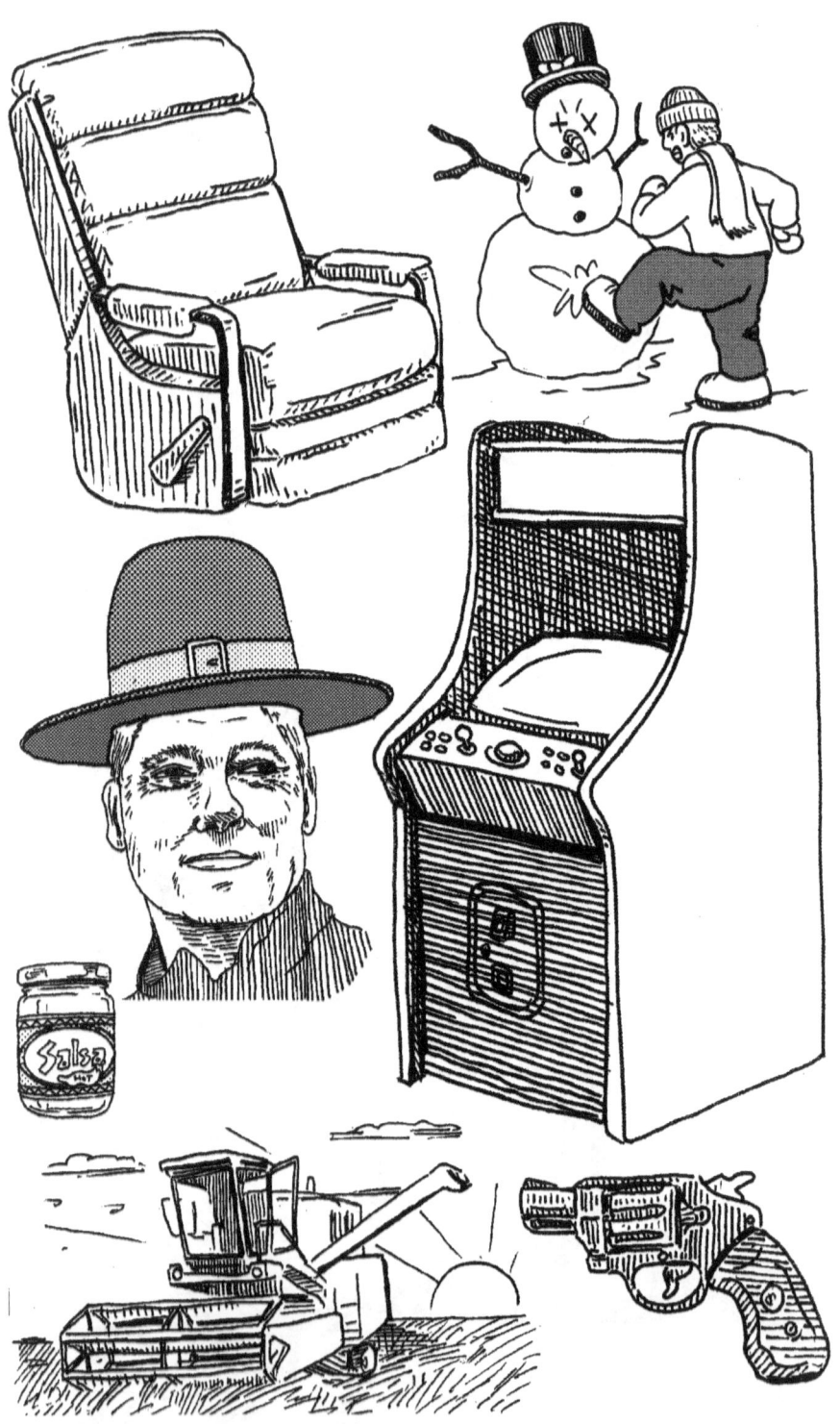

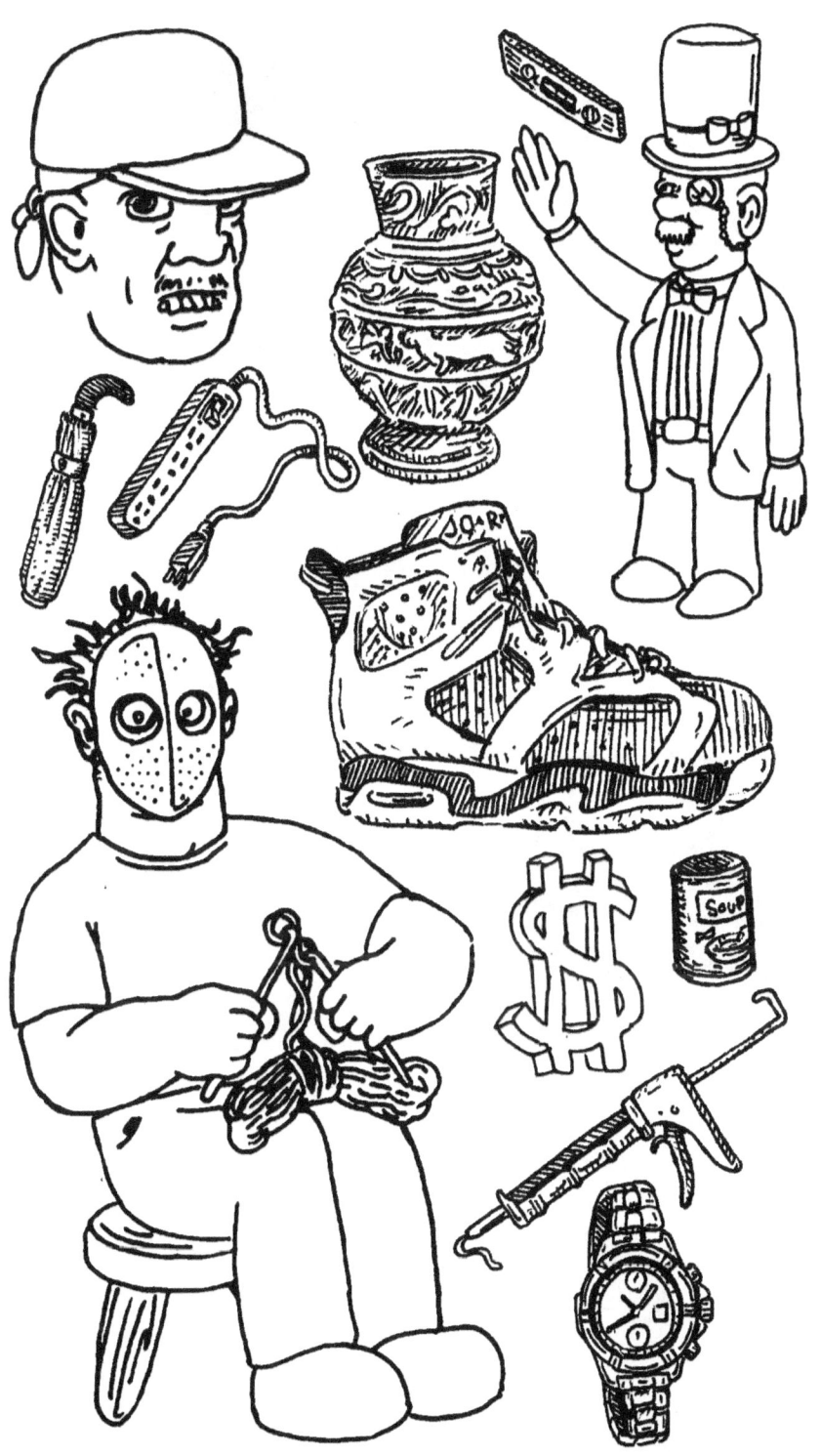

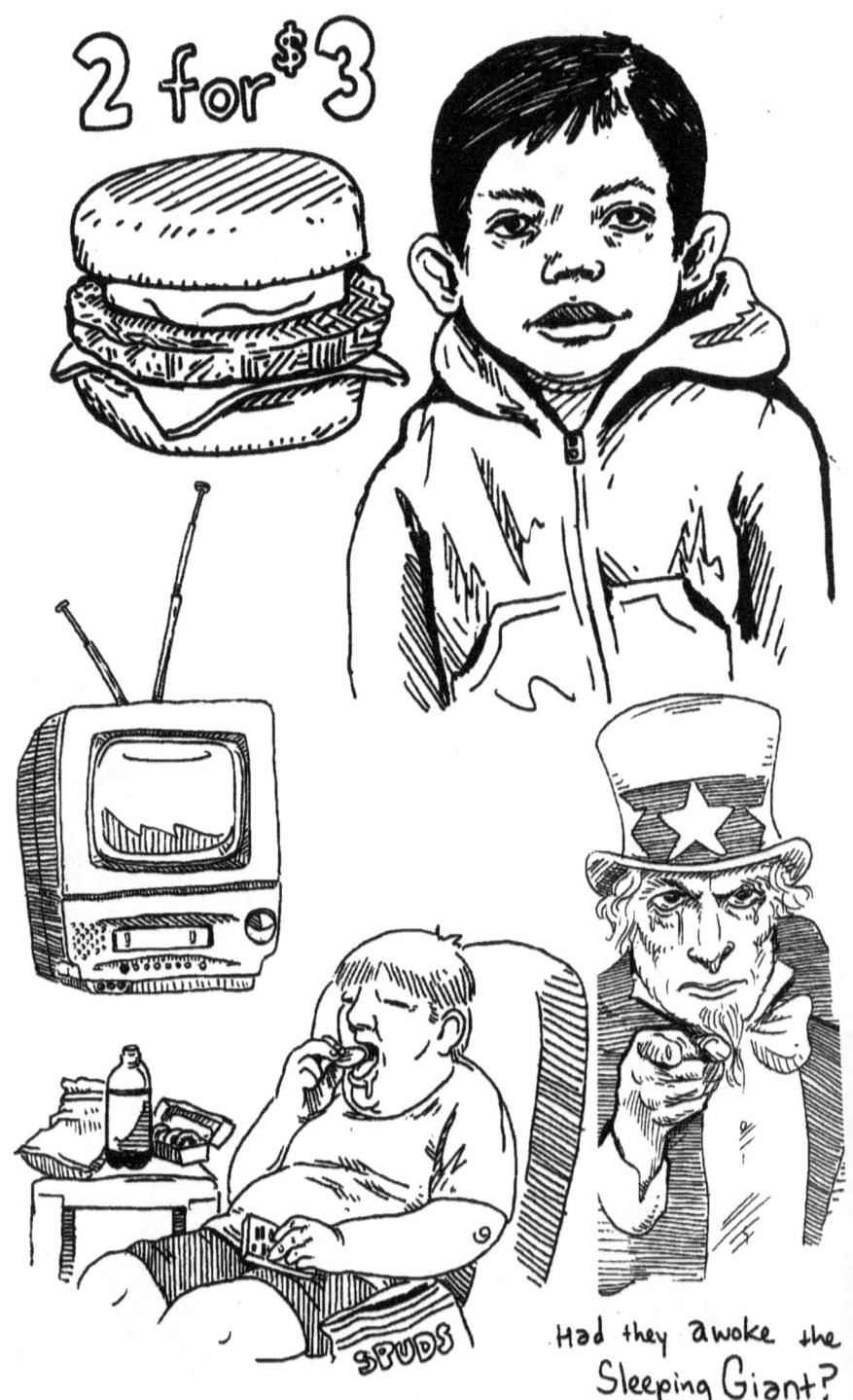

2 for $3

SPUDS

Had they awoke the
Sleeping Giant?

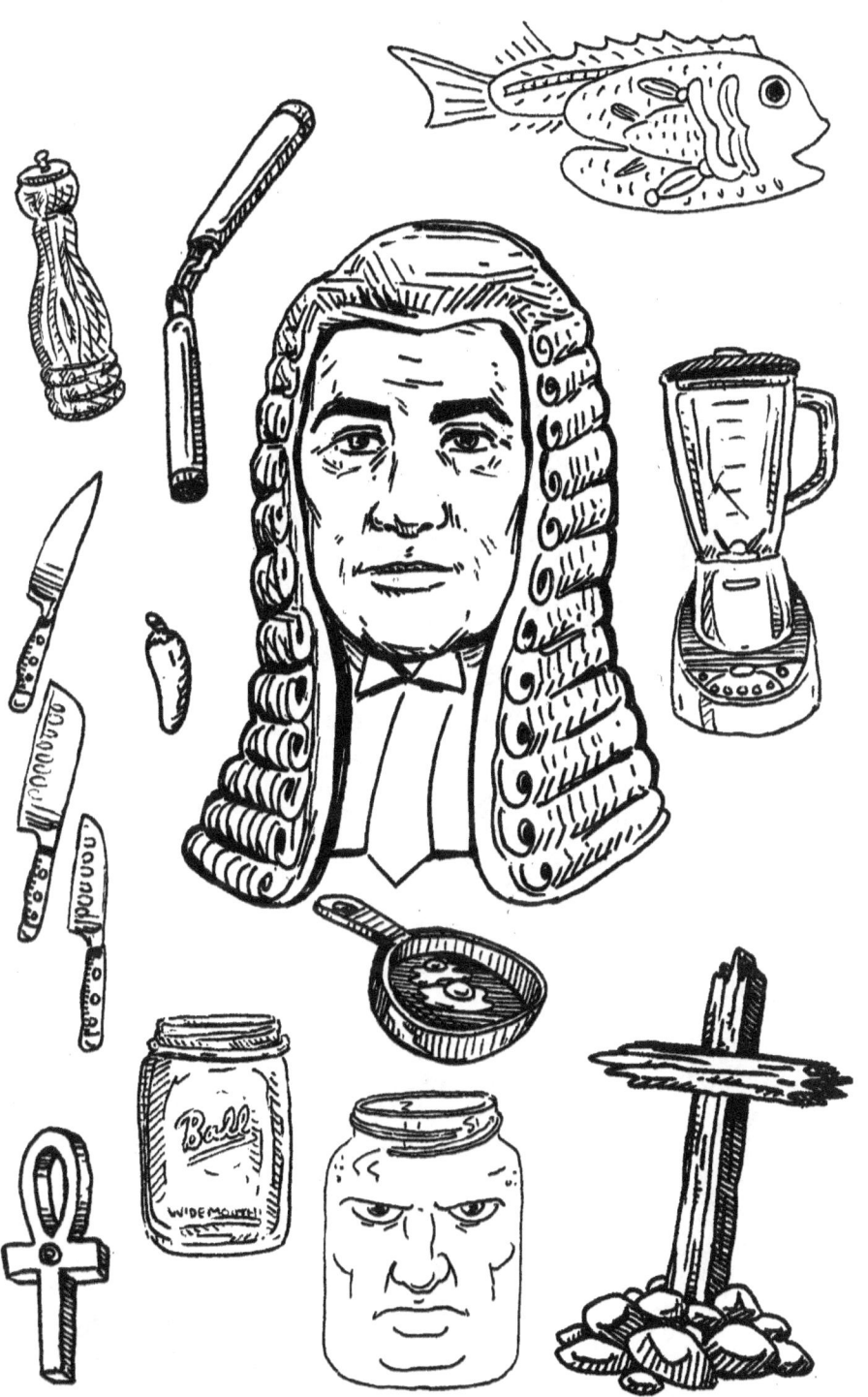

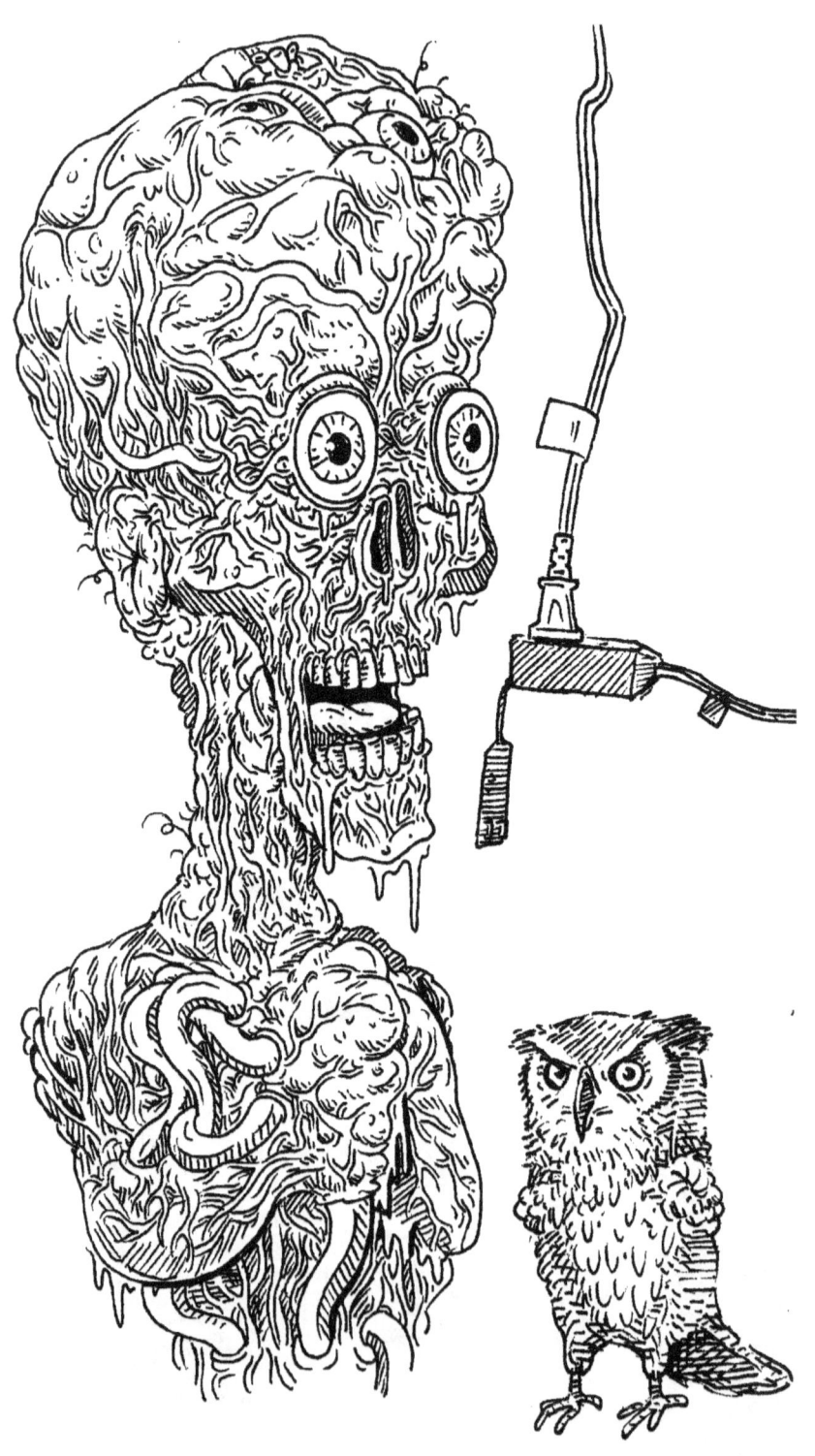

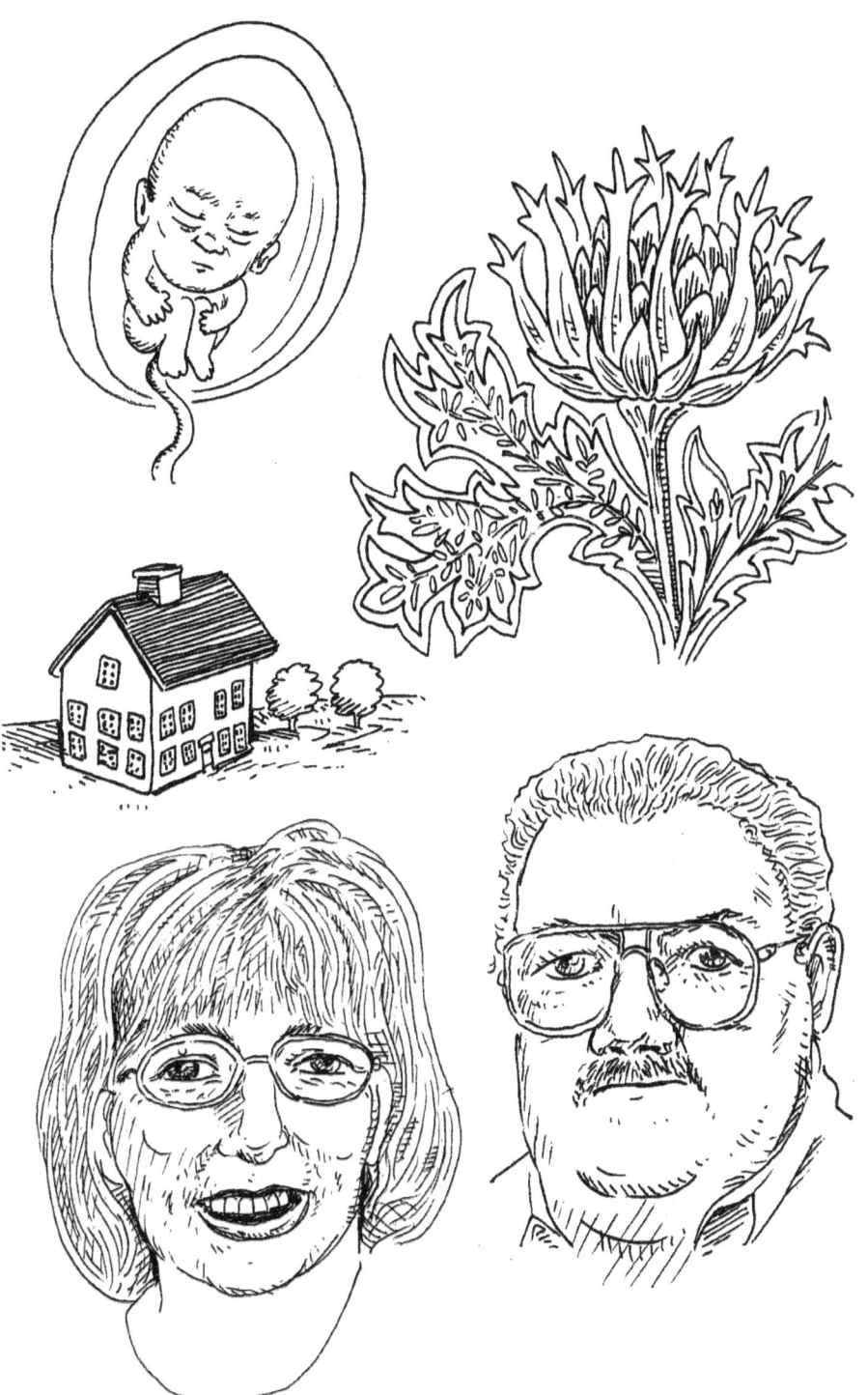

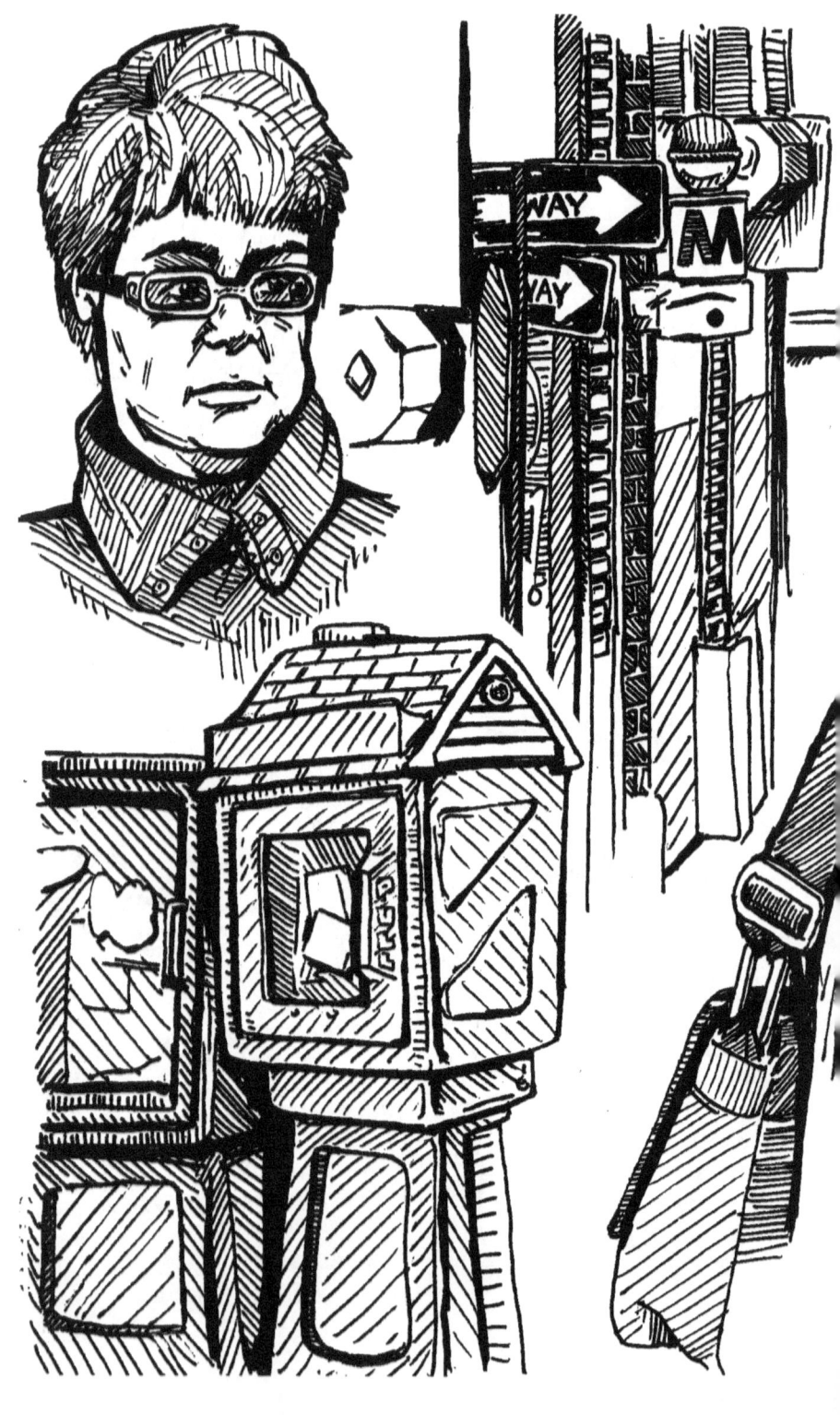

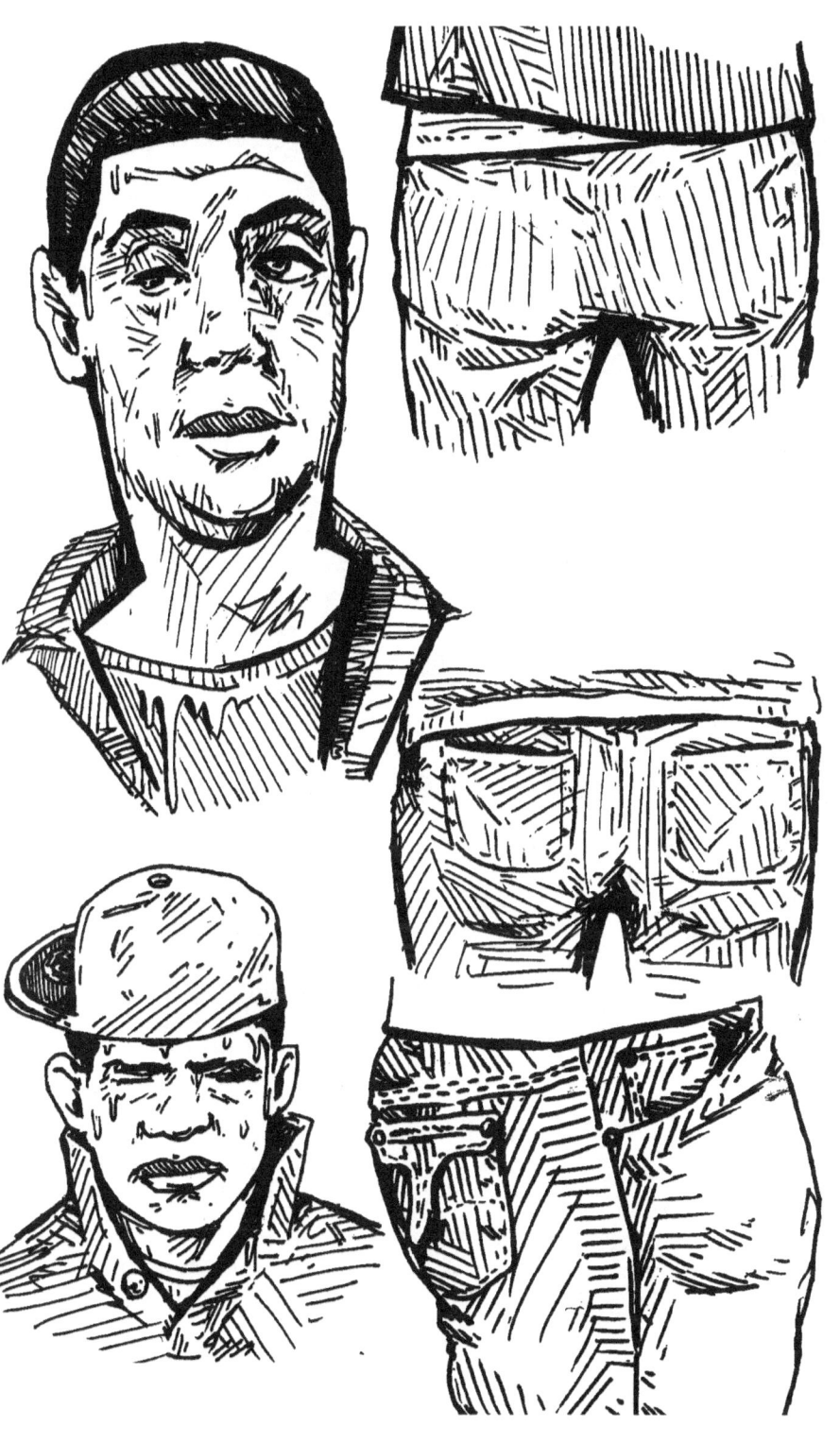

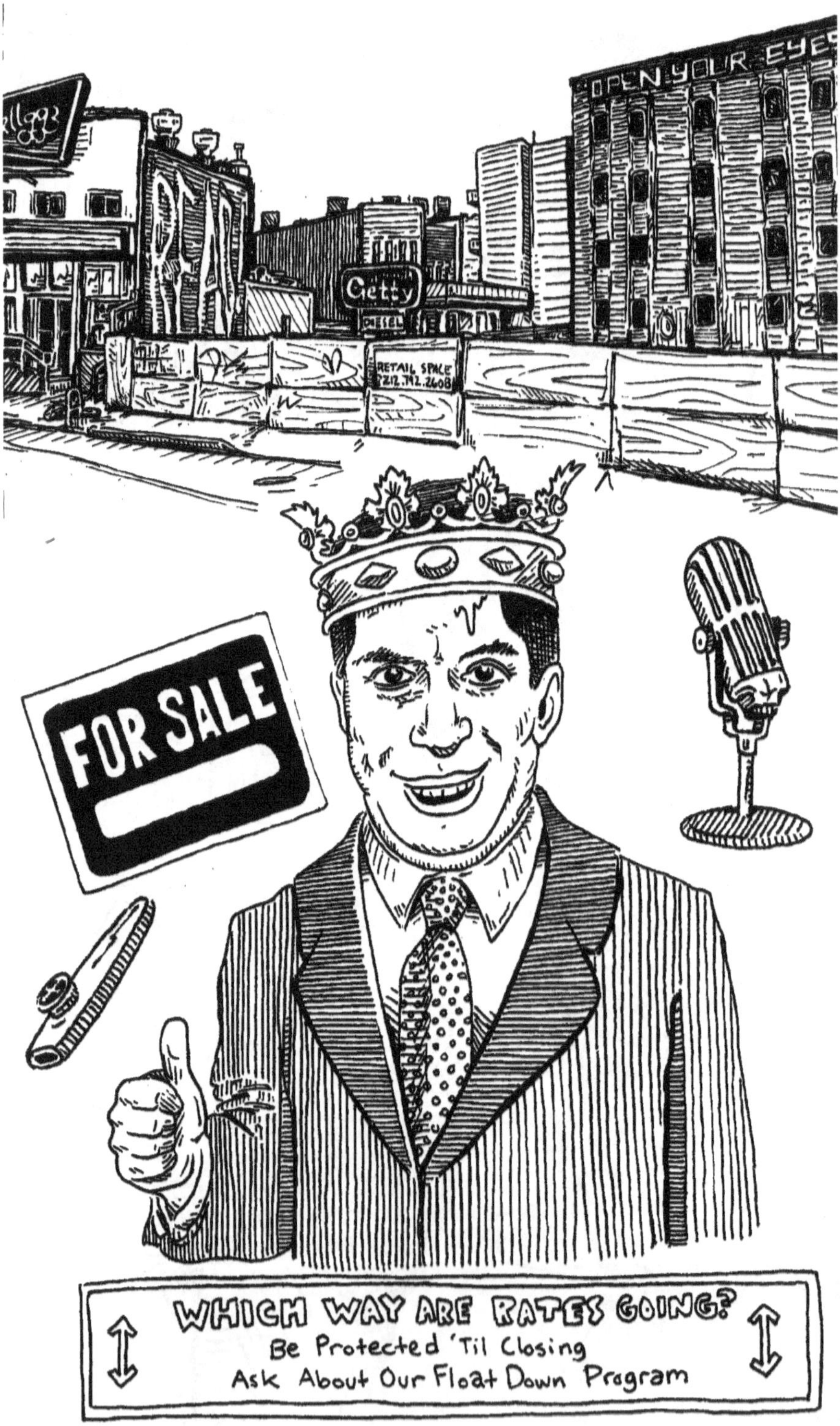

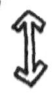

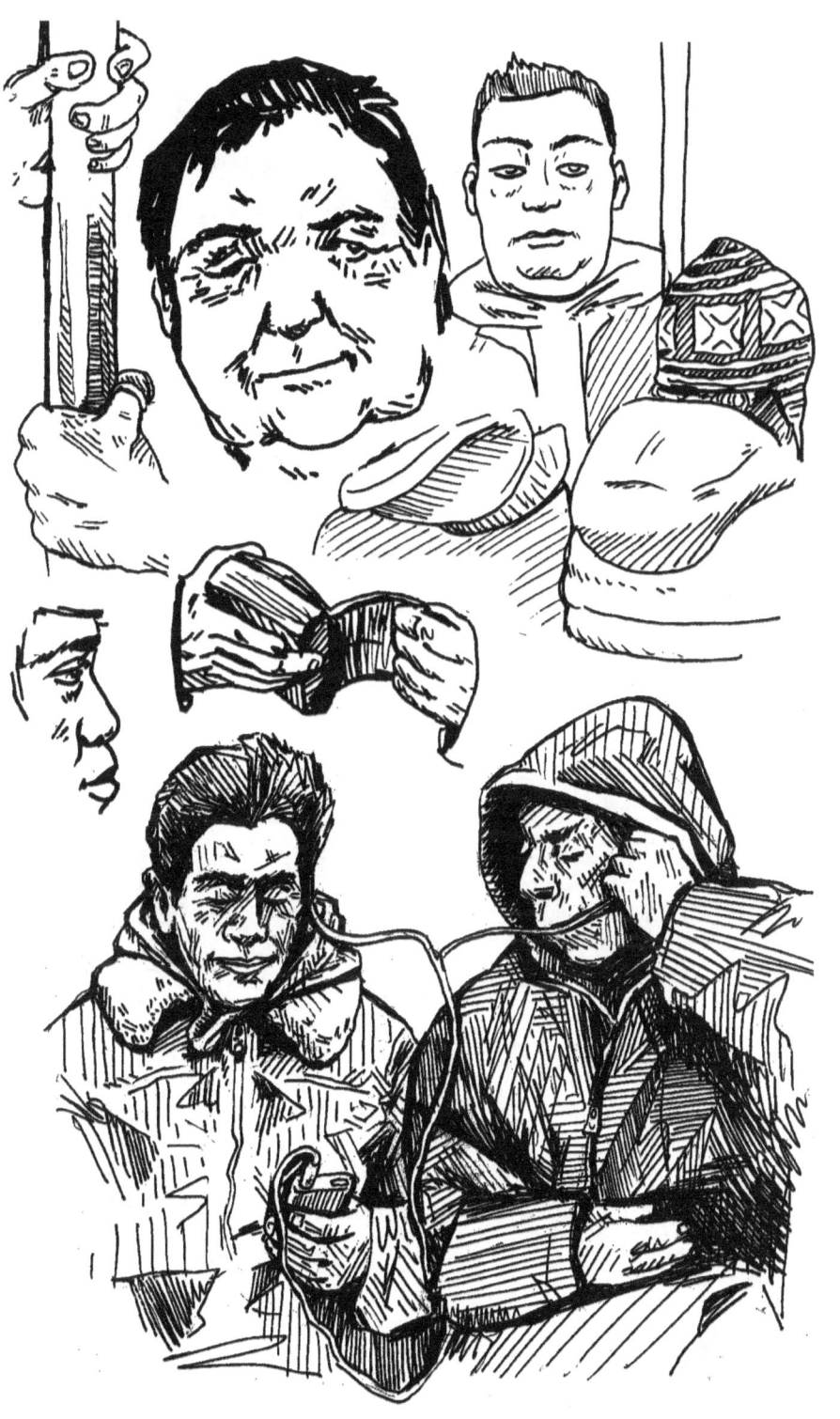

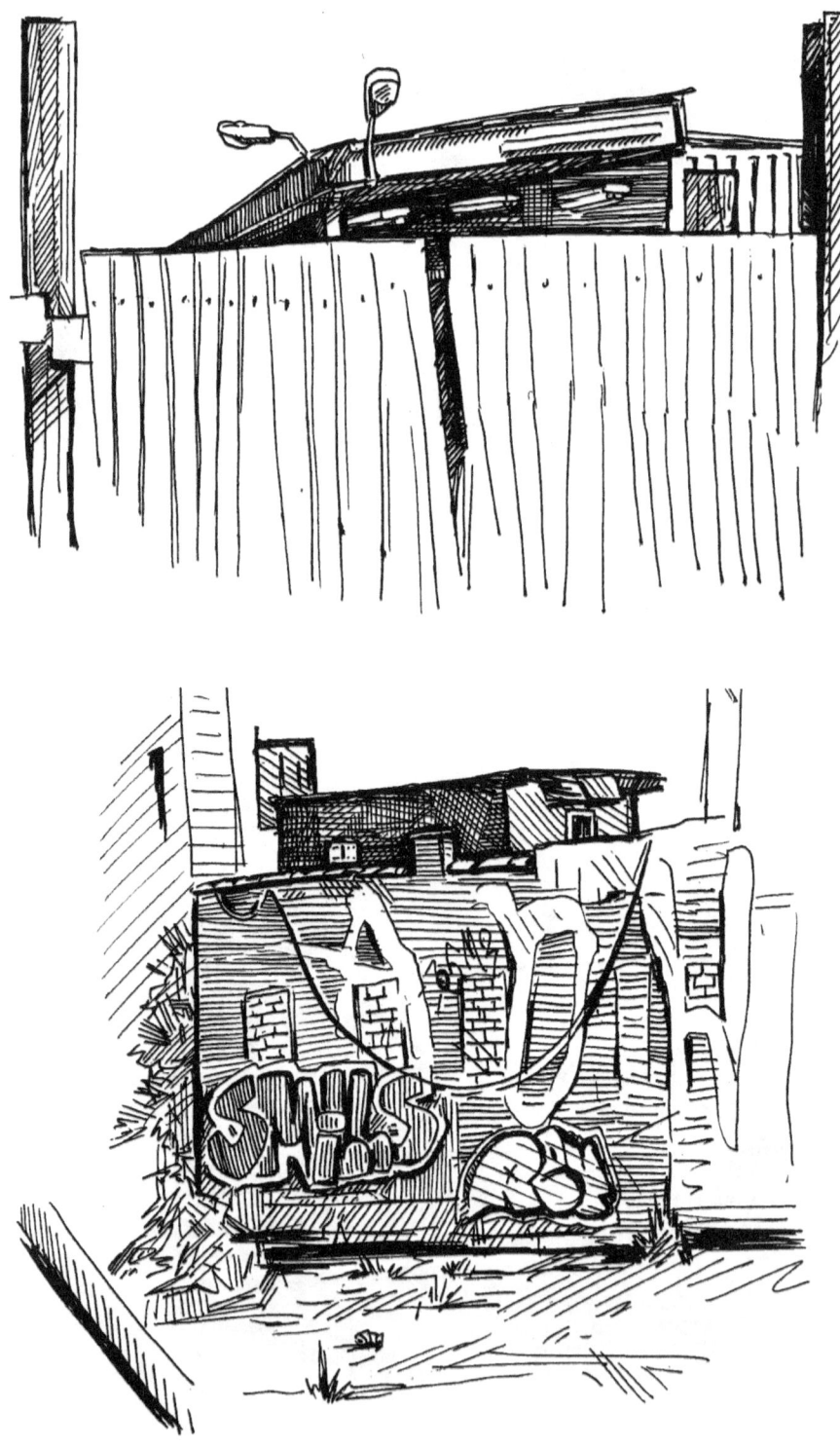

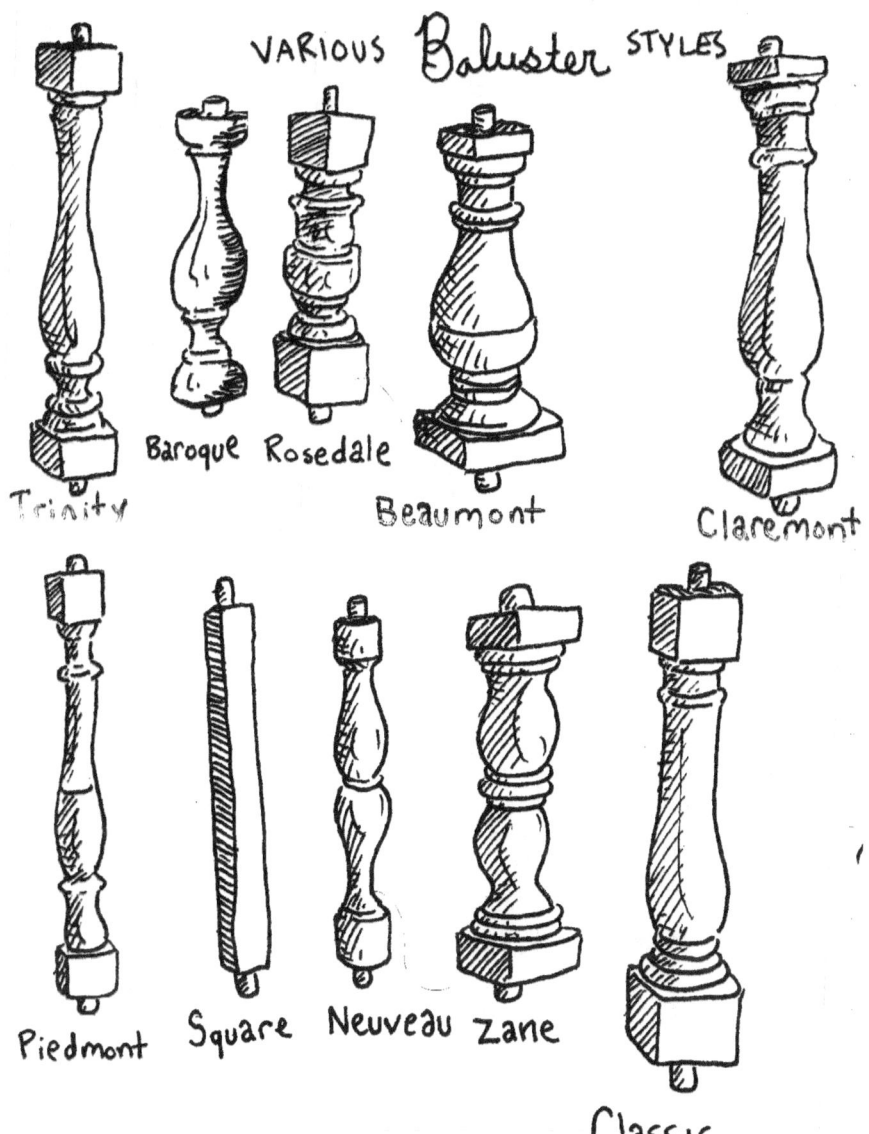

VARIOUS *Baluster* STYLES

Trinity

Baroque   Rosedale

Beaumont

Claremont

Piedmont   Square   Neuveau   Zane

Classic

Charlotte

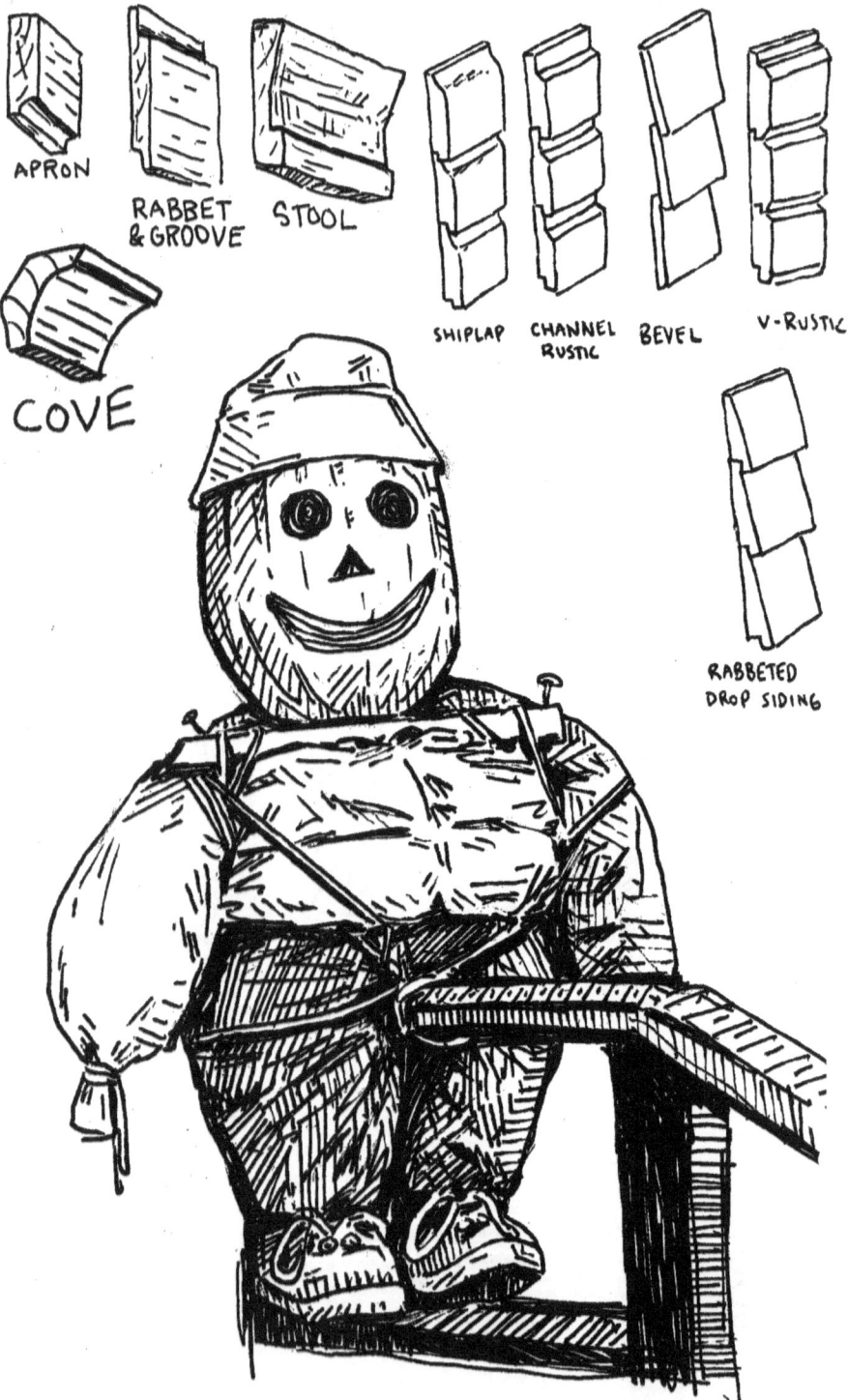

APRON

RABBET & GROOVE

STOOL

COVE

SHIPLAP

CHANNEL RUSTIC

BEVEL

V-RUSTIC

RABBETED DROP SIDING

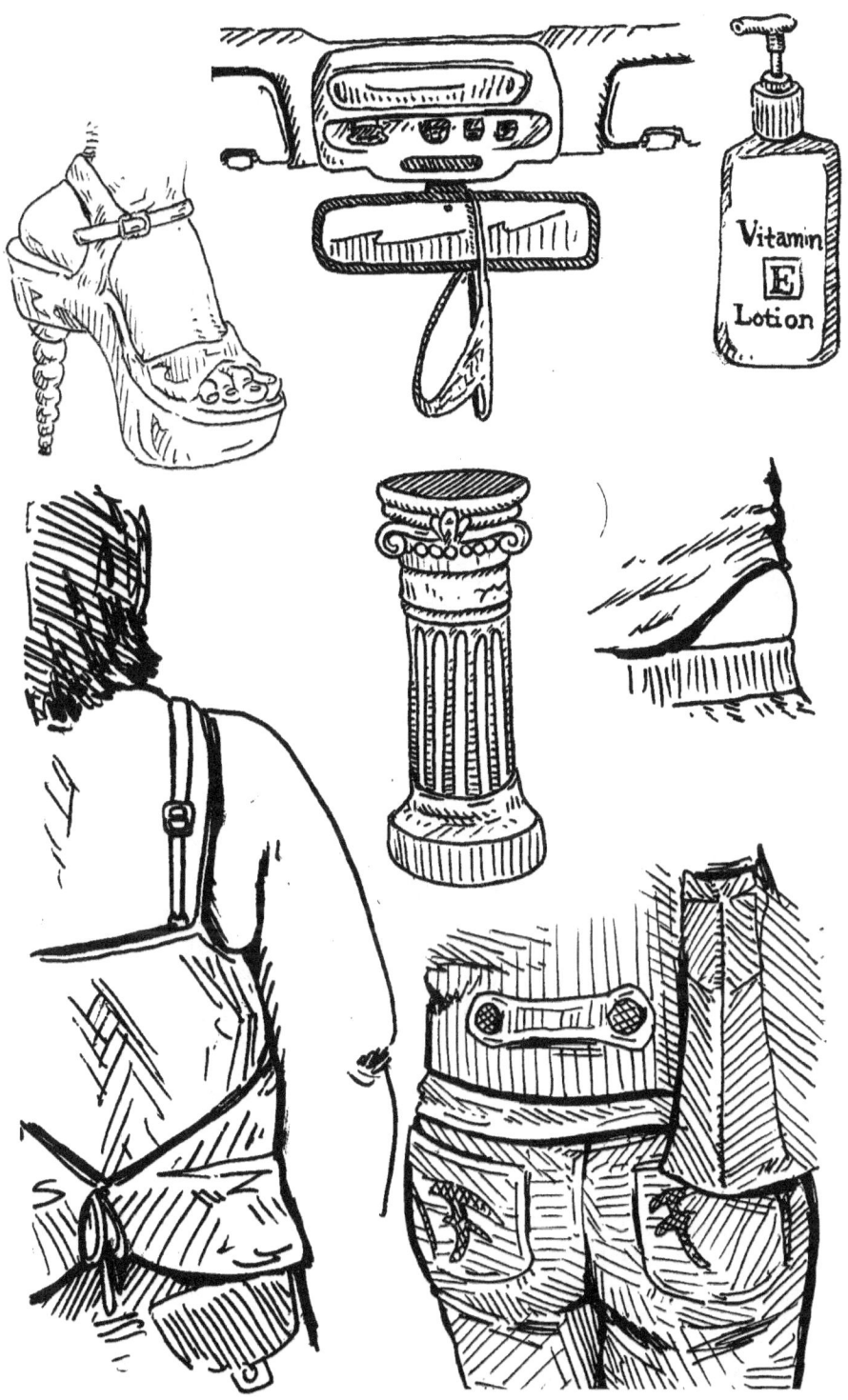

Vitamin
E
Lotion

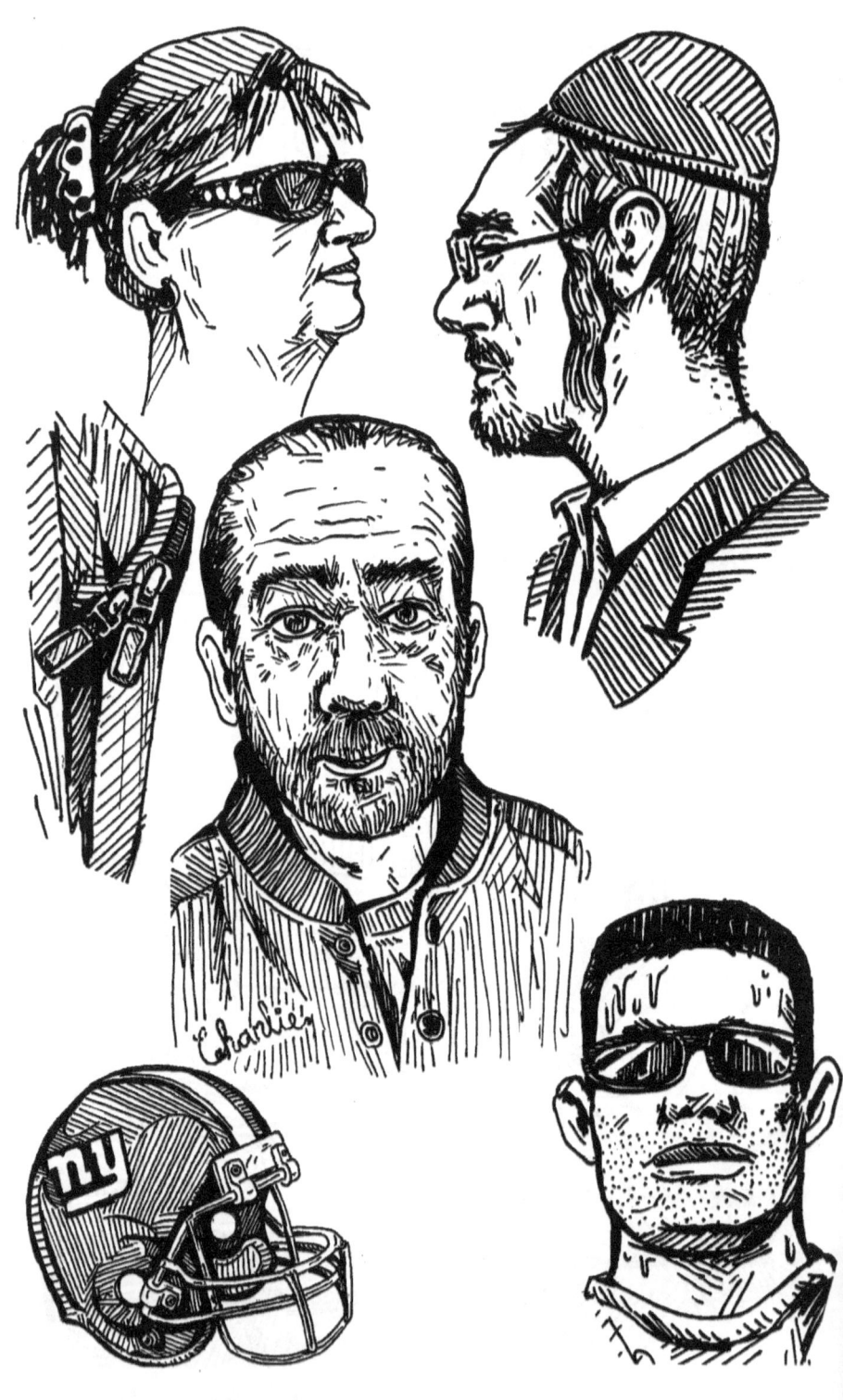

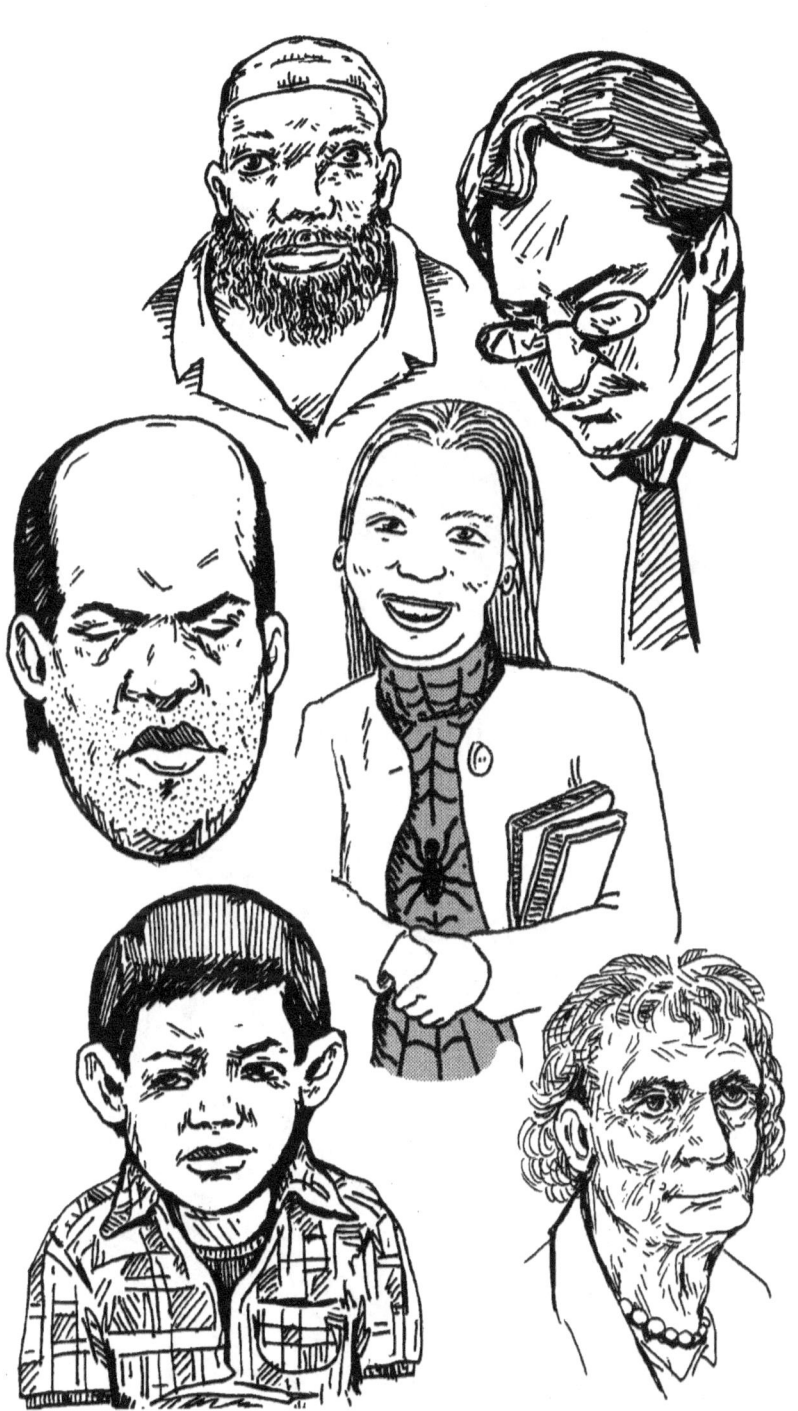

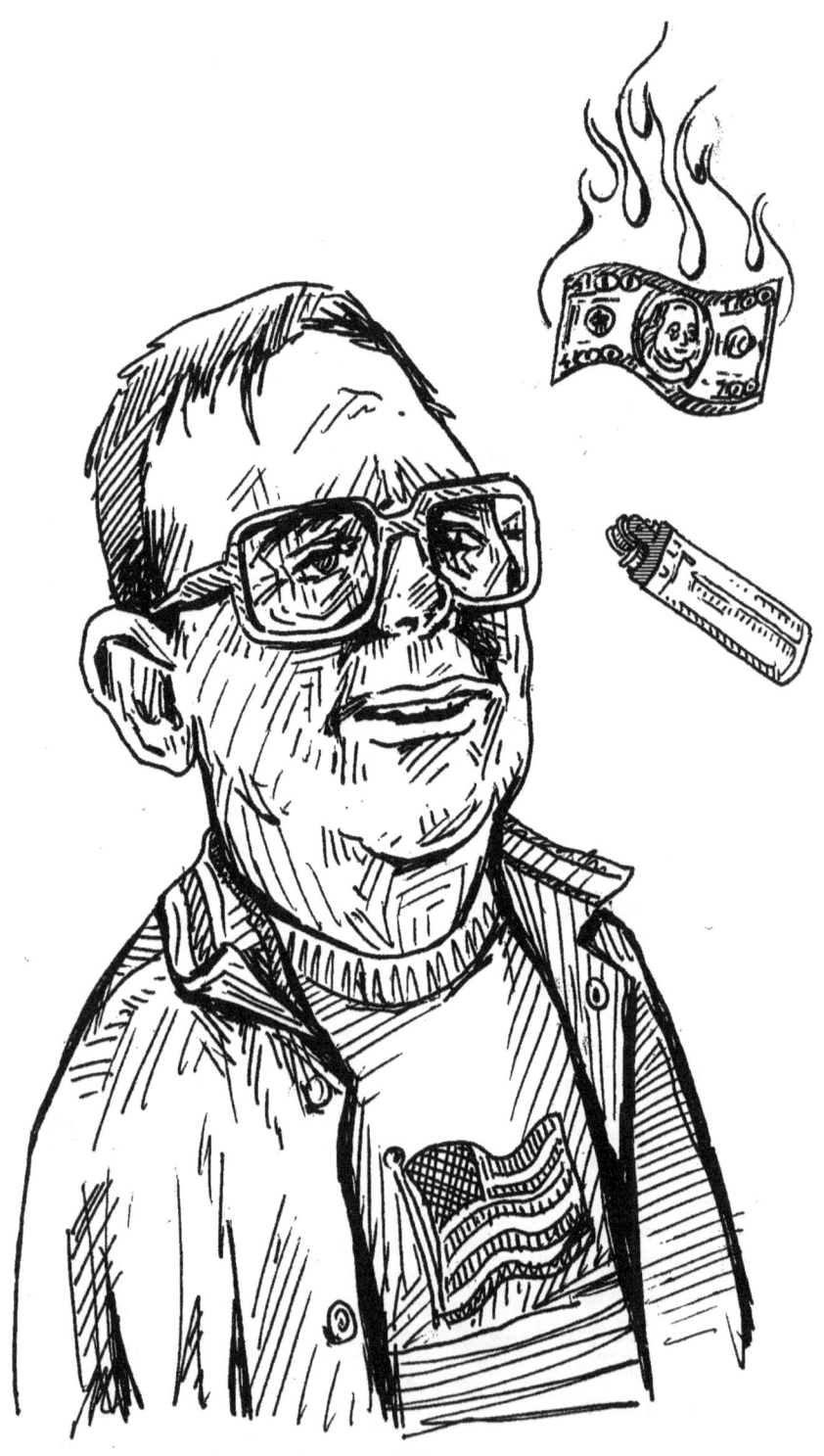

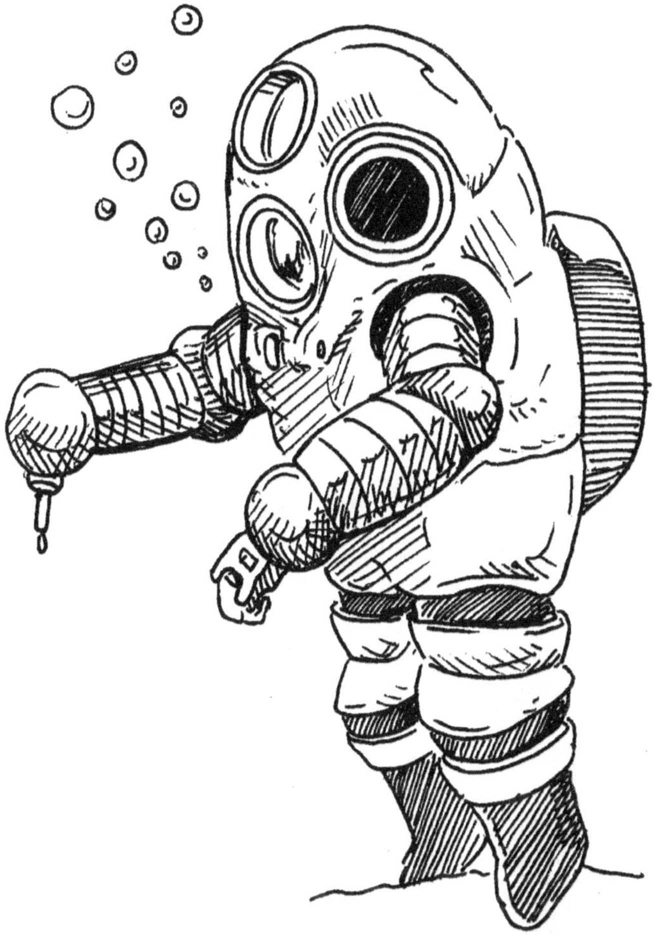

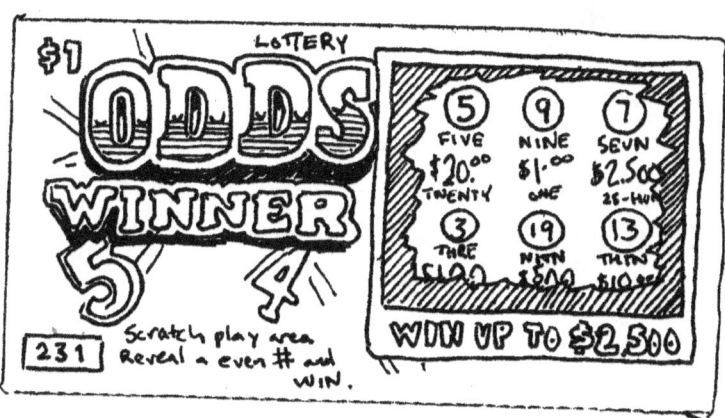

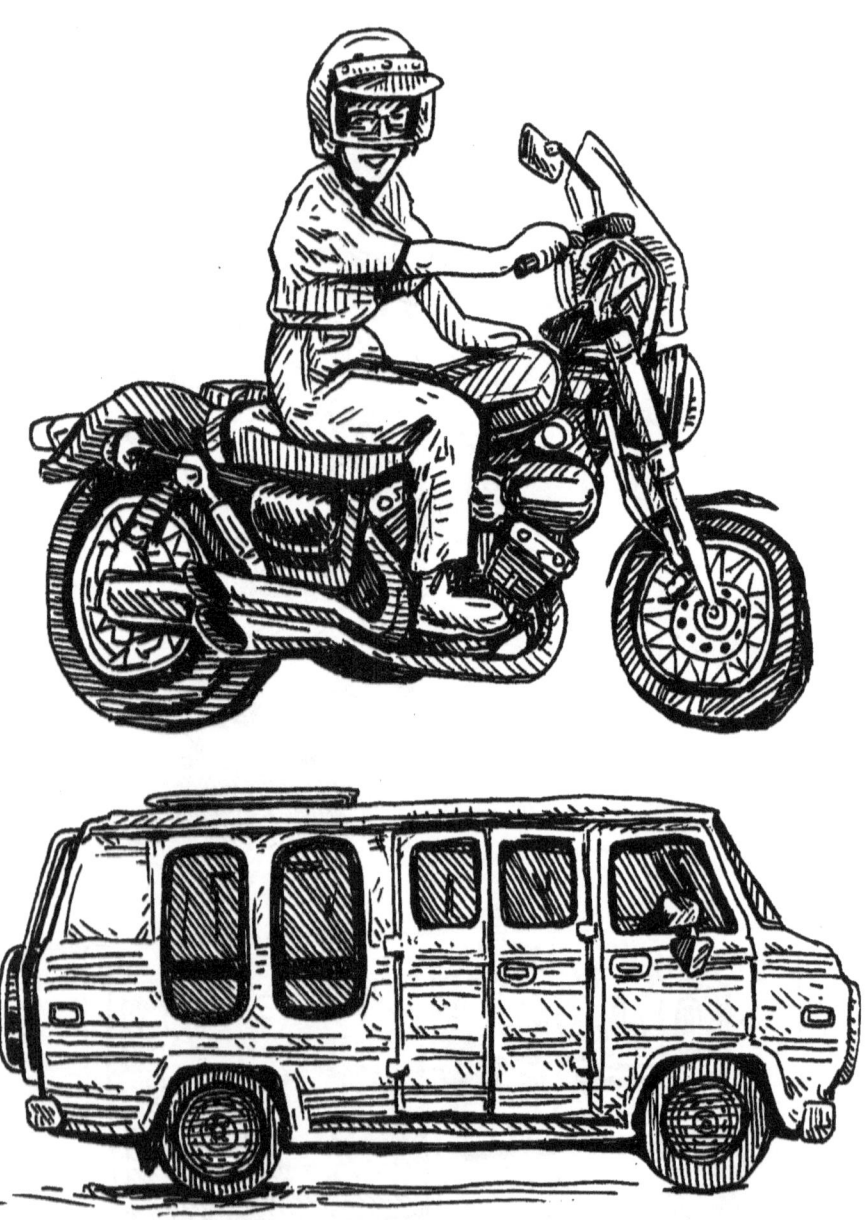

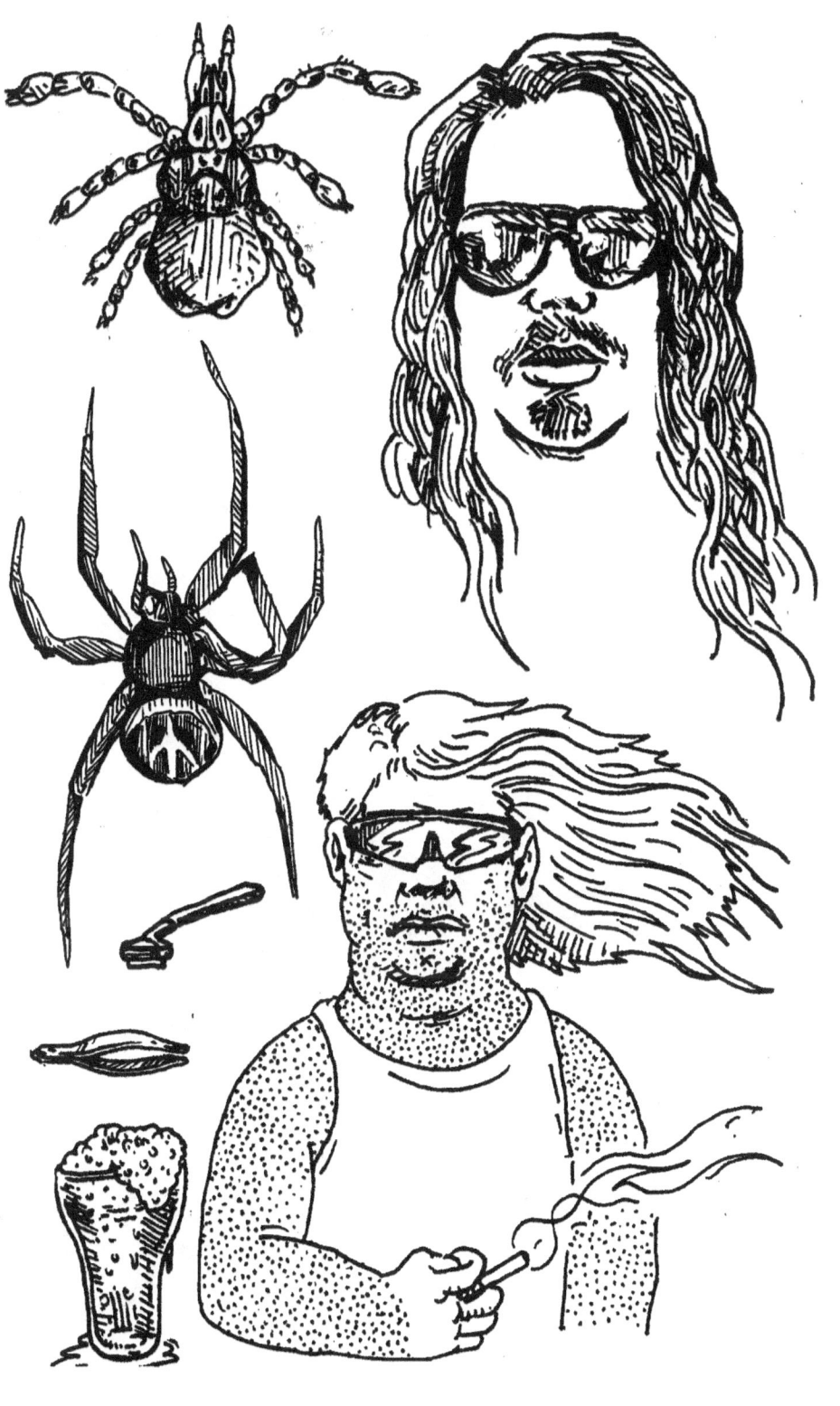

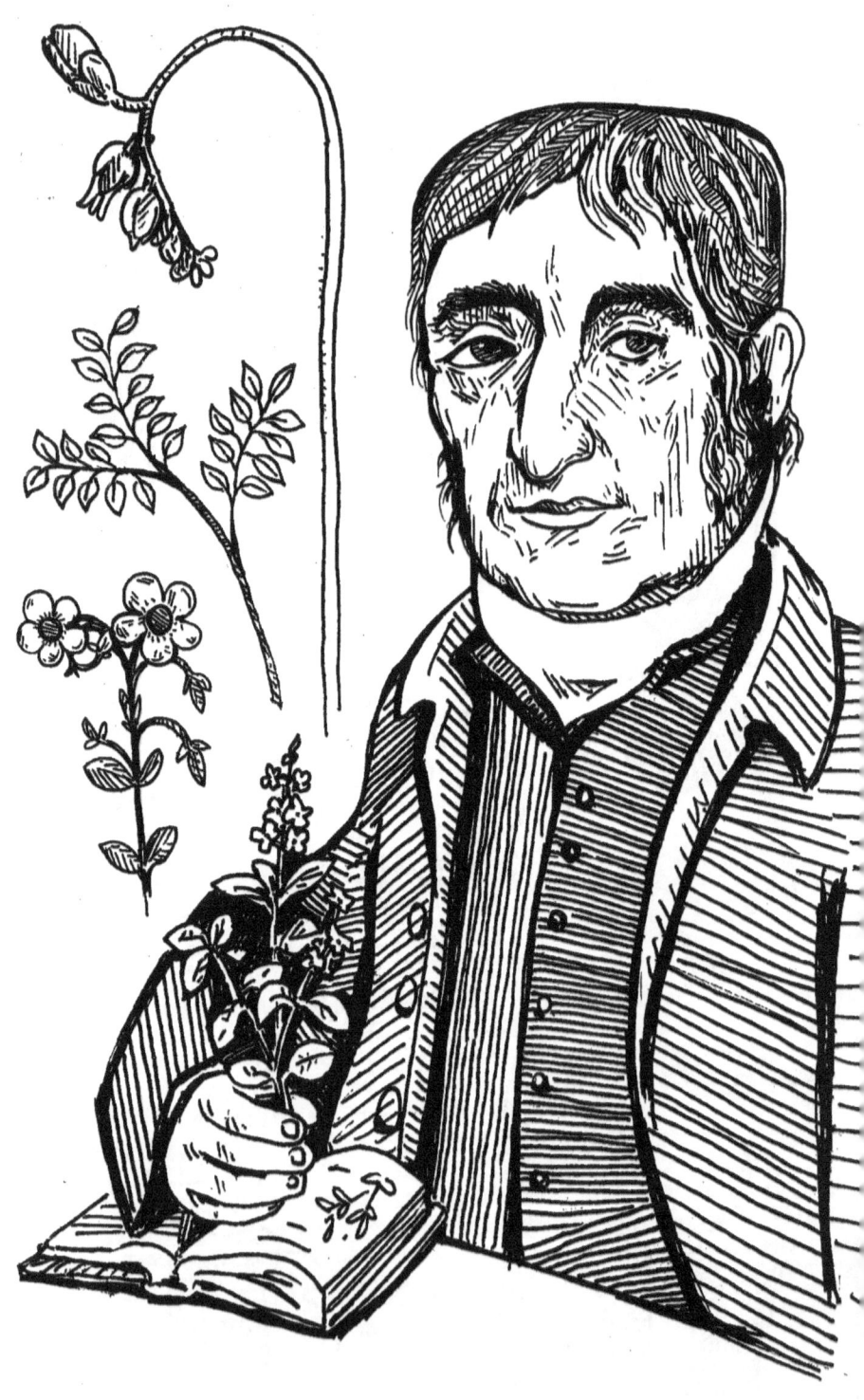

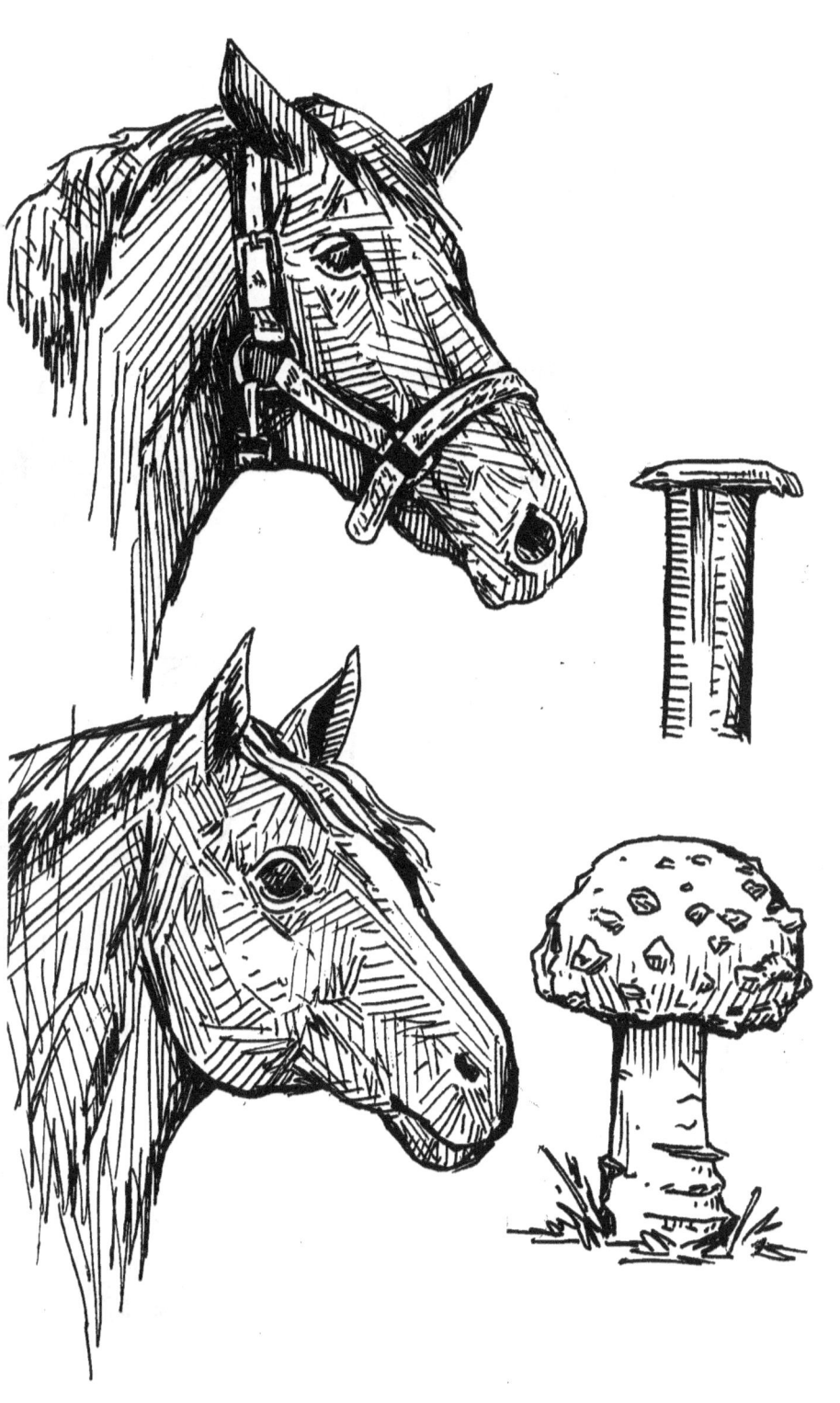

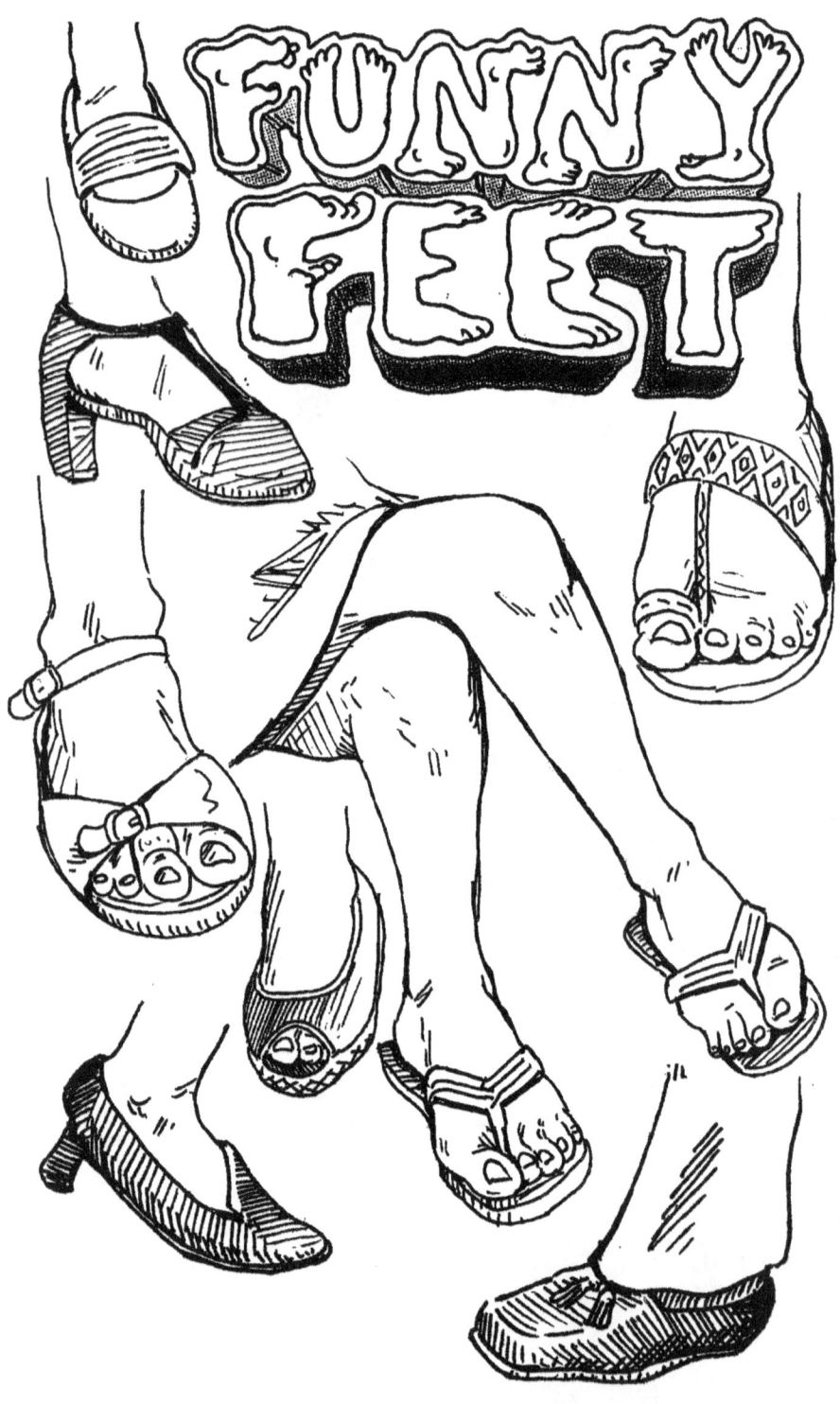

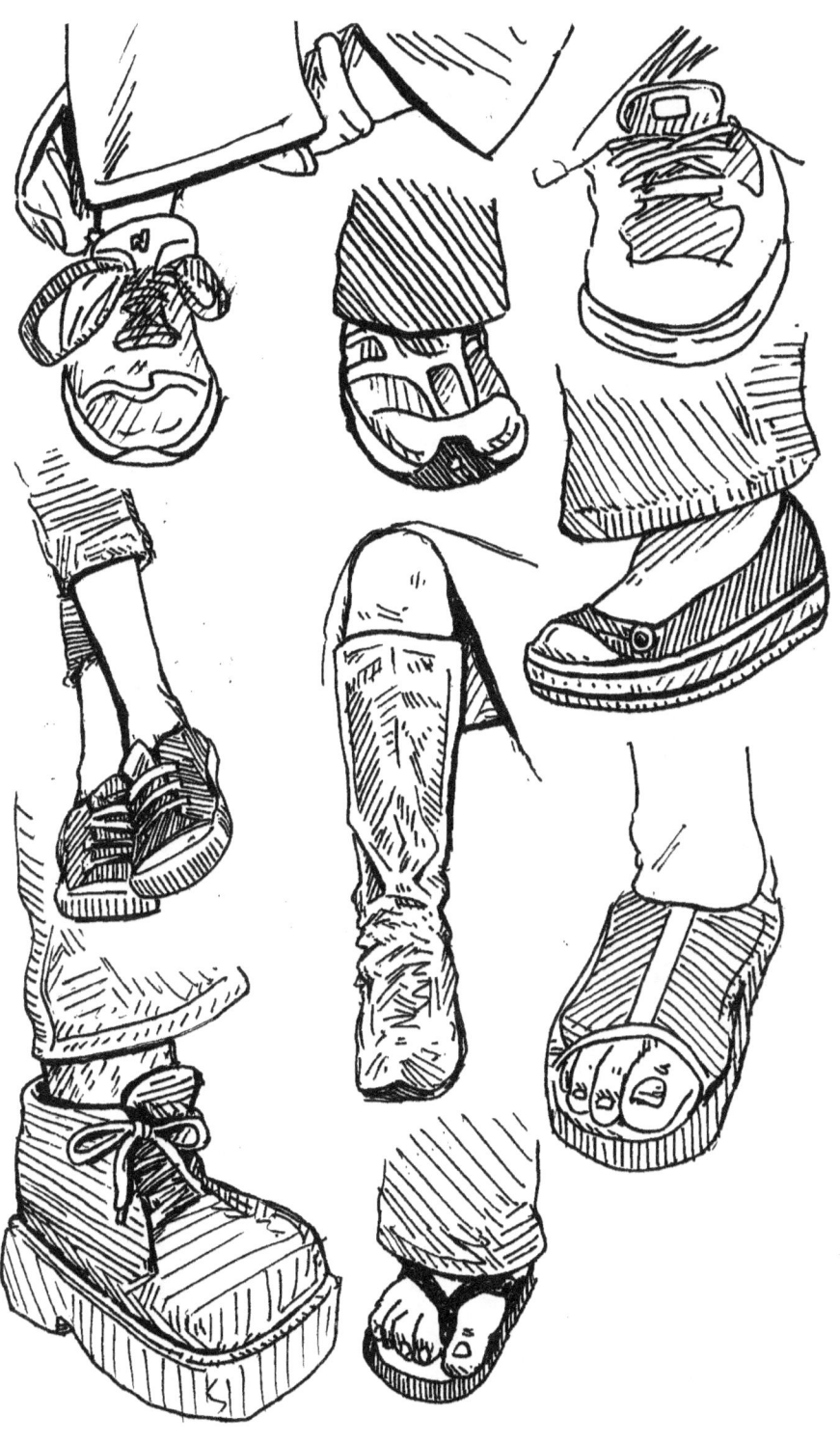

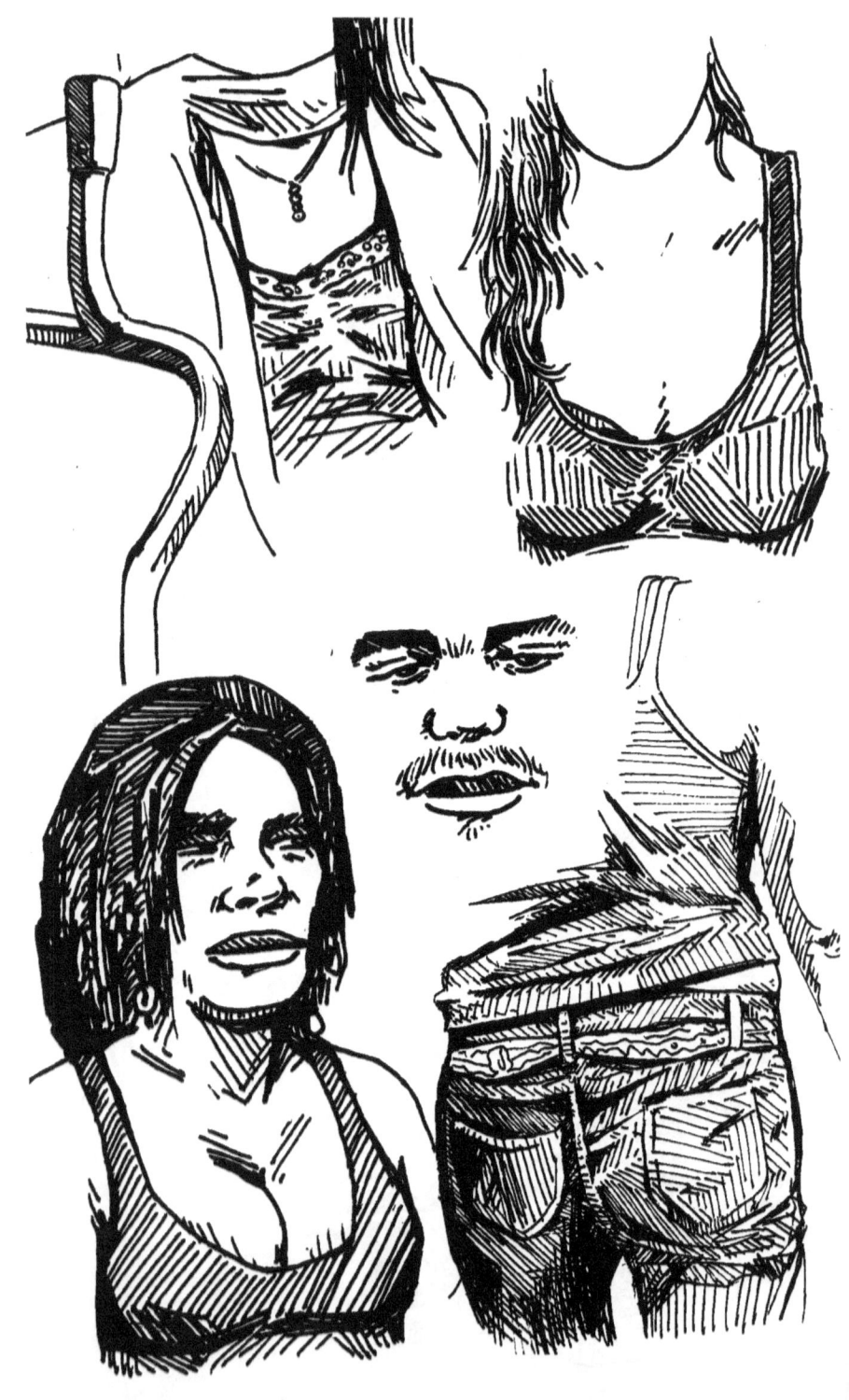

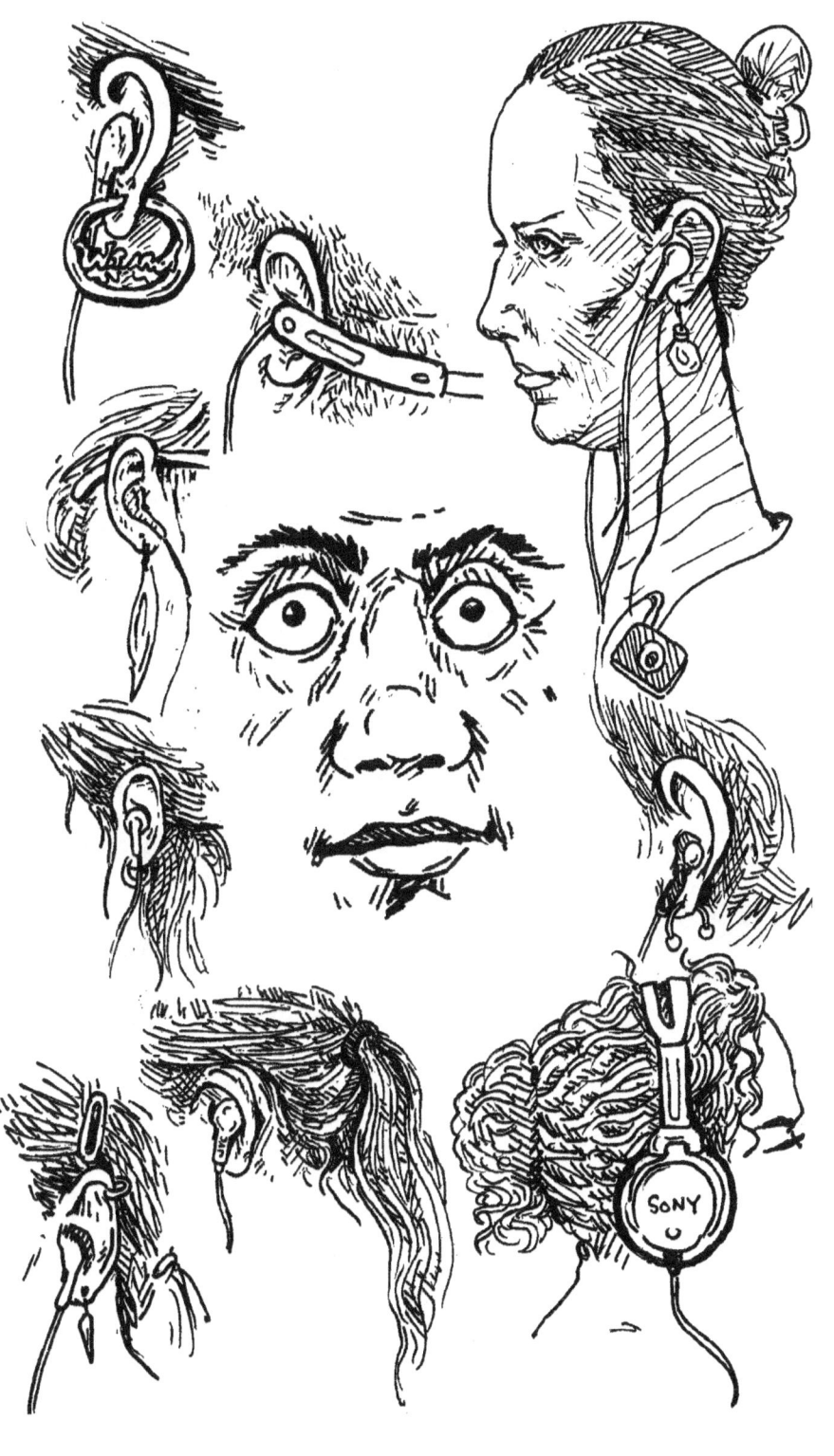

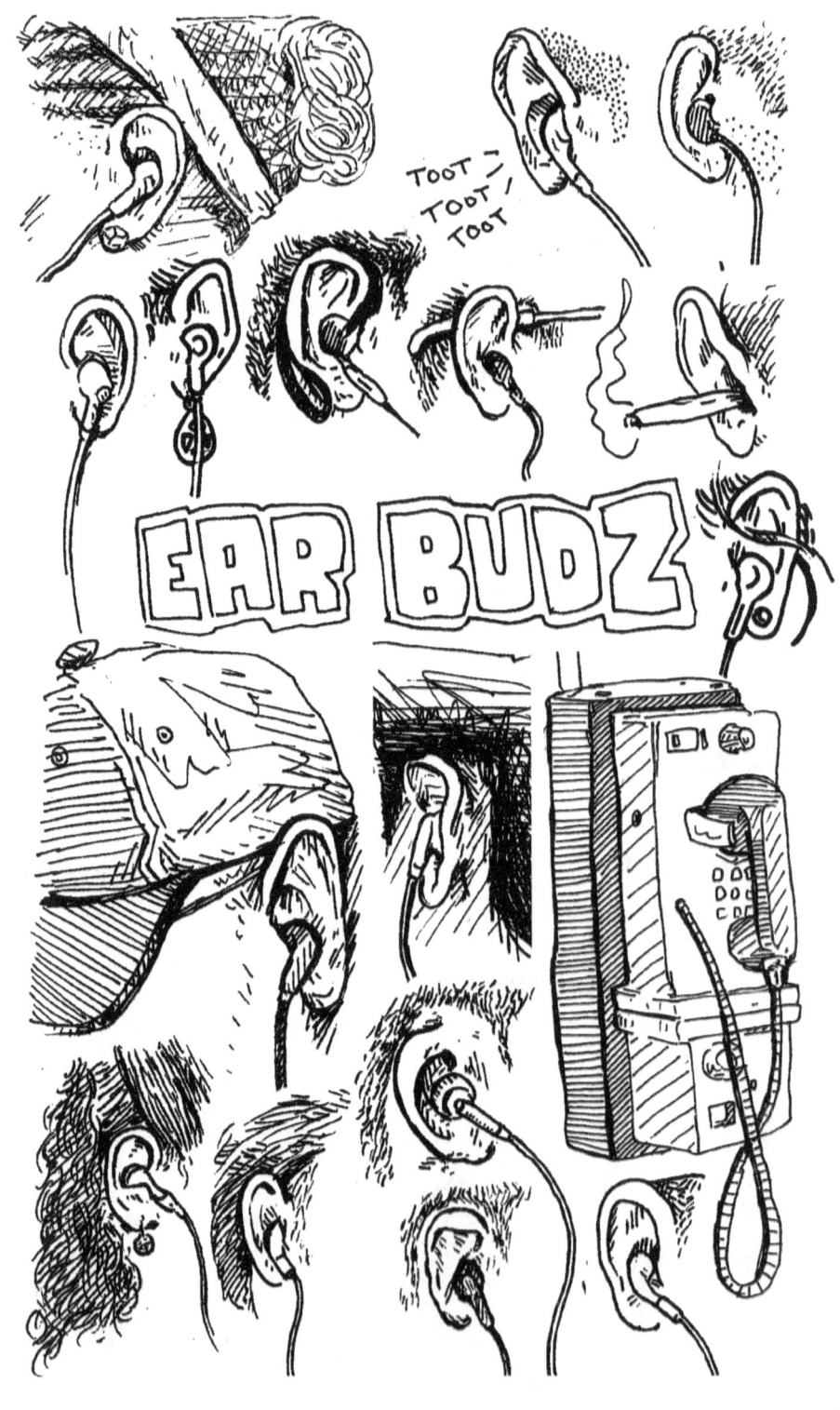

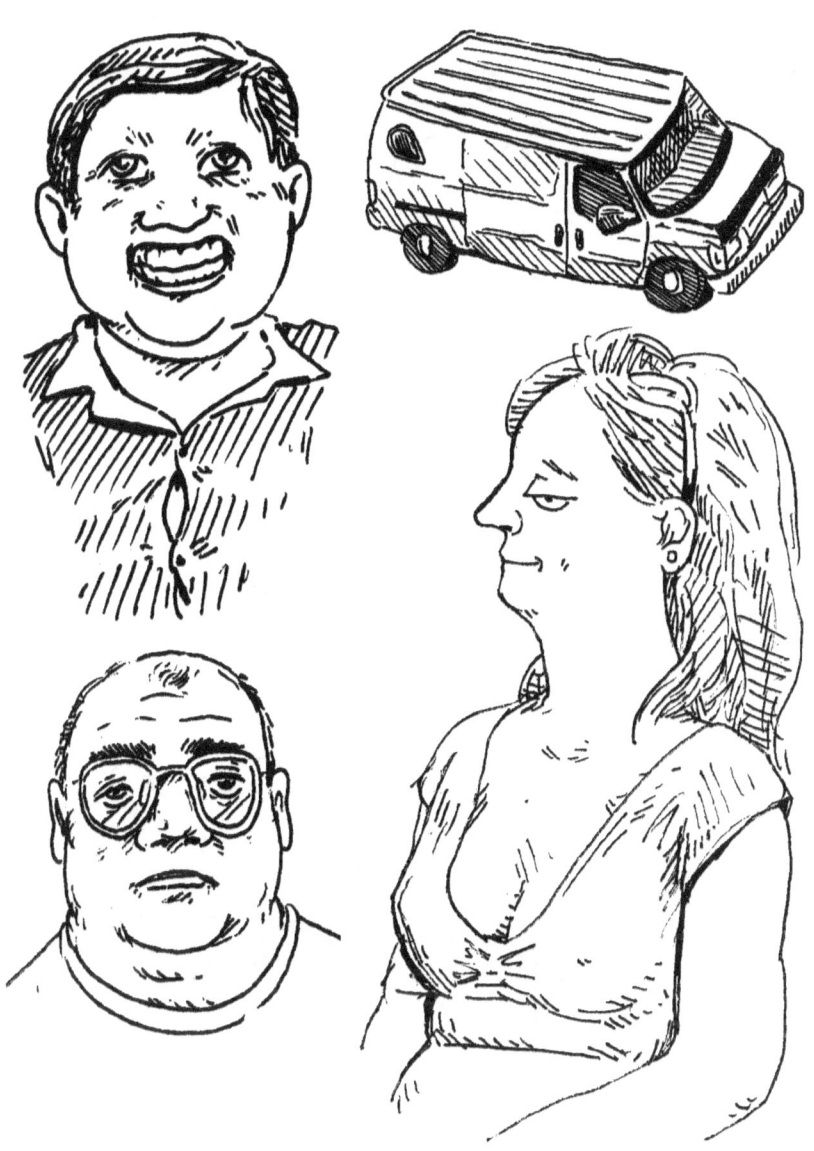

YOU KNOW YOU HAVE
ARRIVED WHEN YOUR
EARS POP.

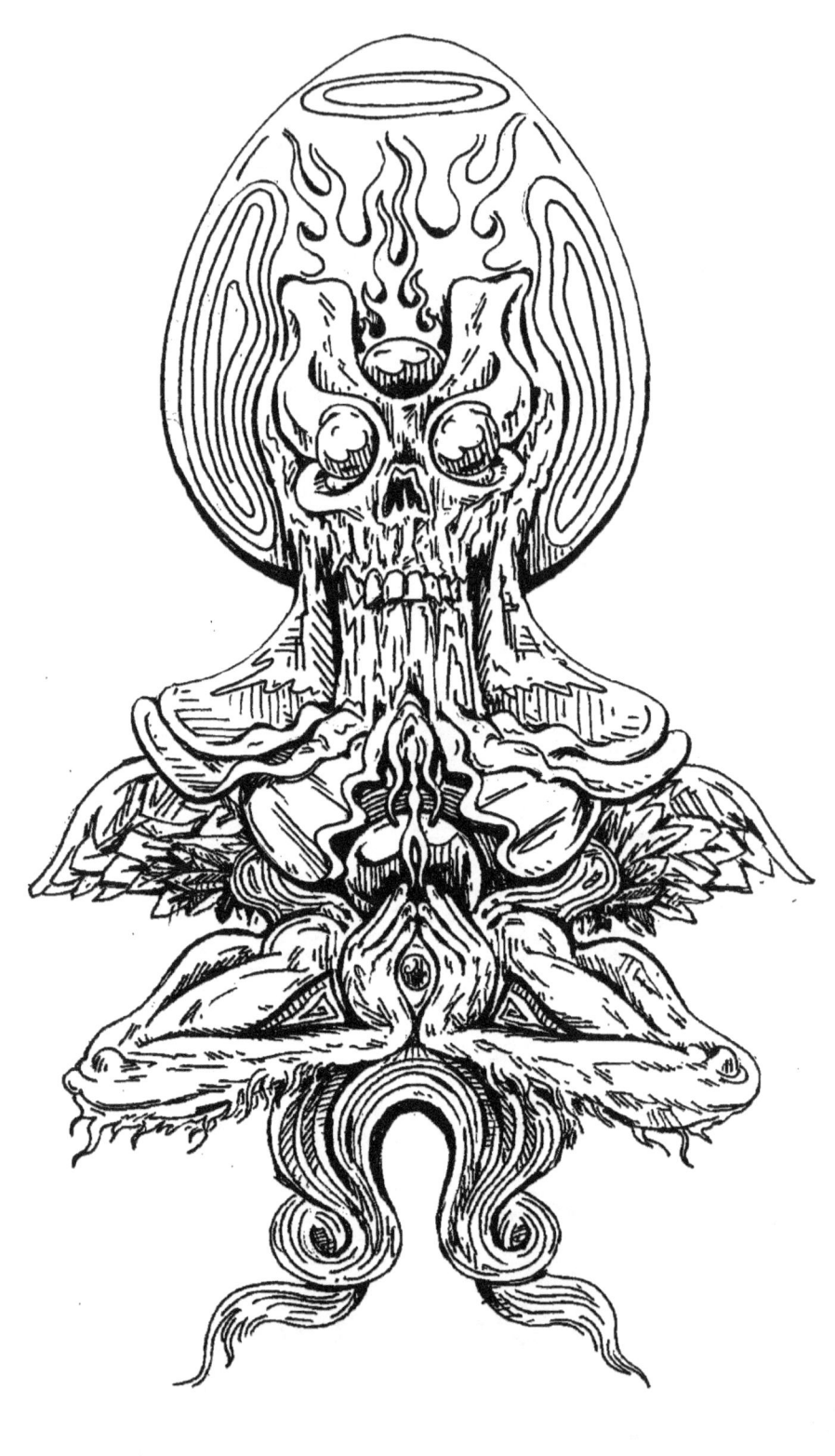

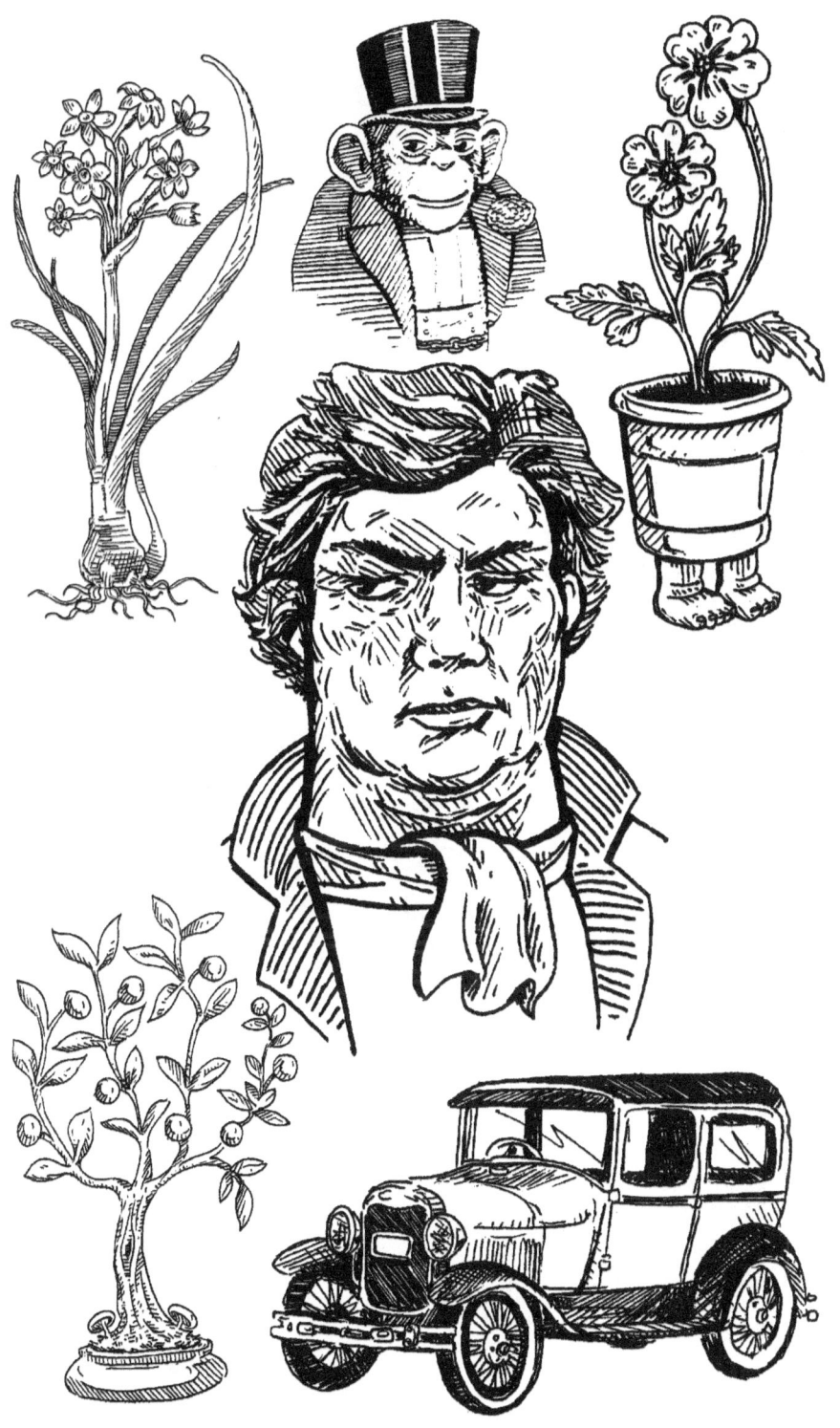

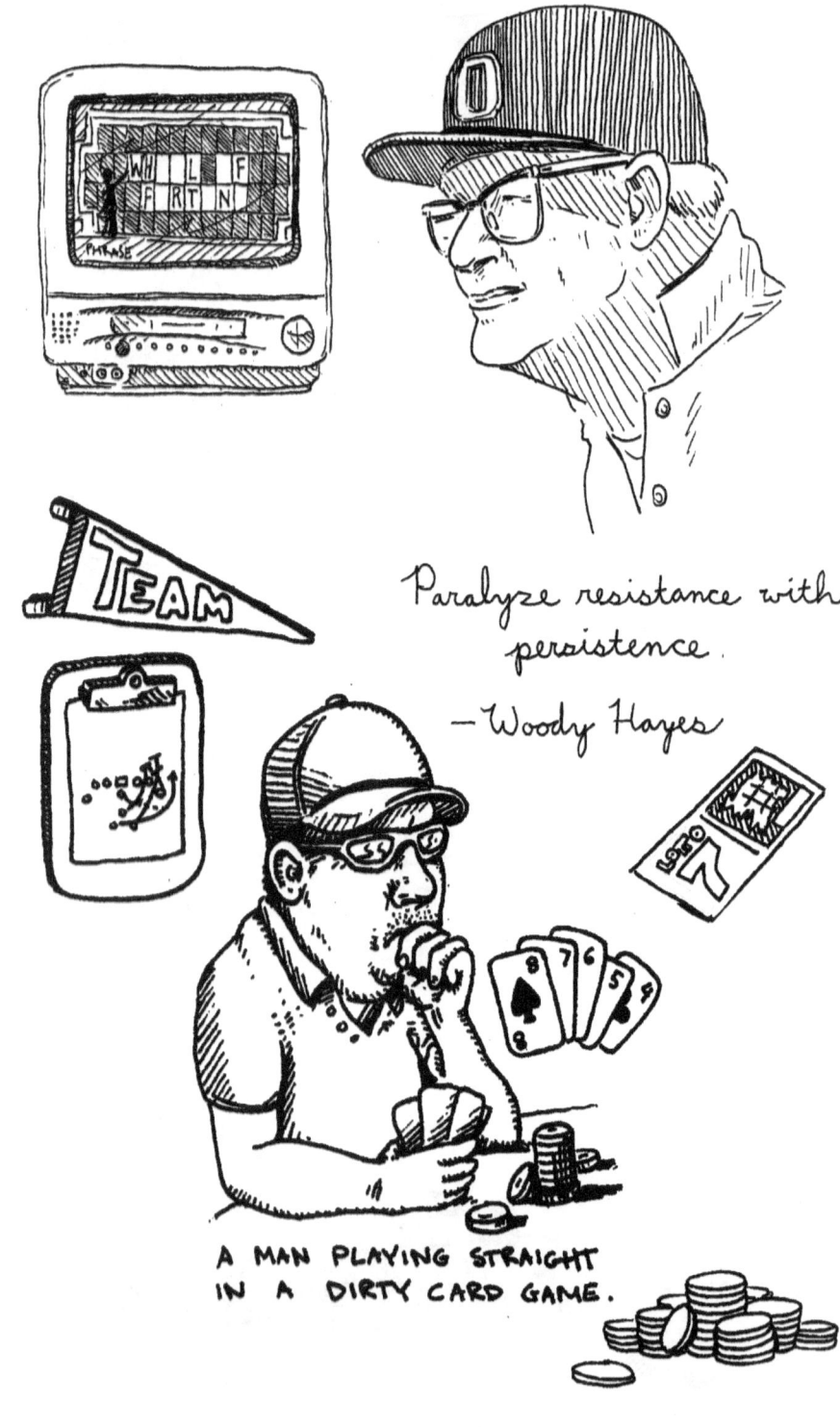

Paralyze resistance with persistence.

—Woody Hayes

A MAN PLAYING STRAIGHT IN A DIRTY CARD GAME.

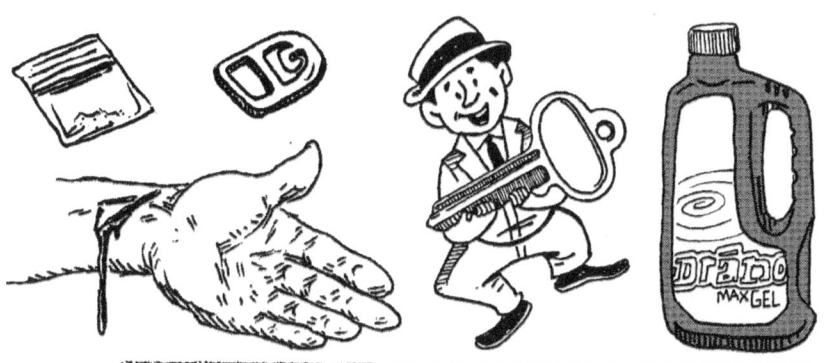

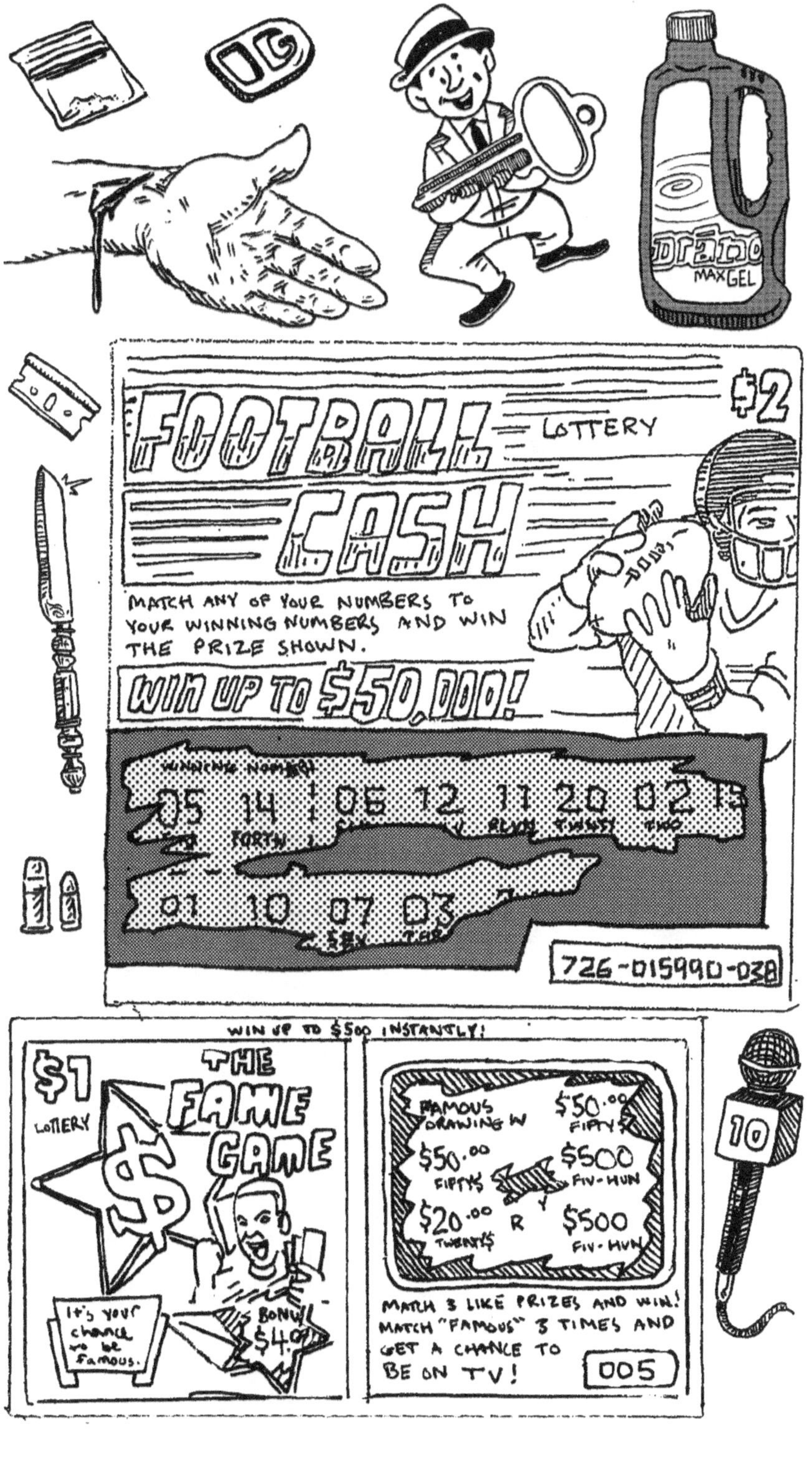

FOOTBALL CASH

LOTTERY

$2

MATCH ANY OF YOUR NUMBERS TO YOUR WINNING NUMBERS AND WIN THE PRIZE SHOWN.

WIN UP TO $50,000!

05 14 06 12 11 20 02 19

01 10 07 03

726-015990-038

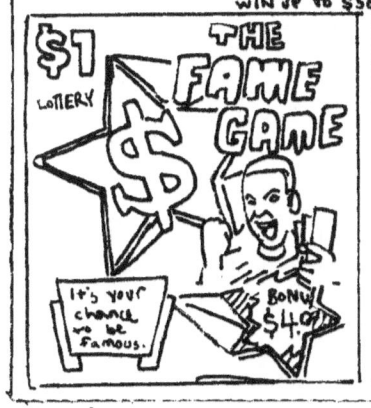

WIN UP TO $500 INSTANTLY!

$1 LOTTERY

THE FAME GAME

$

It's your chance to be famous.

BONUS $4.00

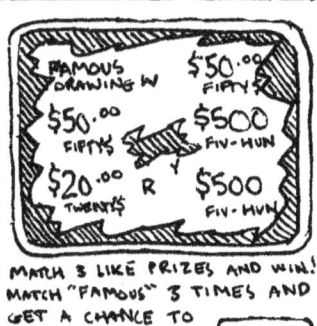

FAMOUS DRAWING W

$50.00 FIFTY$

$50.00 FIFTY$

$500 FIV-HUN

$20.00 TWENTY$

R

$500 FIV-HUN

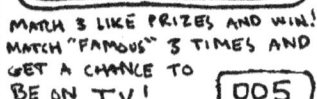

MATCH 3 LIKE PRIZES AND WIN! MATCH "FAMOUS" 3 TIMES AND GET A CHANCE TO BE ON TV!

005

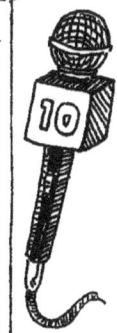

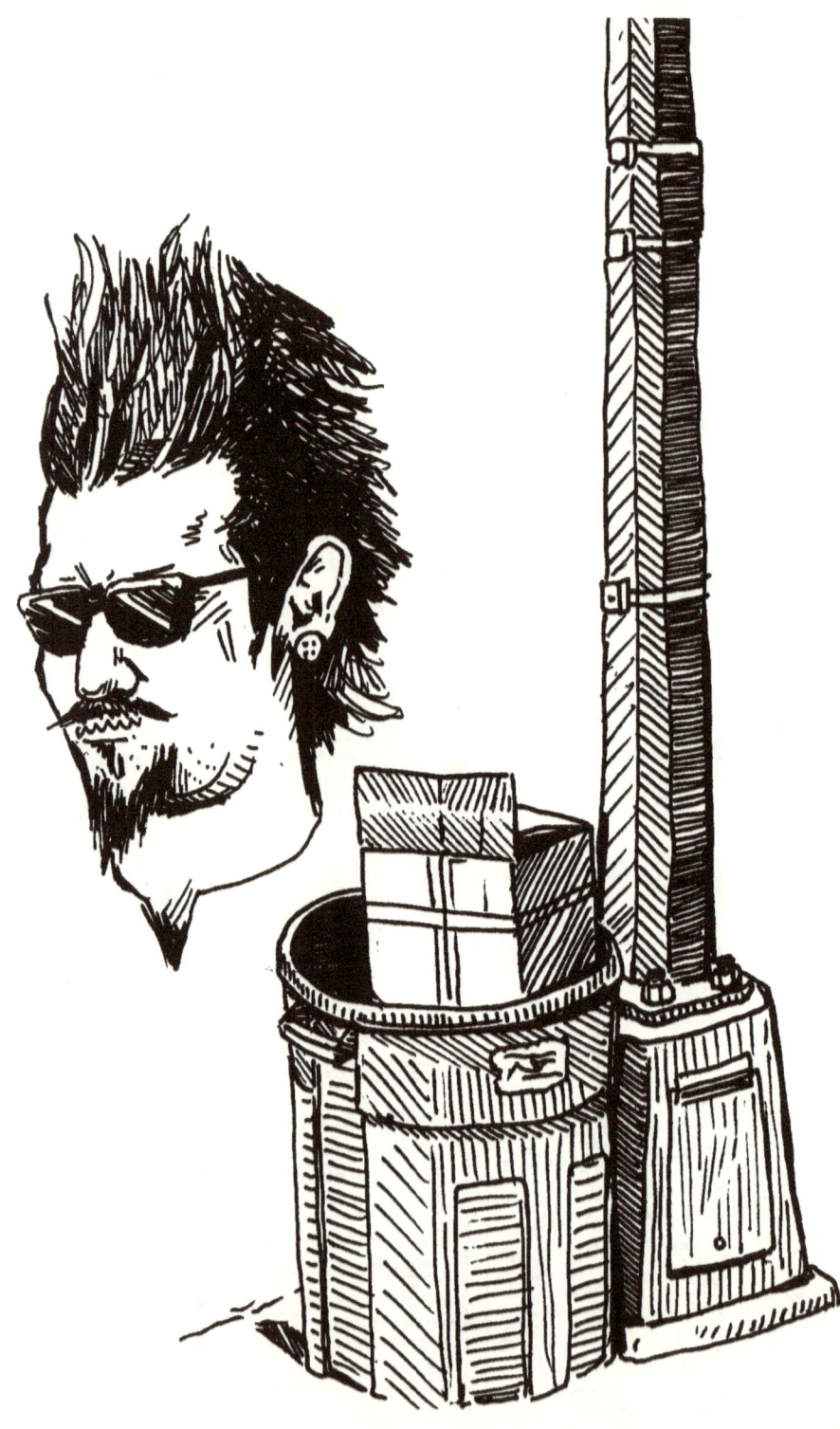

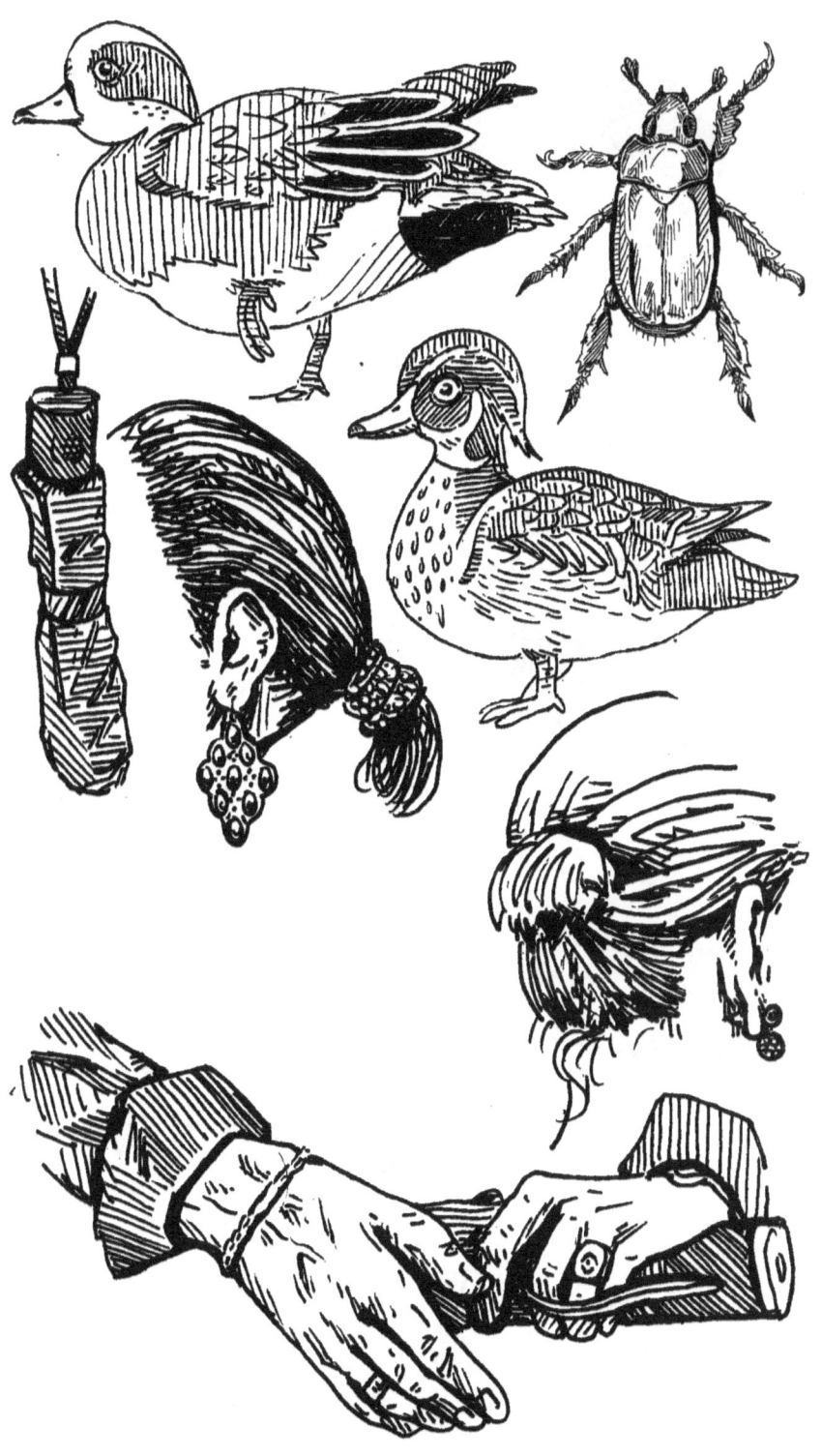

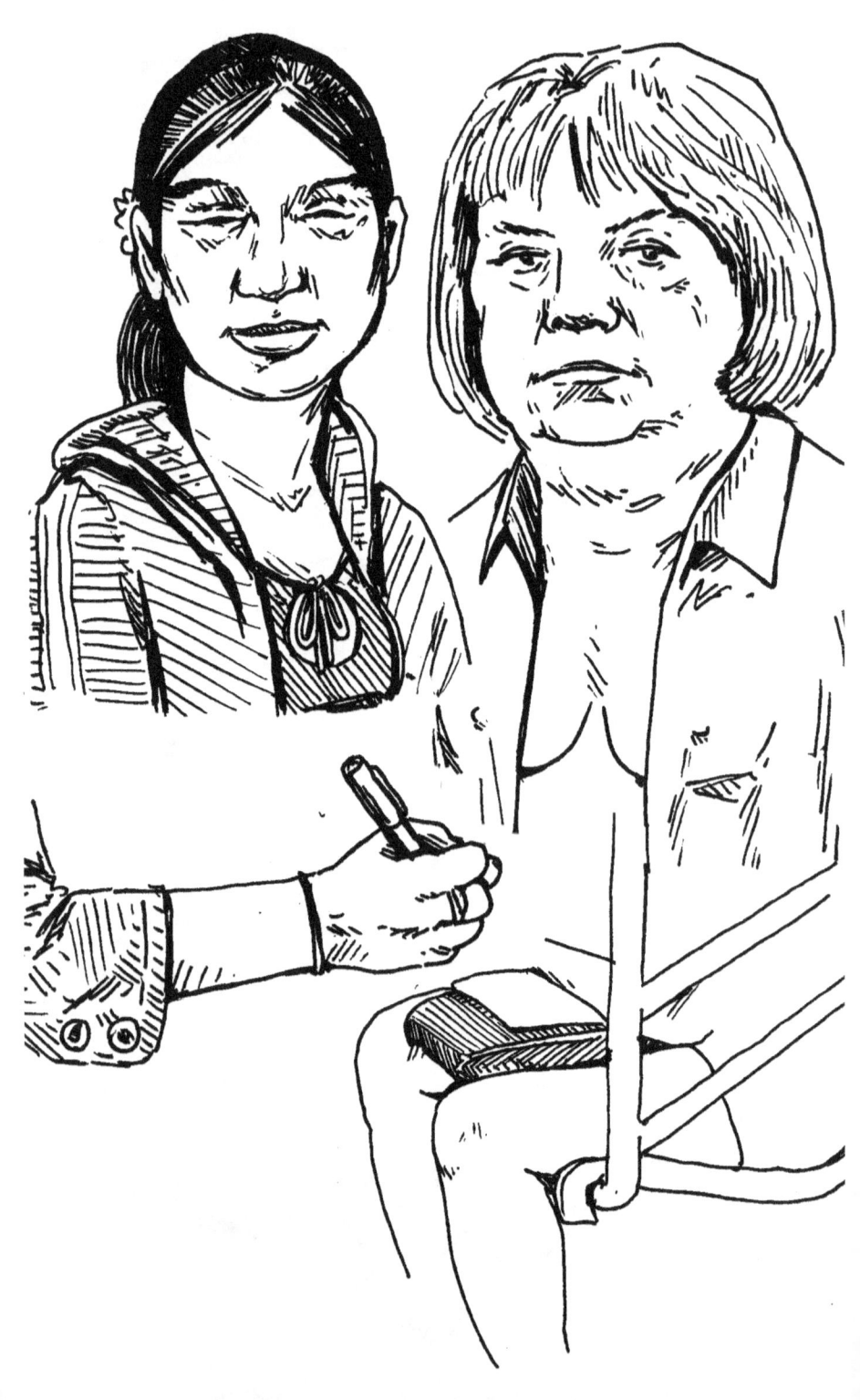

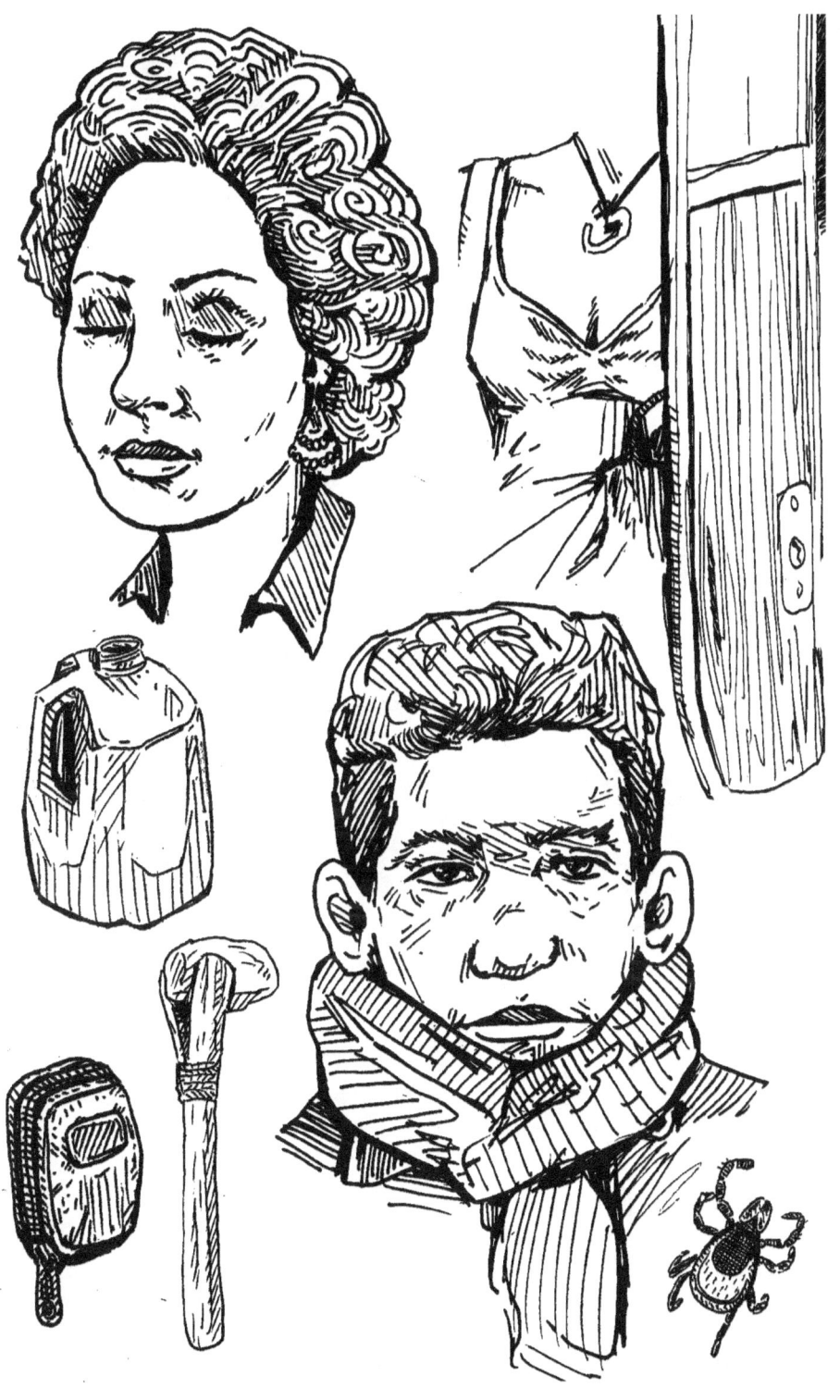

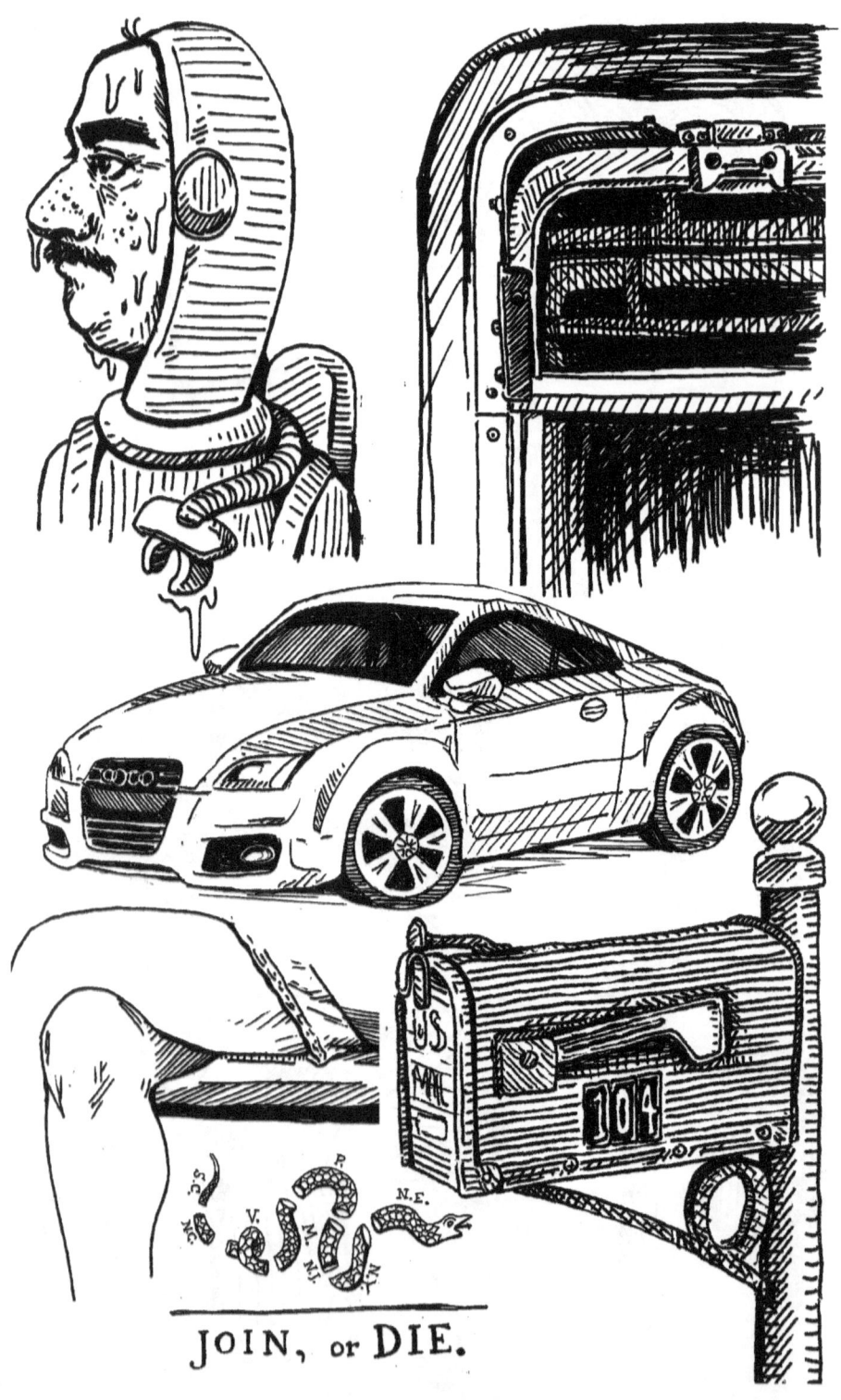

JOIN, or DIE.

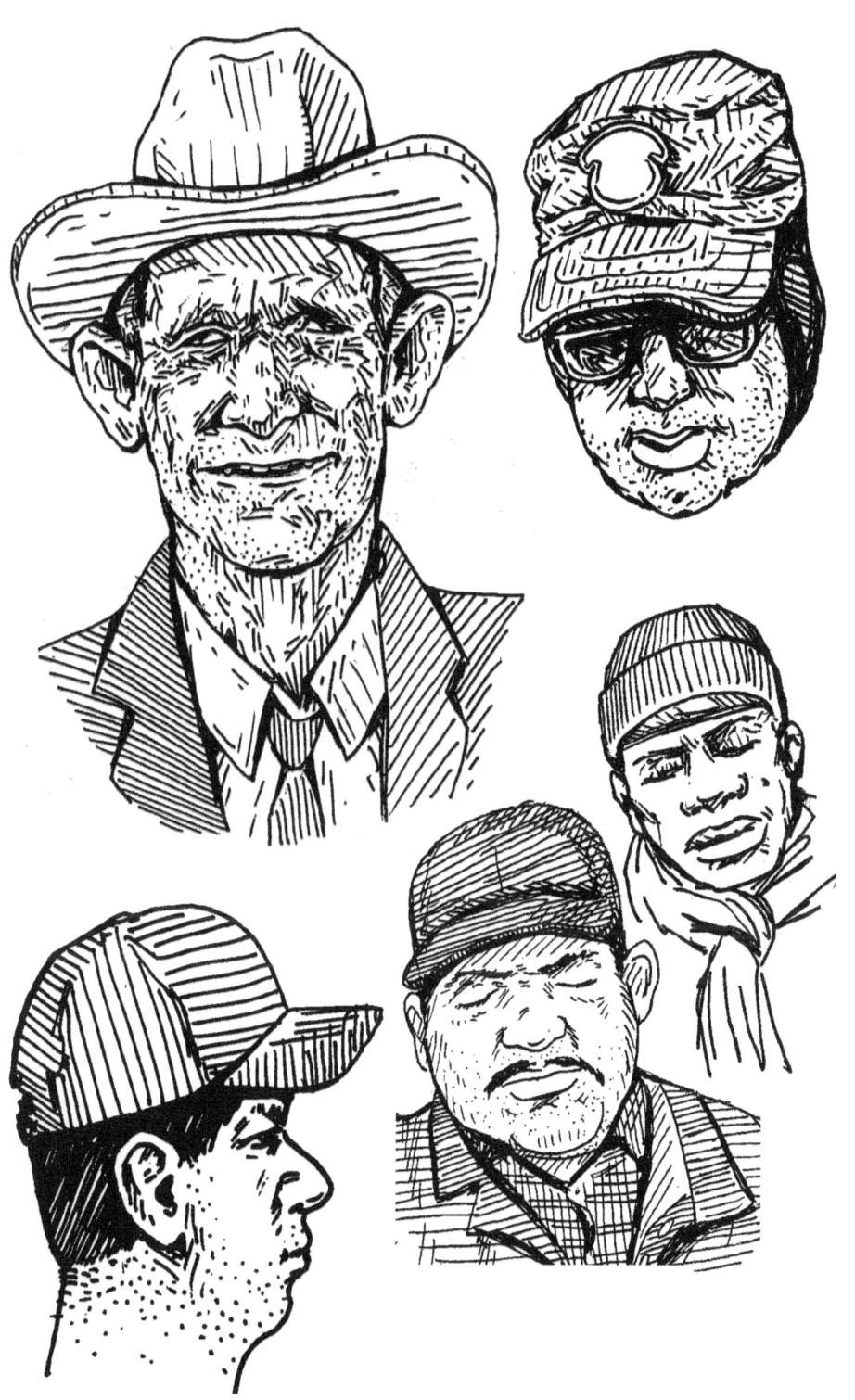

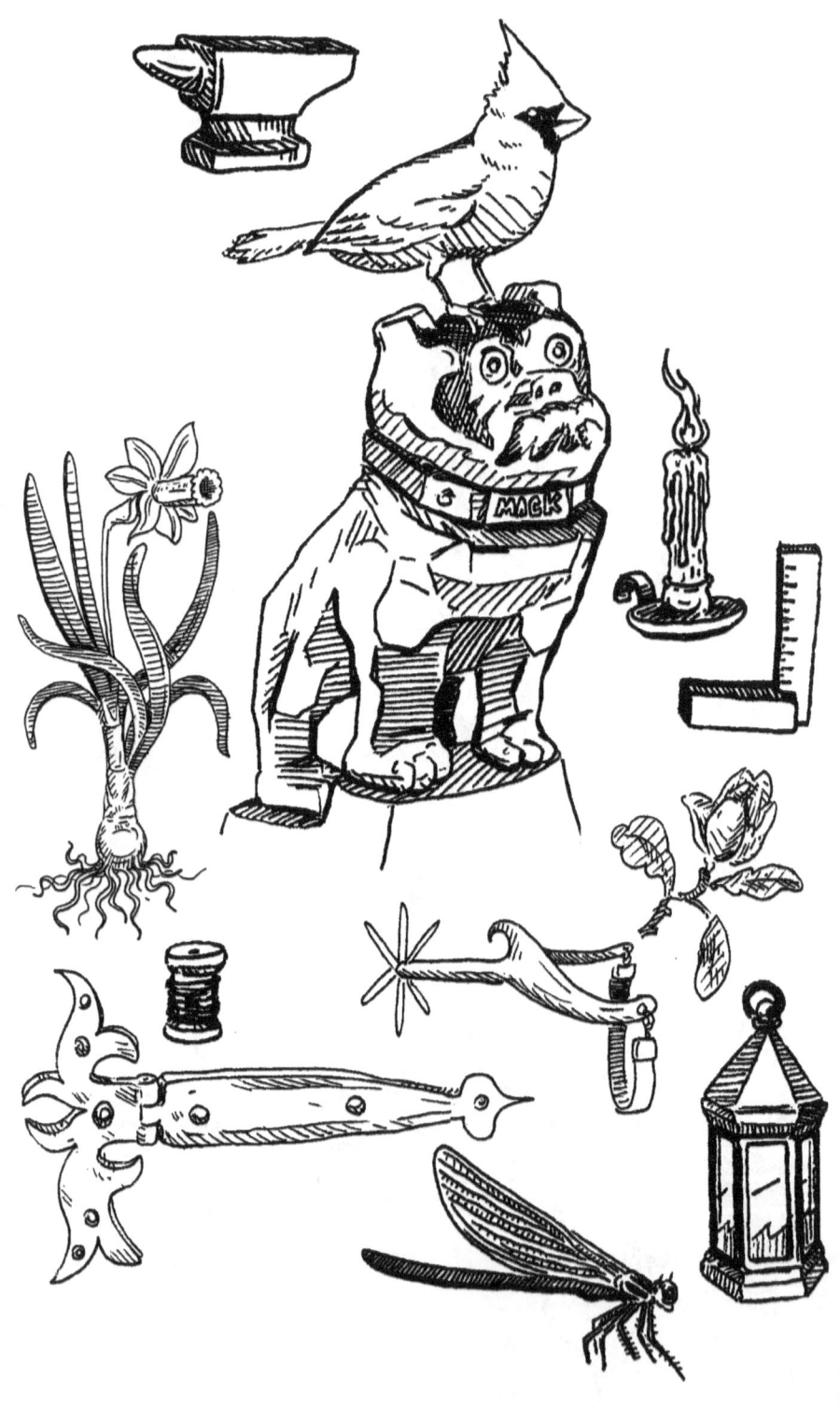

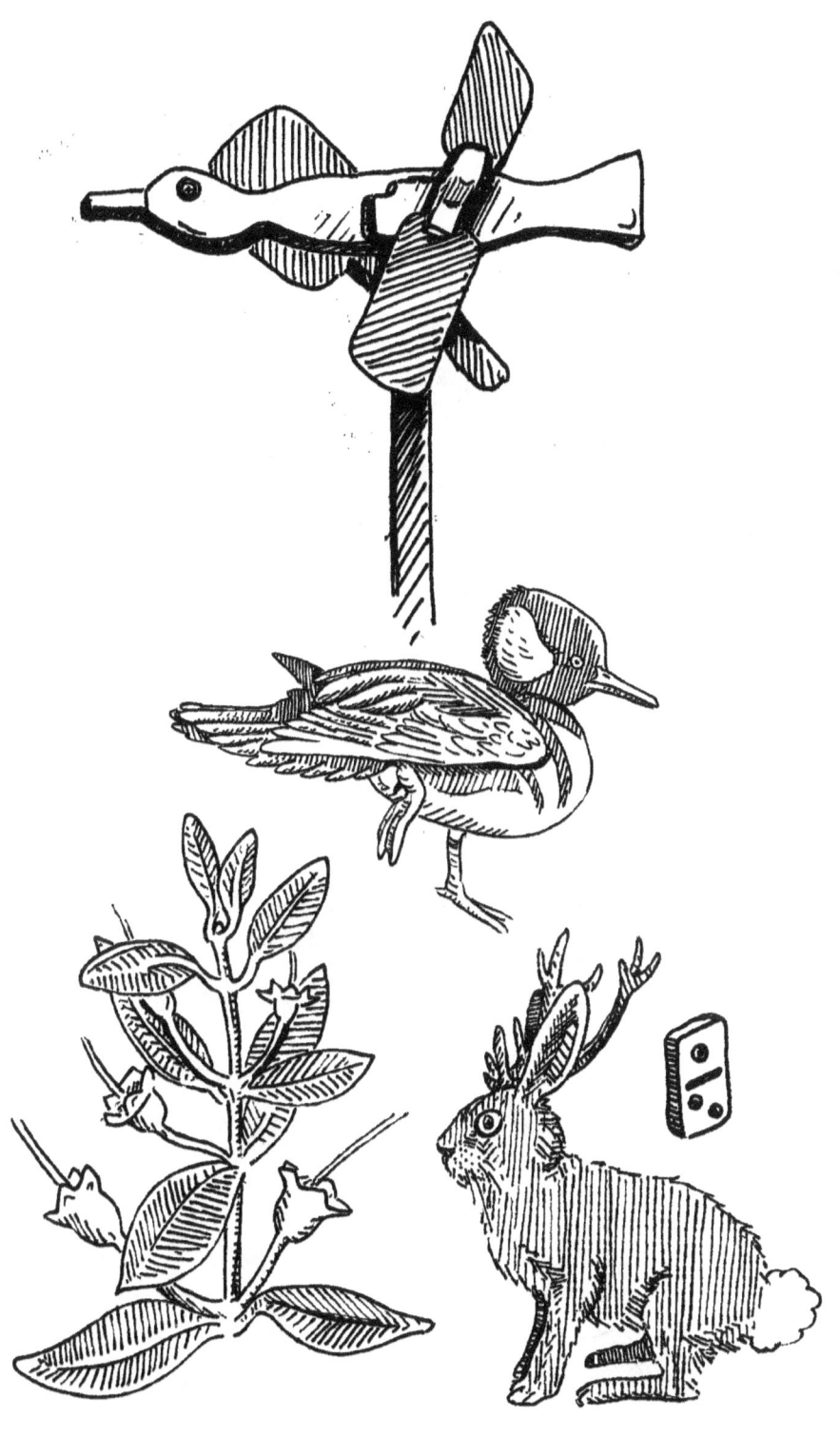

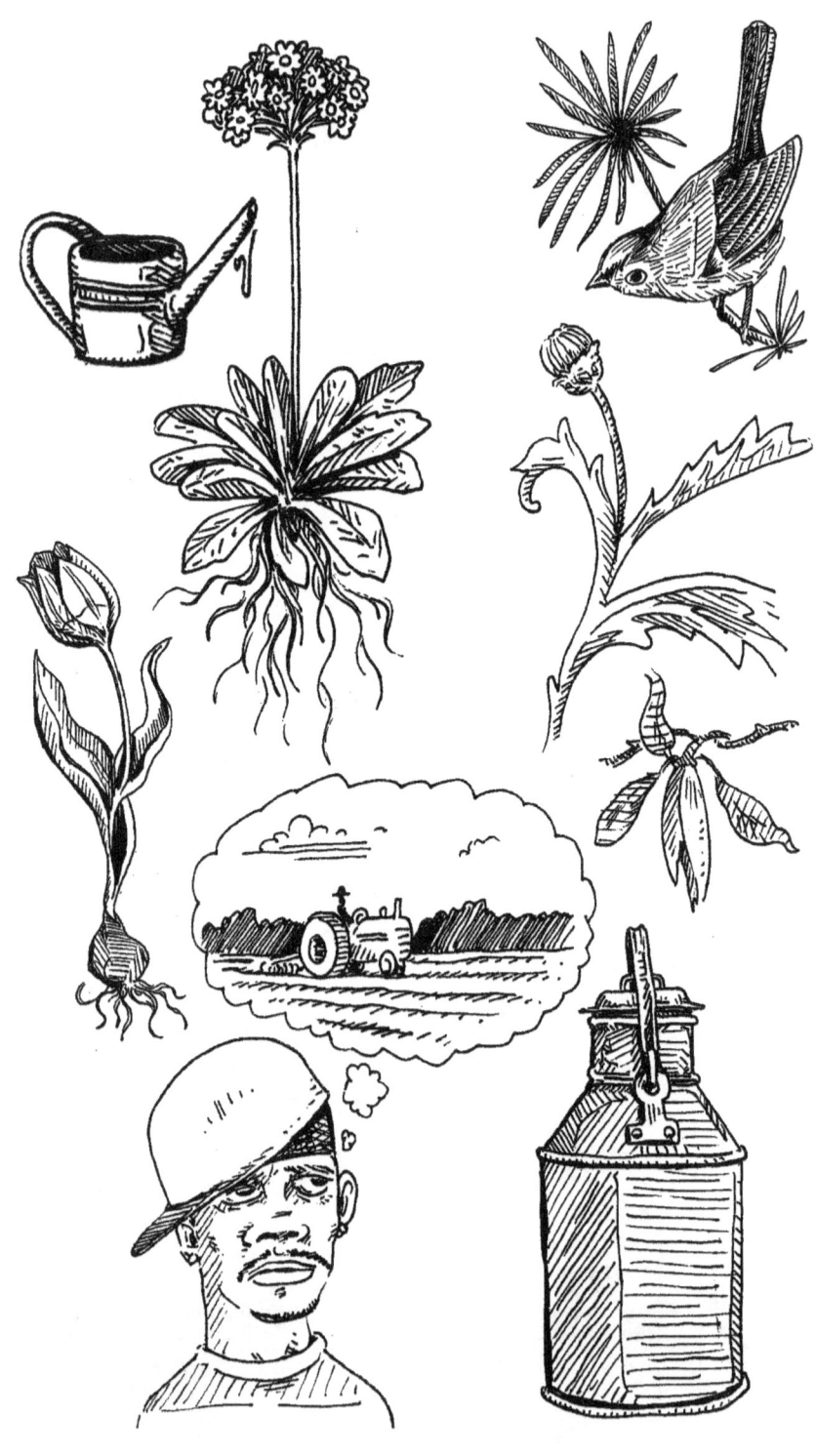

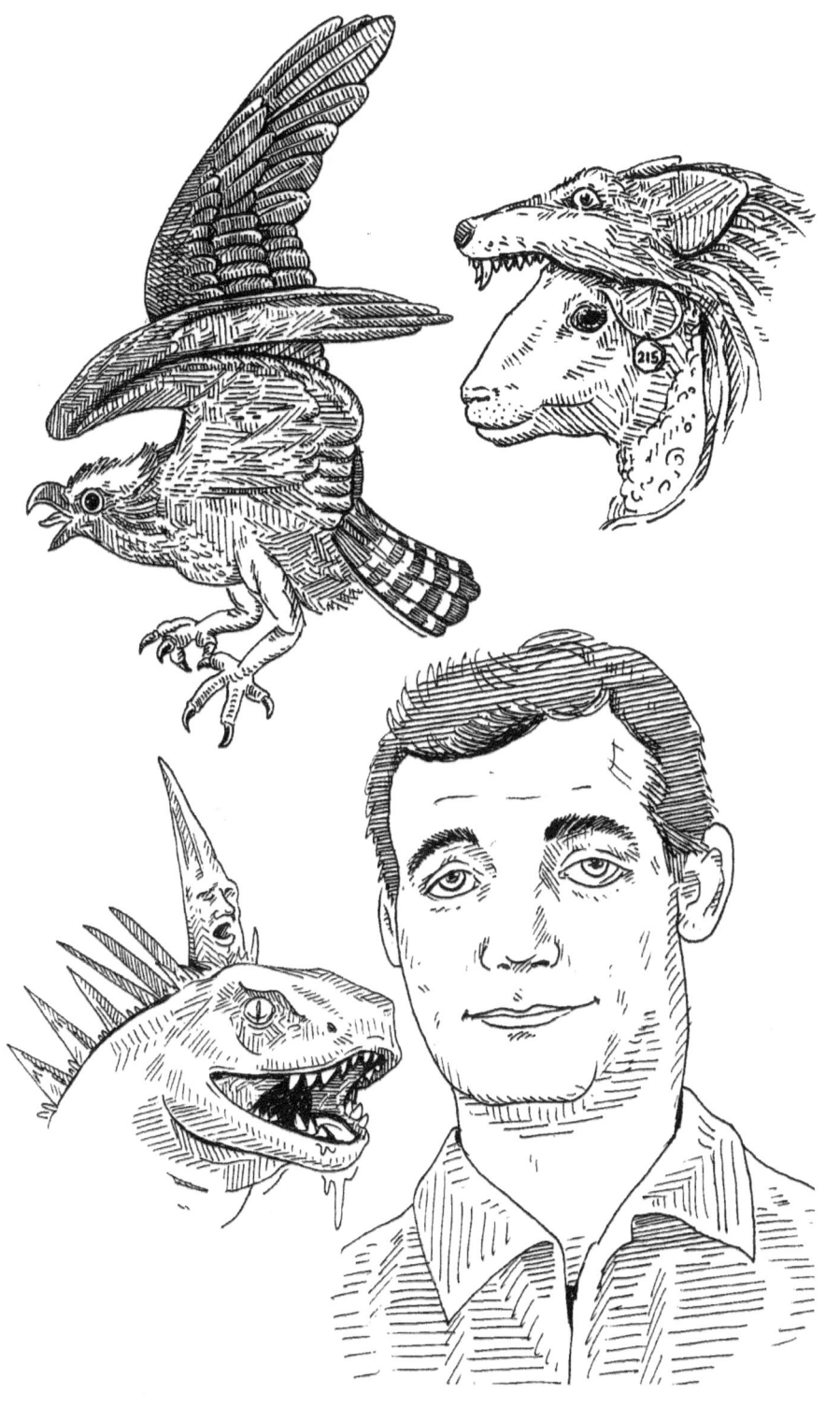

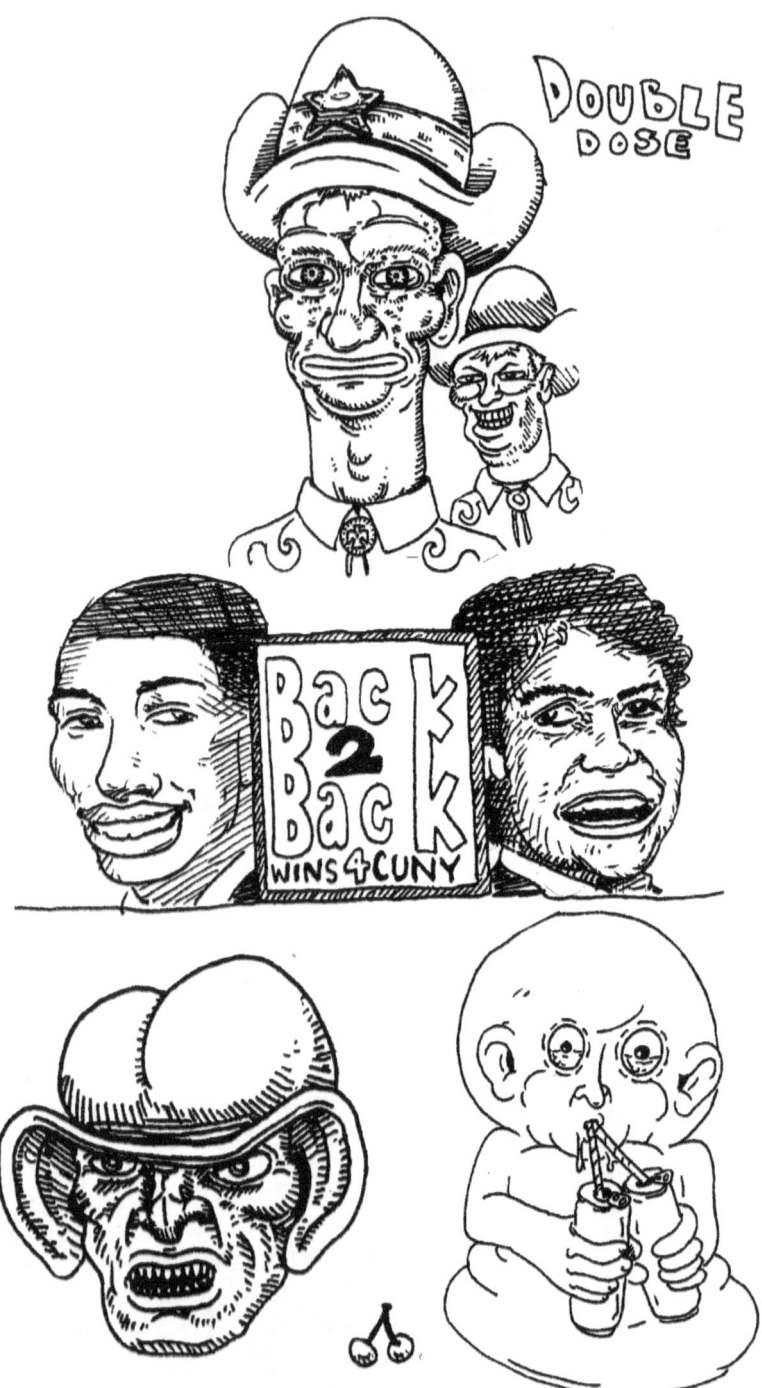

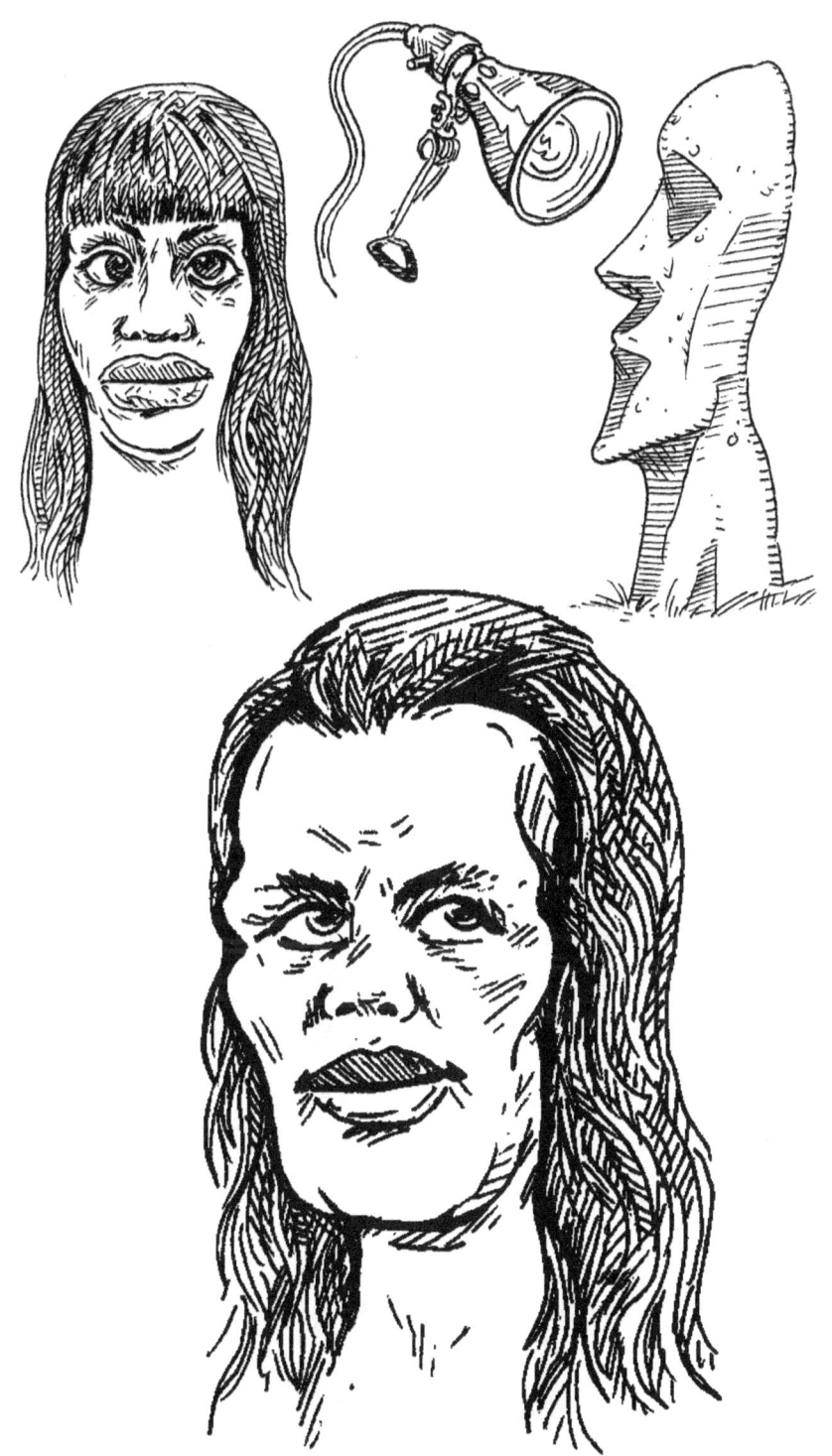

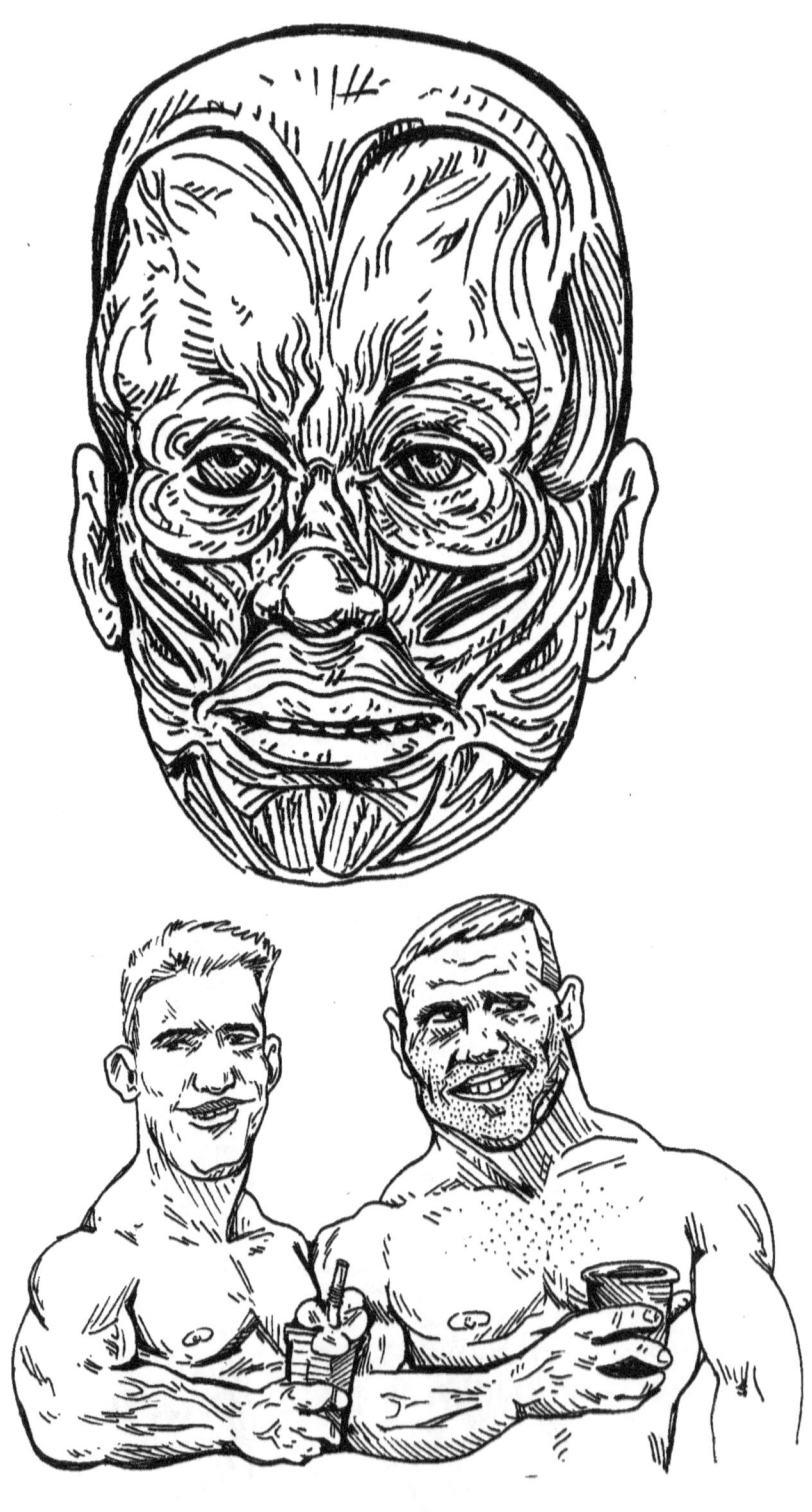

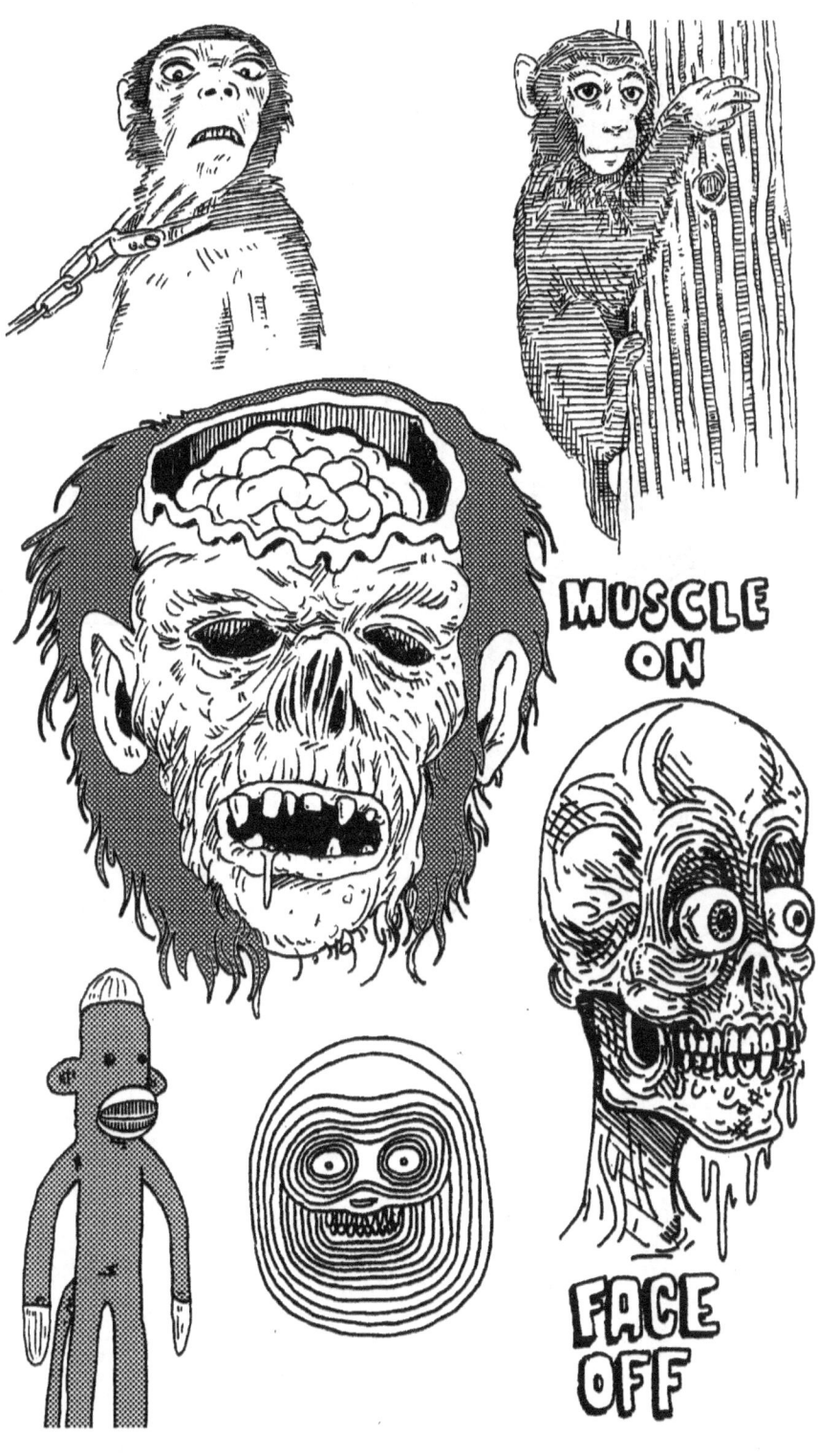

MUSCLE ON

FACE OFF

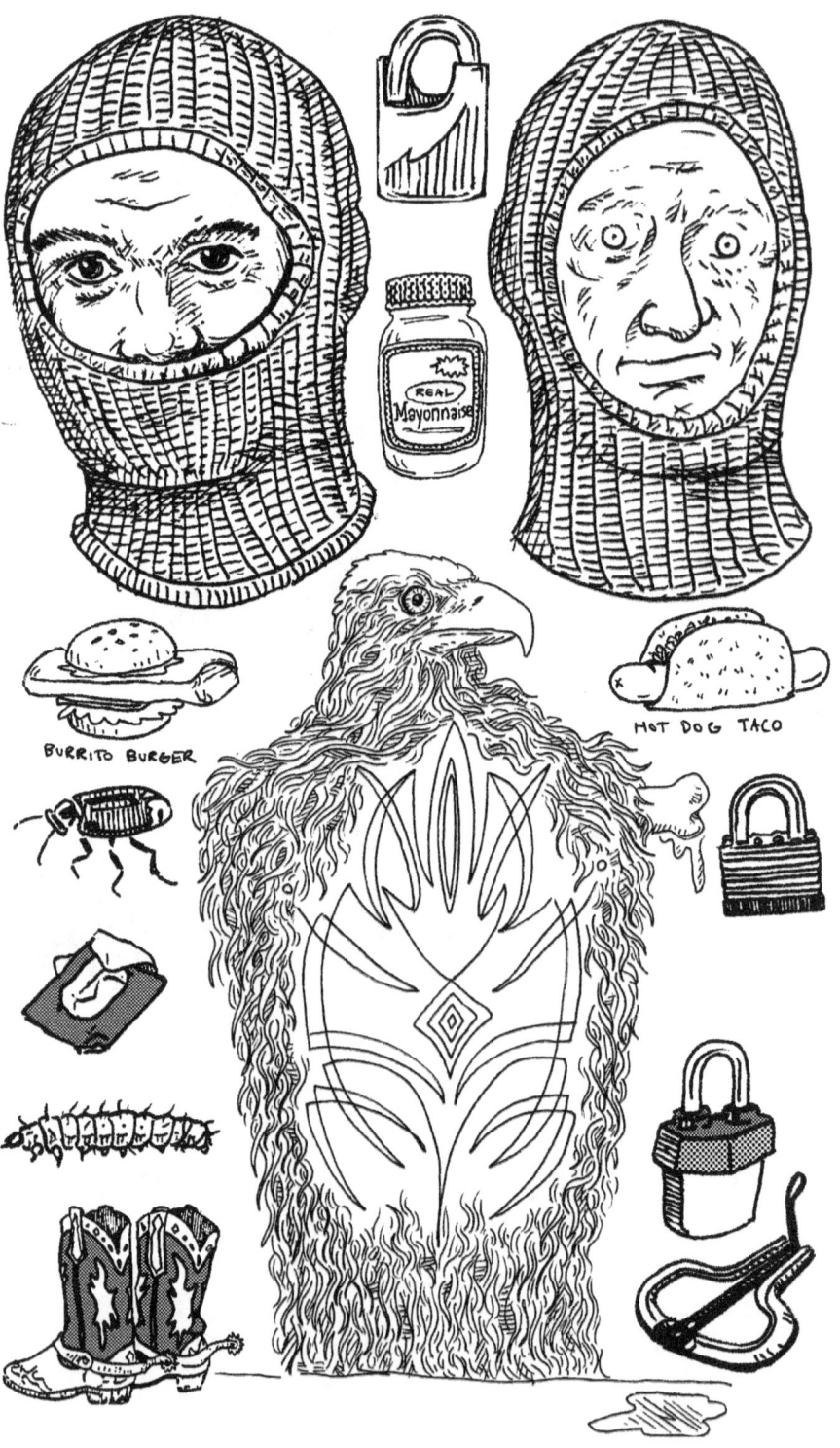

BURRITO BURGER

HOT DOG TACO

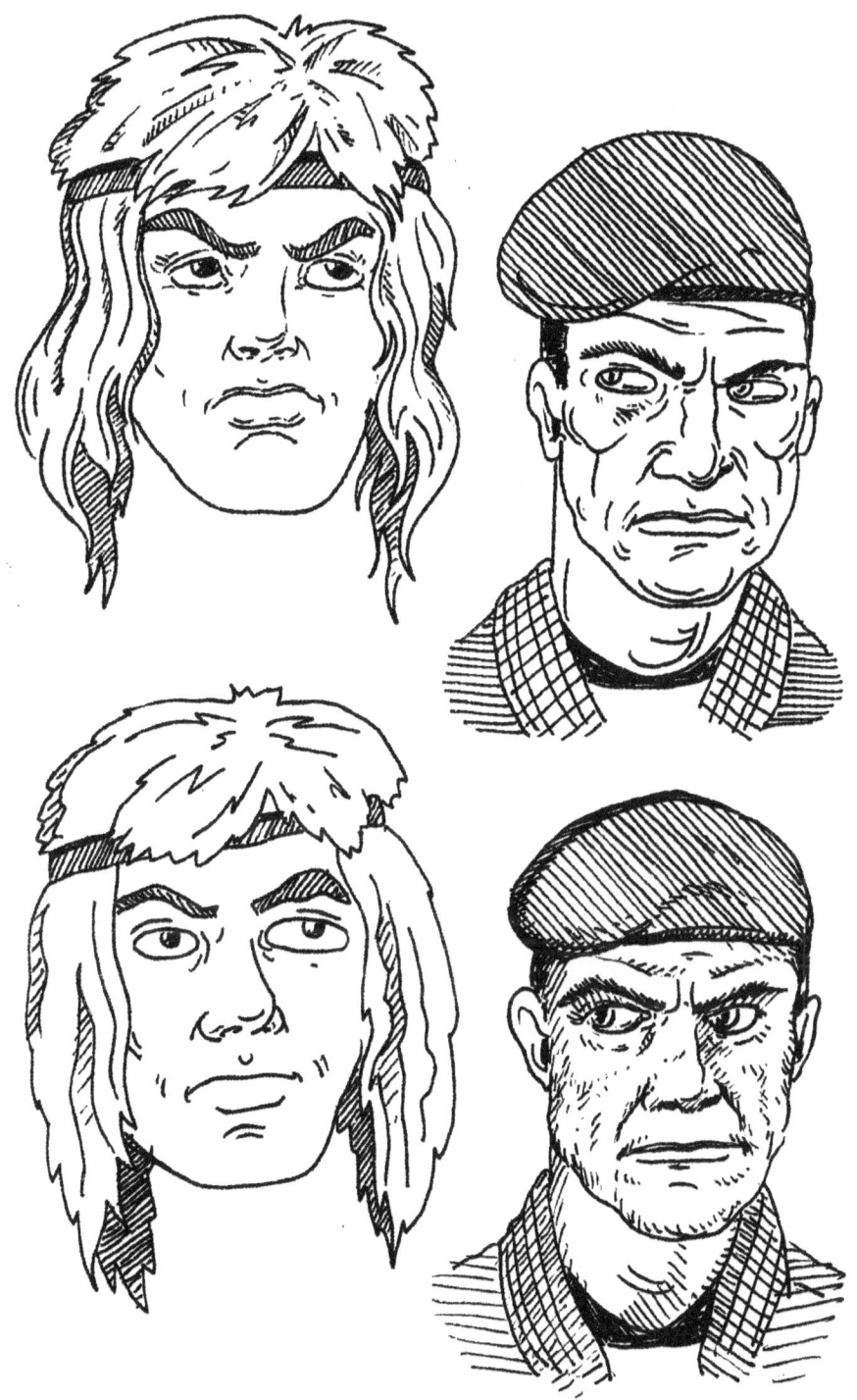

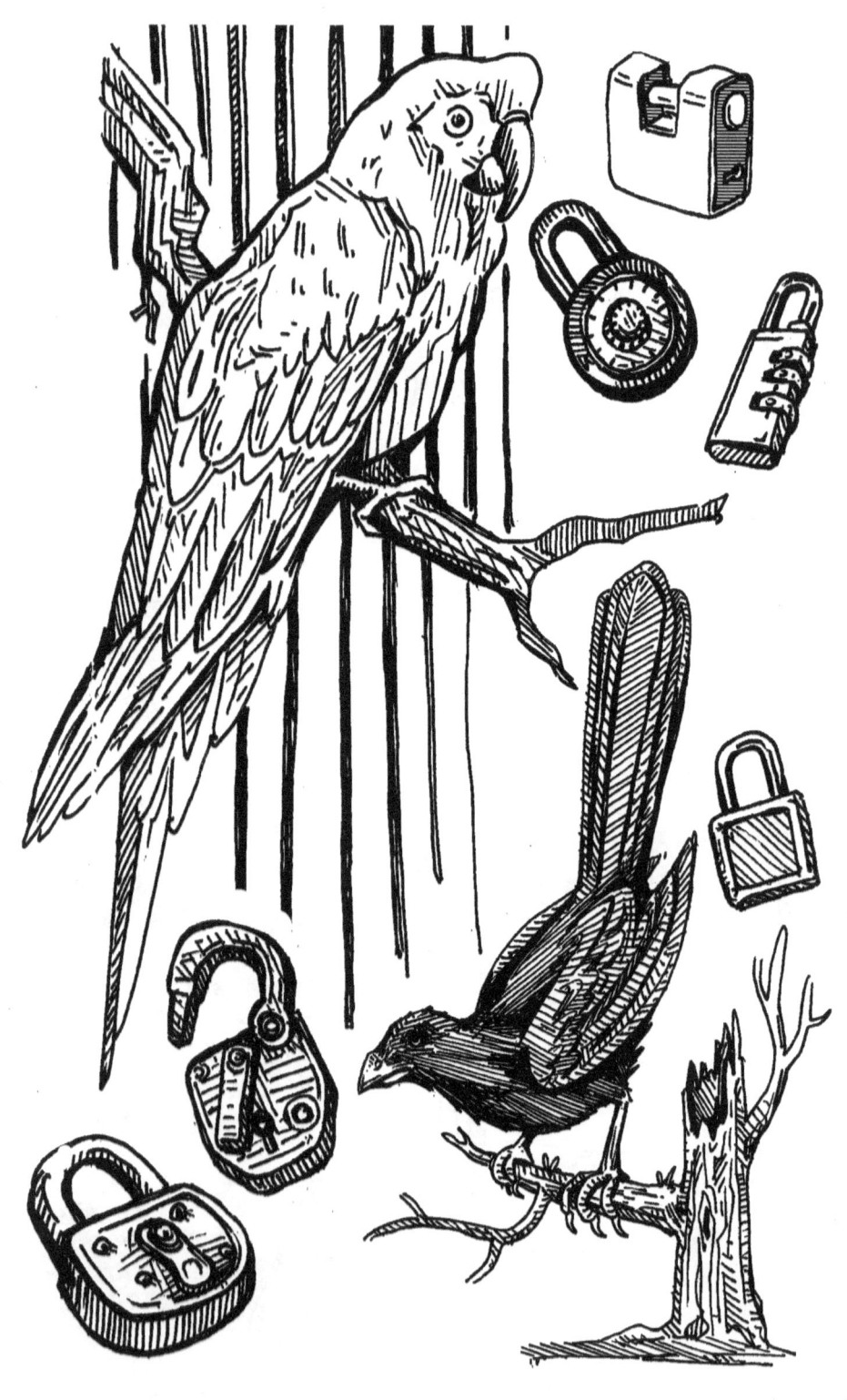

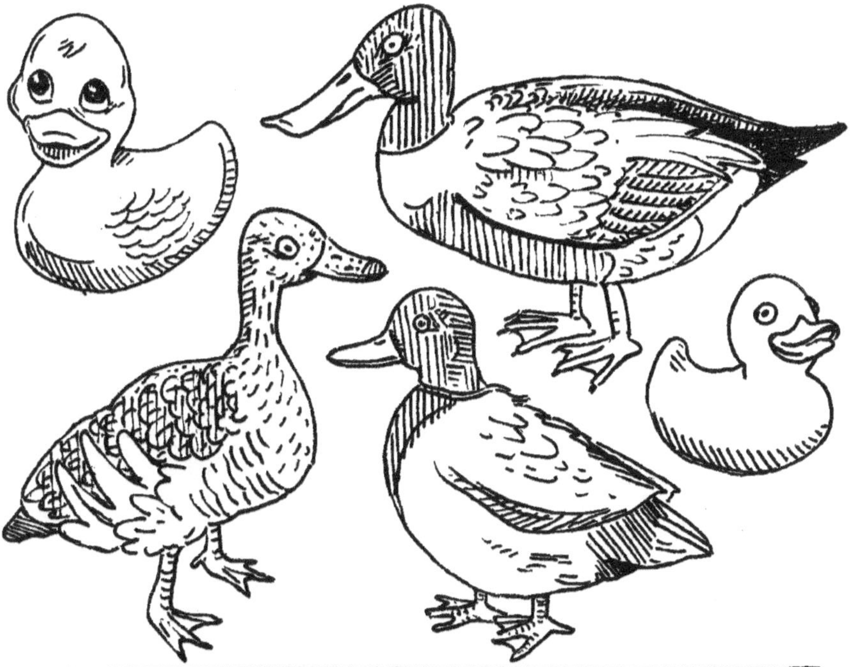

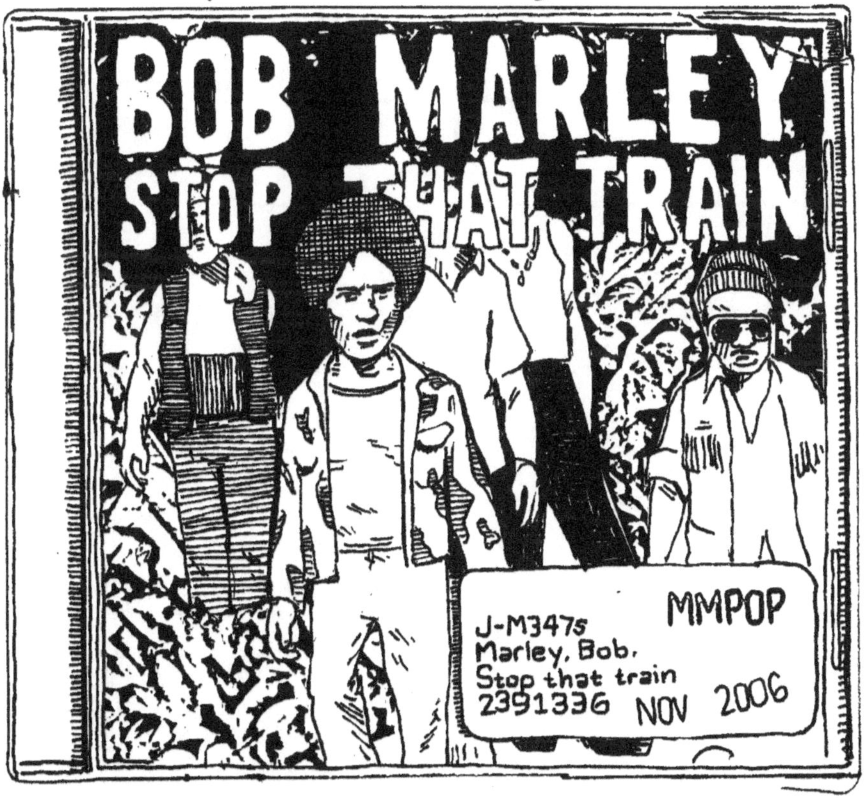
BOB MARLEY
STOP THAT TRAIN
MMPOP
J-M347s
Marley, Bob.
Stop that train
2391336 NOV 2006

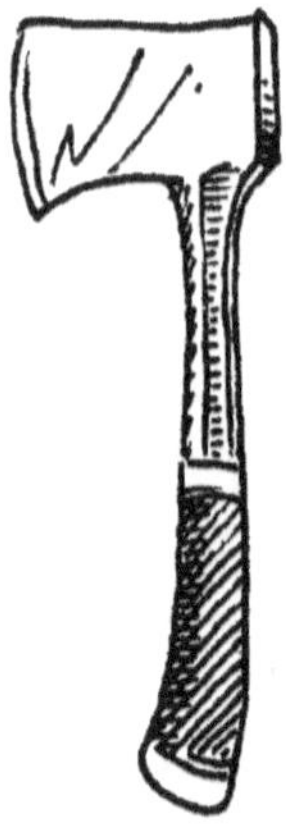

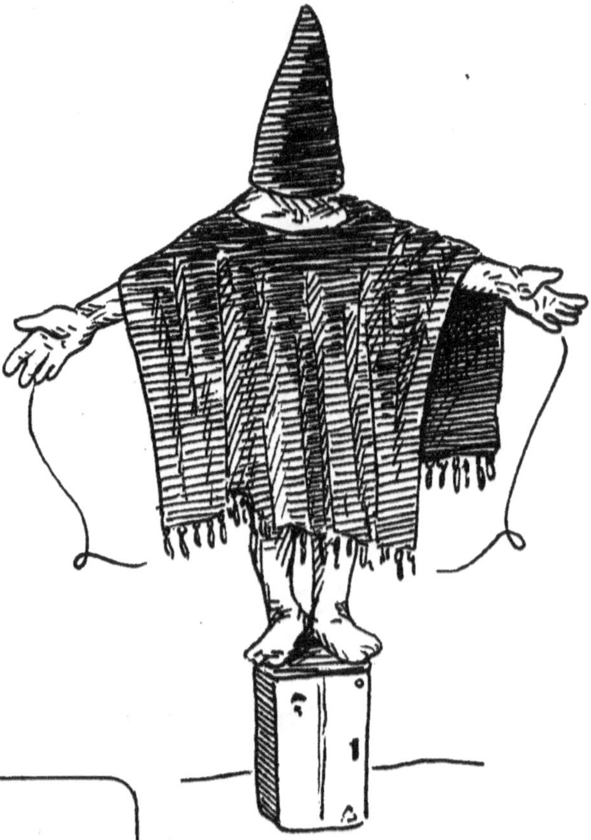

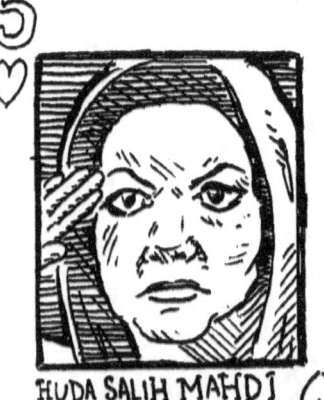

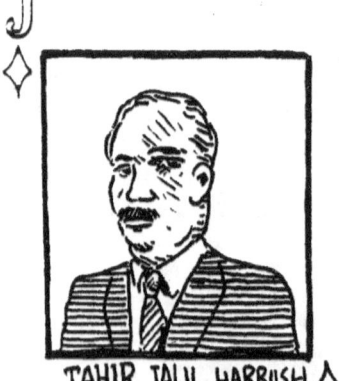

J
♦

TAHIR JALIL HABBUSH
AL-TIKRITI ♦
Iraqi Intelligence Service (IIS)

5
♥

HUDA SALIH MAHDI
AMMASH
WMD Scientist

♥
5

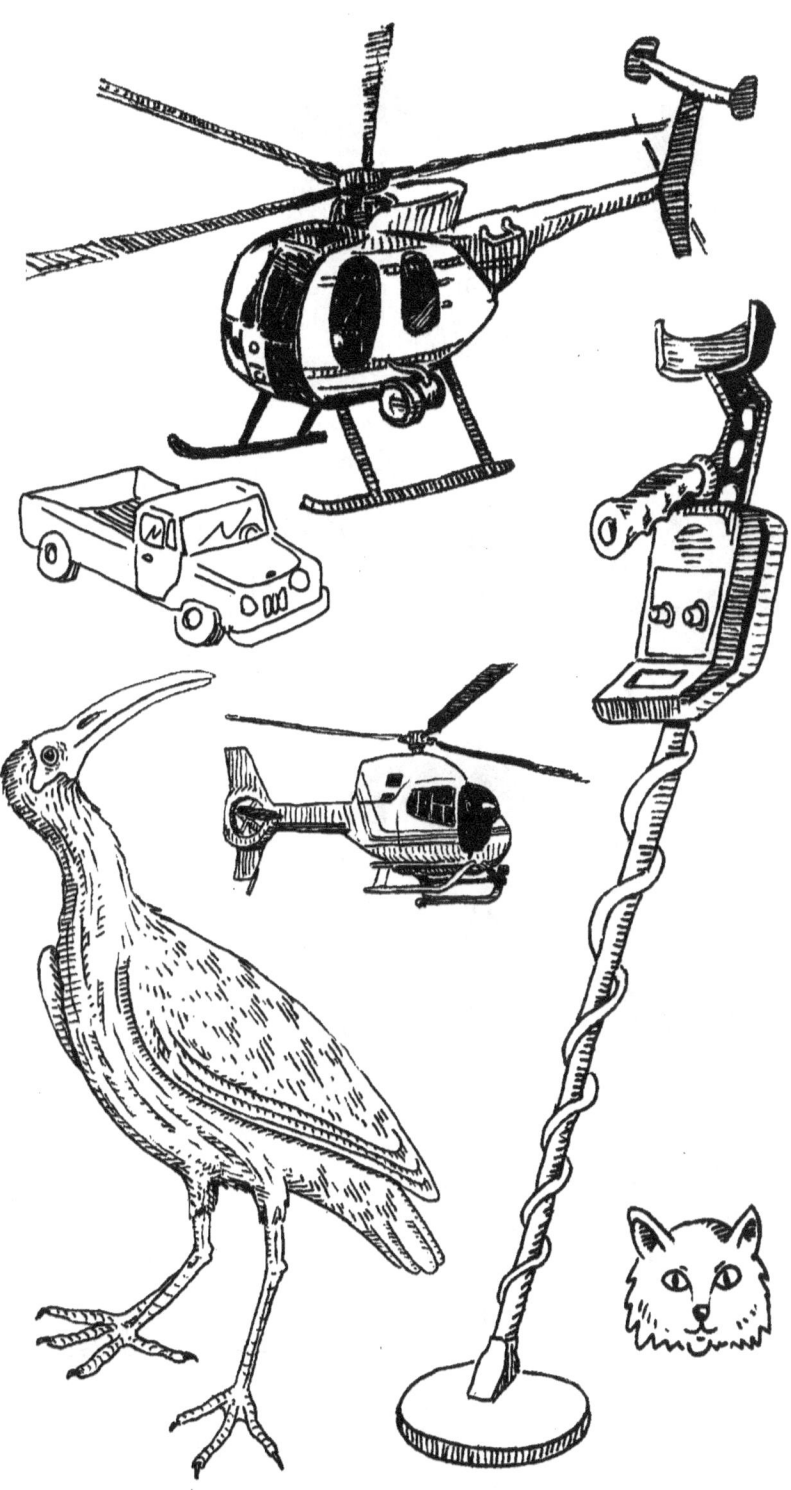

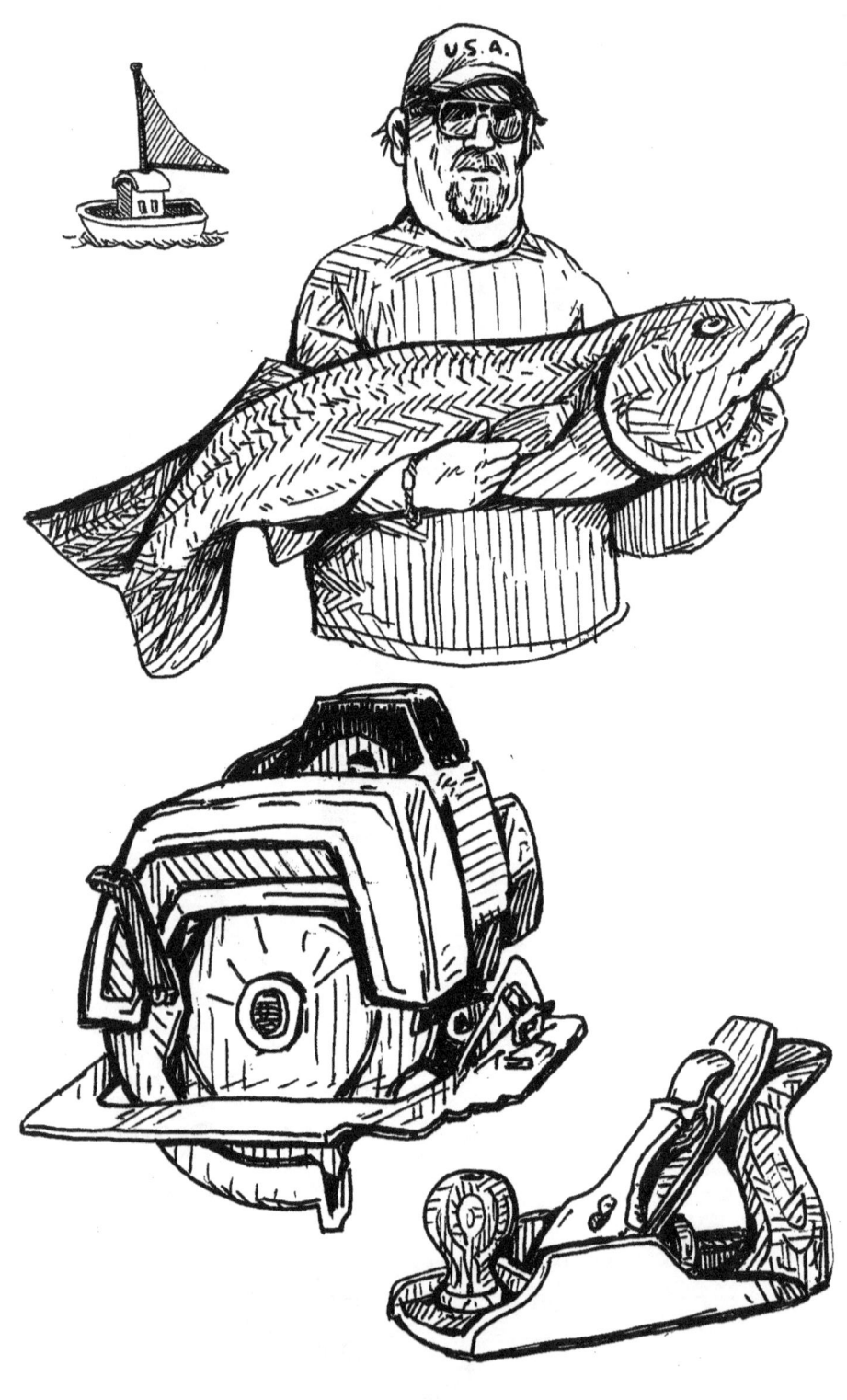

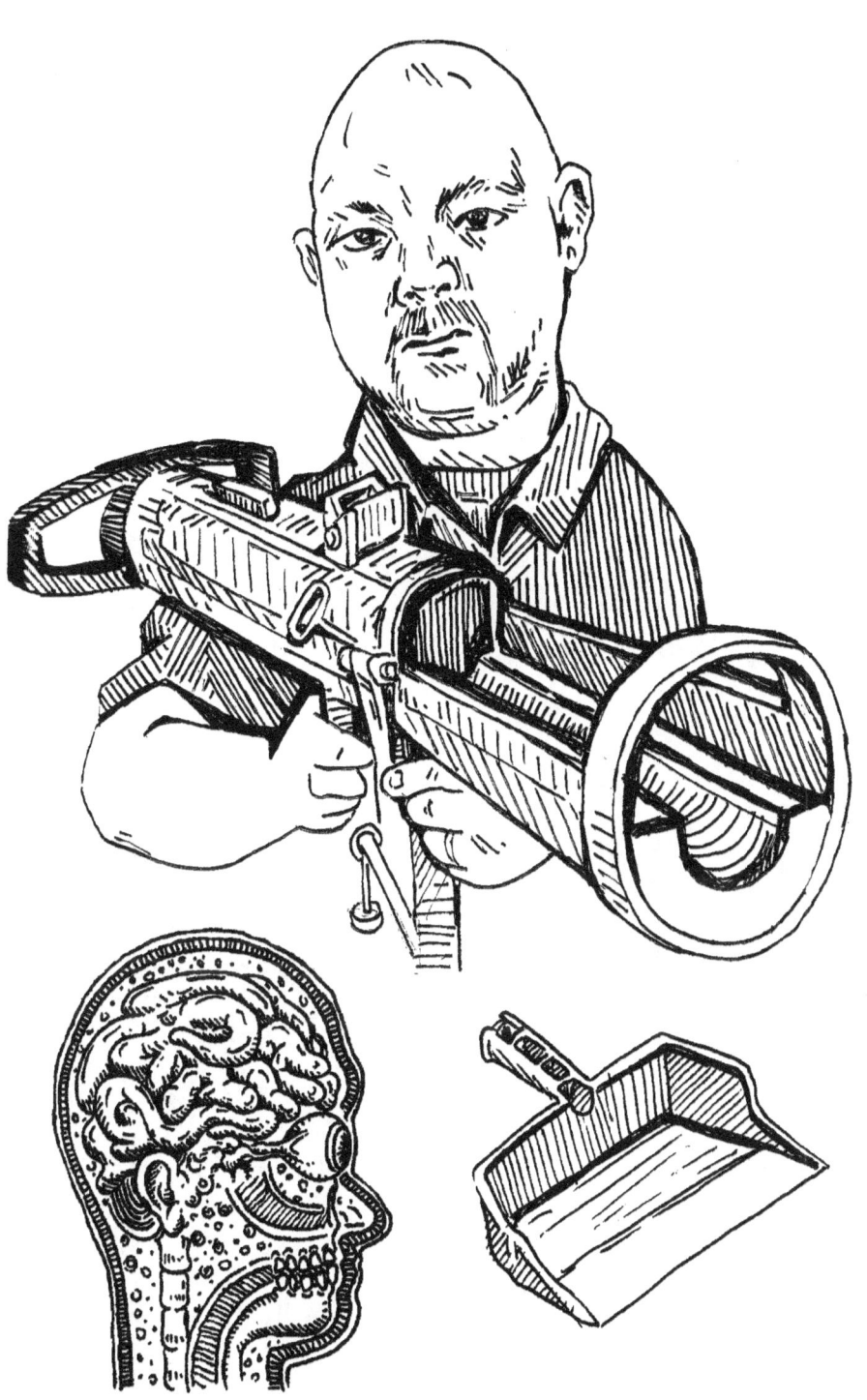

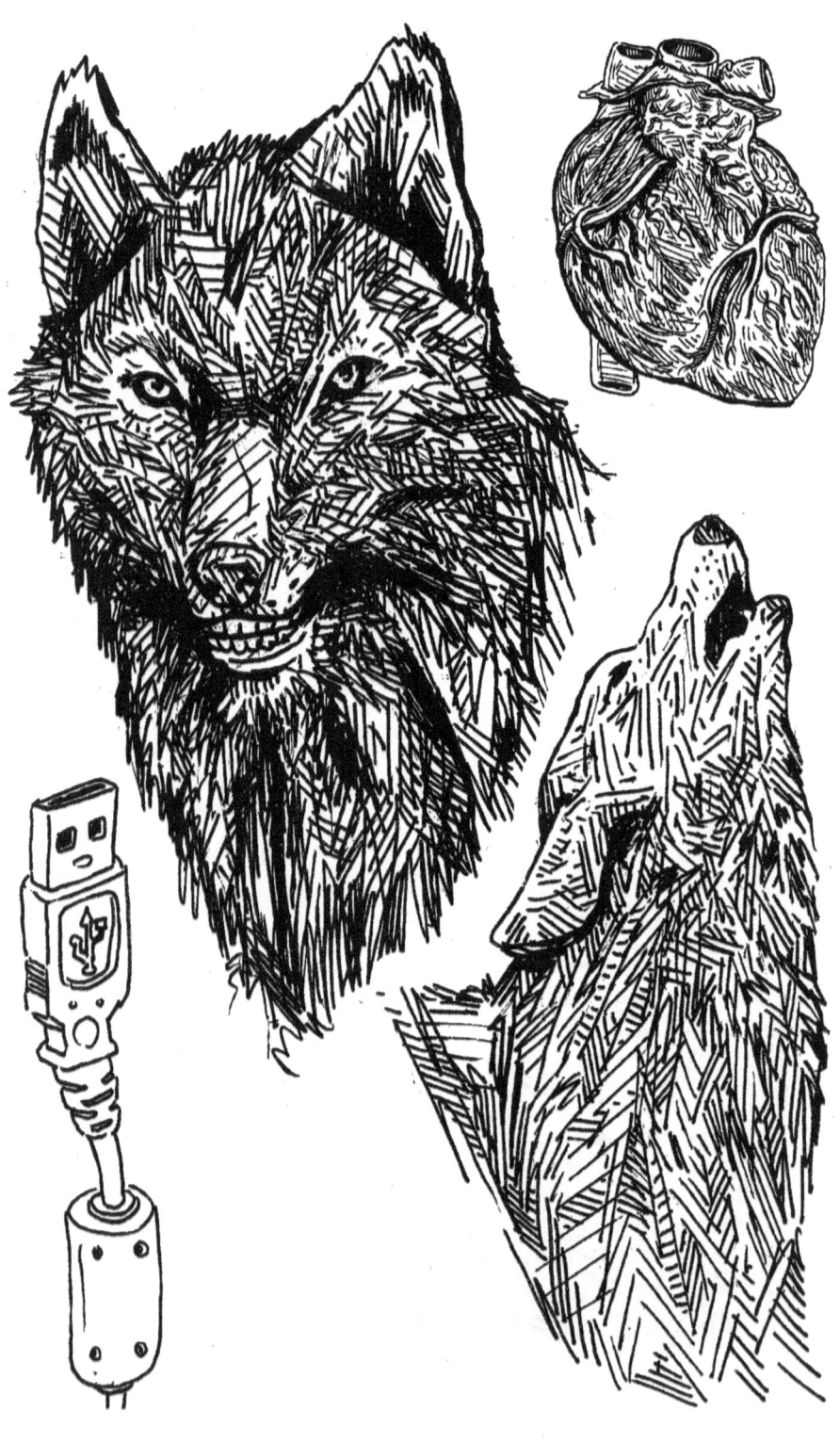

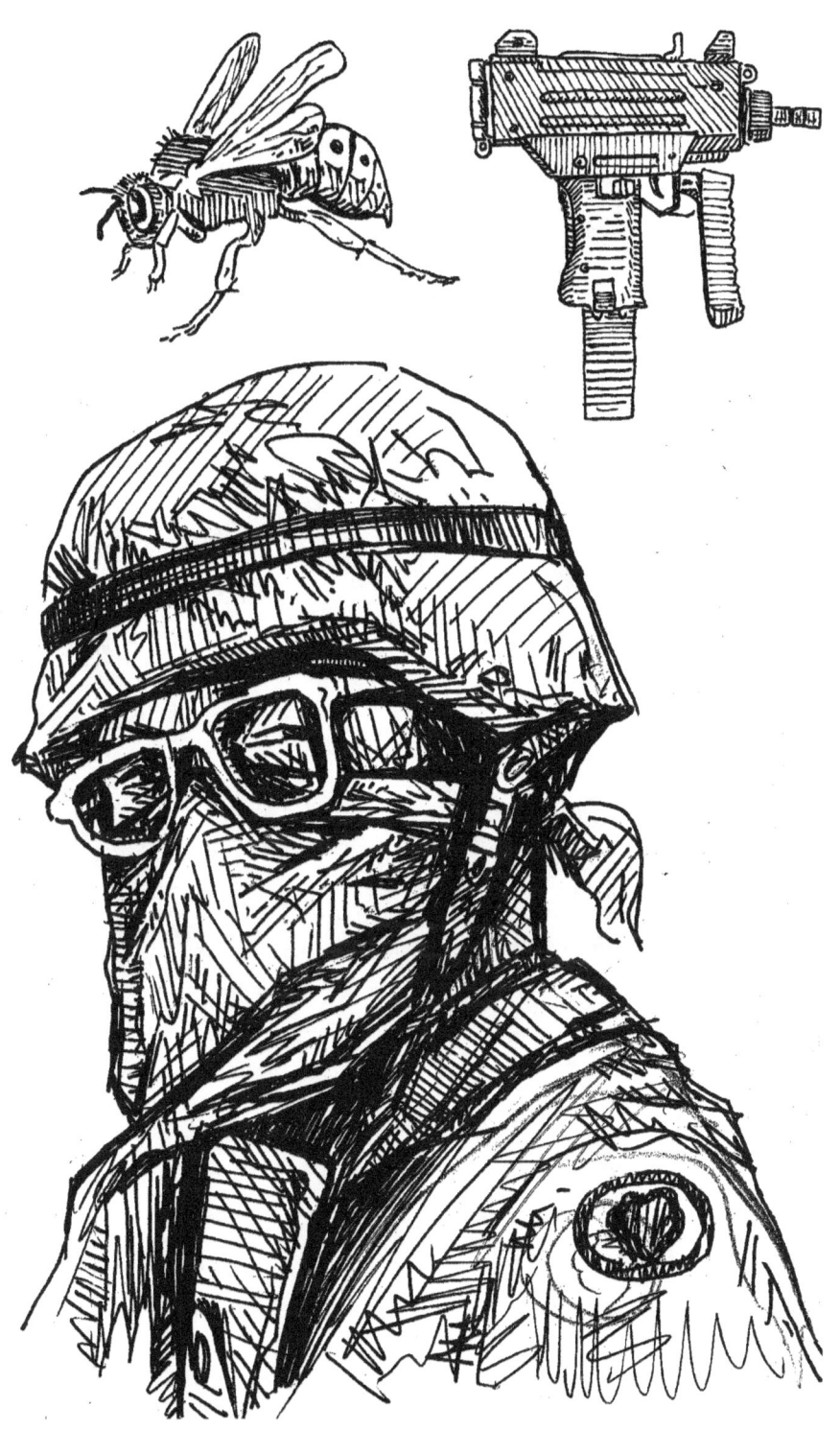

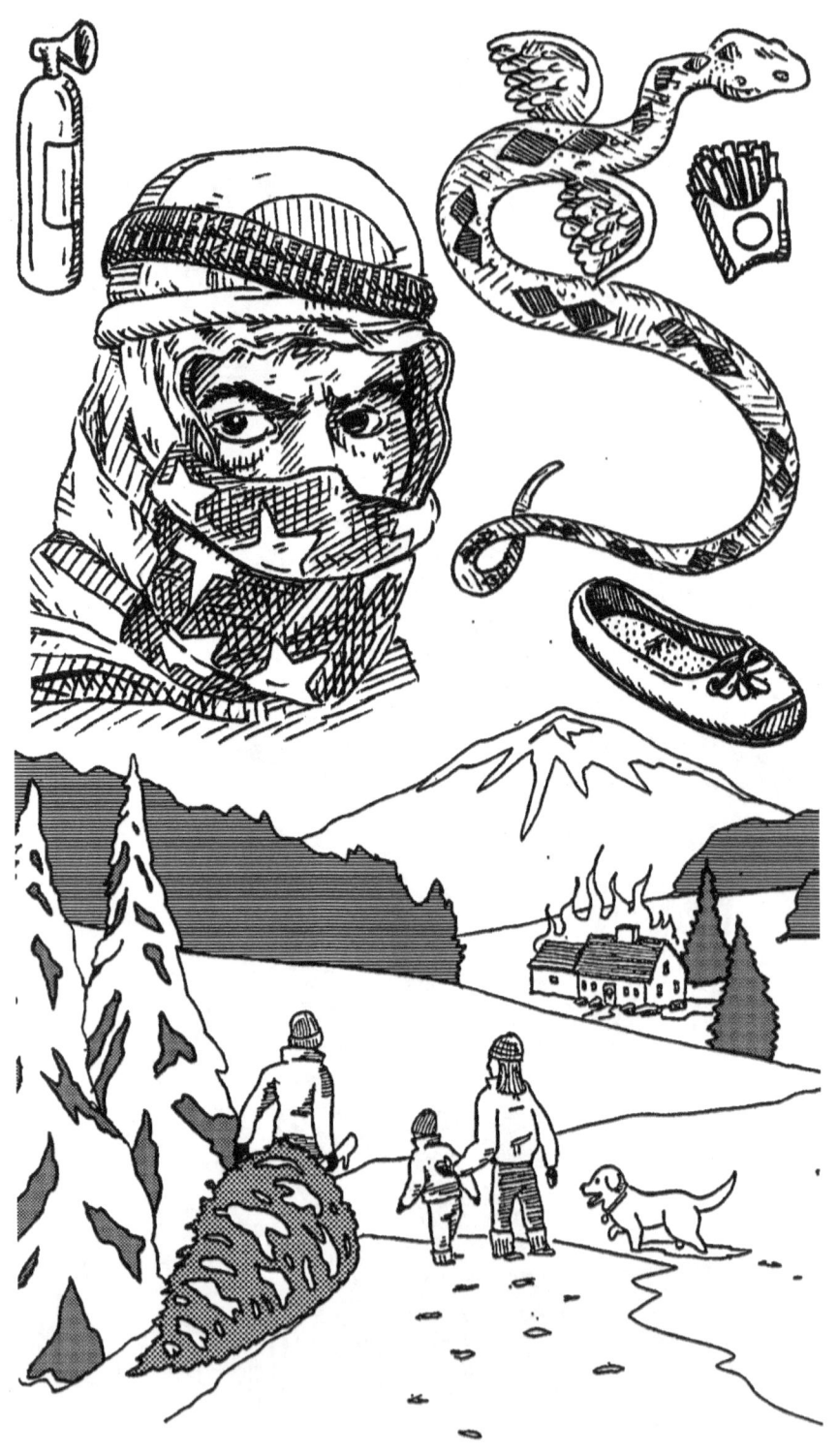

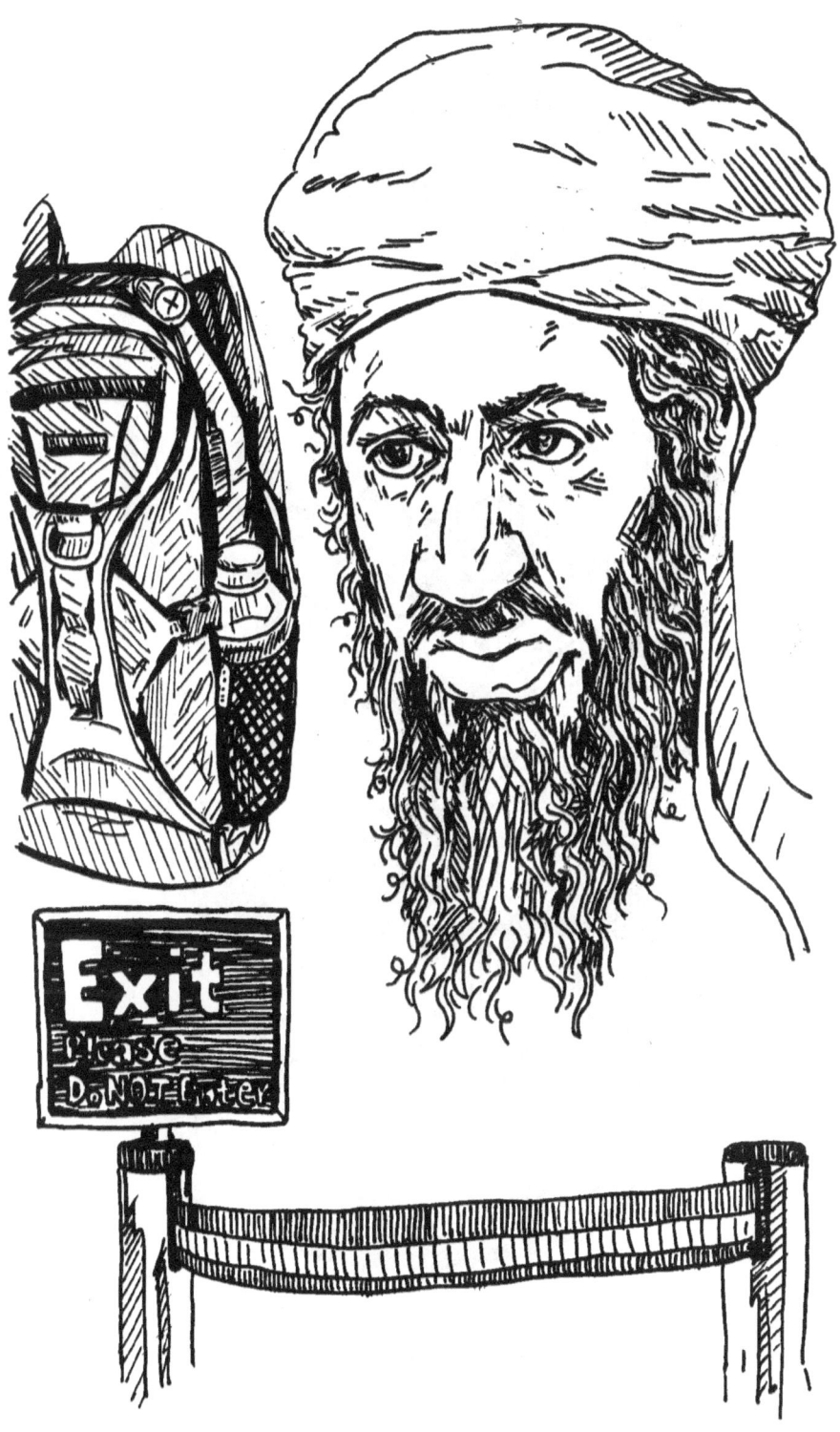

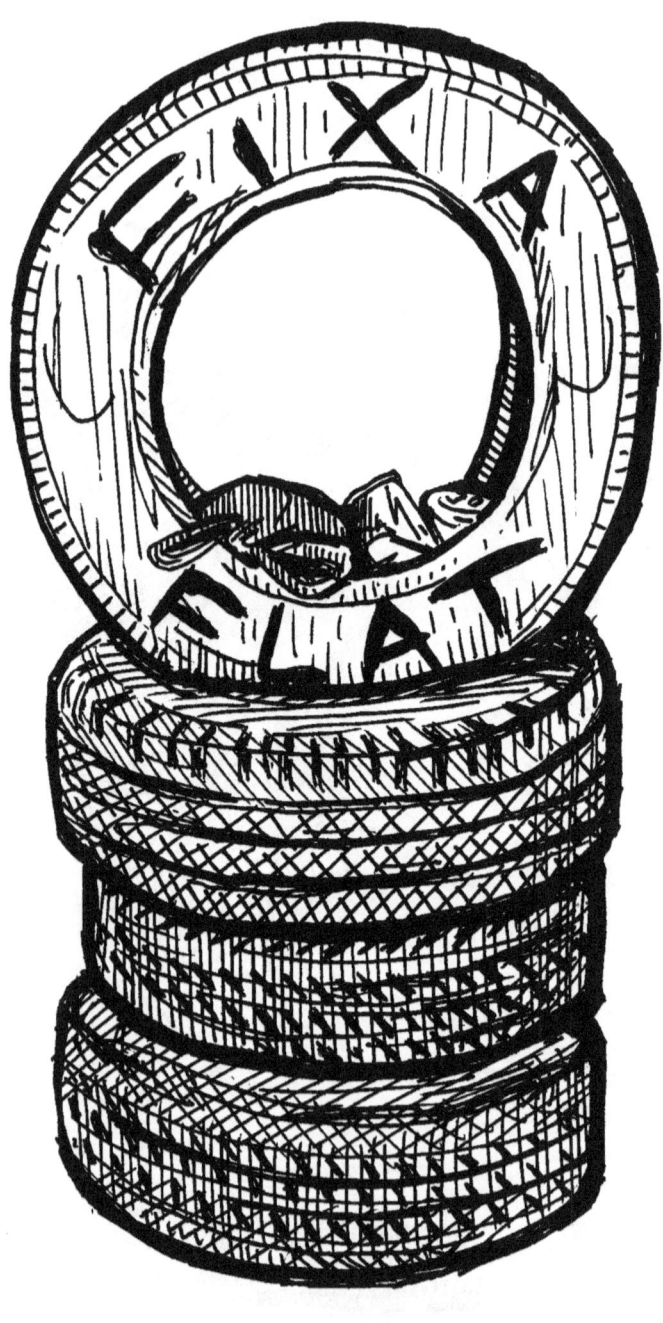

for Laura

www.ingramcontent.com/pod-product-compliance
Lightning Source LLC
Chambersburg PA
CBHW021431170526
45164CB00001B/190